Christopher Warwick was born and educated in London. Before taking up a freelance writing career in 1980, he worked as assistant to the distinguished author Noël Barber, and in publishing.

His work has appeared internationally and he has often taken part in television and radio programmes. His earlier books include several best-sellers, among them the authorized biography of Princess Margaret.

THE UNIVERSAL USTINOV

Christopher Warwick

PAN BOOKS
LONDON, SYDNEY AND AUCKLAND

First published 1990 by Sidgwick & Jackson Limited

This edition published 1992 by Pan Books Ltd
a division of Pan Macmillan Publishers Limited
Cavaye Place London SW10 9PG
and Basingstoke

Associated companies throughout the world

ISBN 0 330 32340 7

The author would like to thank Sir Peter Ustinov for
permission to quote from his autobiography *Dear Me*.
These extracts are also reprinted by permission of
William Heinemann Ltd.

1 3 5 7 9 8 6 4 2

A CIP catalogue record for this book is available from
the British Library

Typeset by Macmillan Production Limited
Printed in England by Clays Ltd, St Ives plc

CONTENTS

ACKNOWLEDGEMENTS

Since our first meeting in September 1987, Peter Ustinov and I have met and talked on innumerable occasions, in London, in Paris and at his home near Geneva. I am enormously grateful to him, not only for all his time, but also for his generosity, his interest and, indeed, his hospitality. My first and very warmest thanks, therefore, are due in full measure to him.

I am no less grateful to Hélène Ustinov, to Peter's son, Igor, and to his daughters, Tamara and Andrea, for all their help. To them, as to Liliane Couturier, Peter's secretary, as well as to his cousin, Dimitry Vicheney, of the Association des Benois in Paris, I offer my sincerest thanks.

I should also like to extend my gratitude to each of the following: Sir Richard Attenborough; Brian Auld; Bunny Austin; Lauren Bacall; Robin Bailey; Charlotte Balazs; Dirk Bogarde; Lord Brabourne; the archivists of the British Film Institute; Brenda Bruce; Suzanne Bruno; Faith Buckley; John Cavanagh; Jonathan Cecil; Horst M. Cerni, Unicef, New York; Schuyler Chapin; Peter David, Unicef, New York; Lady Daubeny; Léon Davičo, Unesco, Paris; Fergus Davidson, Teltale Limited, Edinburgh; Yvonne de Valera; the late Robert Eddison; John Field and Valerie St Johnston, Westminster School; Jayne Fincher; Dr Garret FitzGerald; Patrick Fitz-Gibbon; Angela Fox; Francesca Franchi, Royal Opera House, Covent Garden; Bettina K. Fredrick, Boston; Margaret Gardner; Valerie Garner; Dr Ann Geneva; Sir John Gielgud; Sir Alec Guinness; Angela Hawke, Unicef, UK; Clare Head; Sir Edward

Heath KG, MP; S. Mervyn Herbert; King Hussein of Jordan; Stephen M. Kenis; William Morris Ltd, London; Deborah Kerr; Erica Lawrence, University of Durham; Professor Rolf Liebermann; the late Cyril Luckham and Mrs Violet Luckham; Tom McCormick, the Players Theatre, London; John McGreevey, JMP, Toronto; Robin Macwhirter; Sir Yehudi Menuhin; the late Lord (Bernard) Miles; Hayley Mills; Lord Montagu of Beaulieu; Doreen Montgomery; Frank Muir; Julie Murphy, Edinburgh Festival; Anne Neal, Buckingham Palace Press Office; Denis Norden; Michael O'Mara; Dilys Powell; Peter Roberts, *Plays International*; Paul Rogers; Dr Helmut Schmidt; James Sharkey; Ned Sherrin; Carey Smith; Sheamus Smith; Timothy Smith; Irene Swinton, University of Dundee; Judy Tarlo; Ming Tcherepnin; the archivists of the Theatre Museum, Covent Garden; Mr and Mrs J. C. Trewin; Liv Ullmann; Dr Kurt Waldheim, President of Austria; Diana Waterland; Nigel West; Jean Williams; Ian Woodward, and Barbara Young.

At Pan, I should like to offer warmest thanks to Ingrid Connell.

                                      Chris Warwick
                                      June 1990
                                      Revised April 1992

INTRODUCTION

Au Clos du Château, built in the late 1960s, stands on the edge of a small and picturesque village some thirty kilometres outside Geneva. Vineyards on three sides slope away from a terrace built on two levels: the secluded upper part laid out in more or less traditional garden style, the lower designed as a leisure area, complete with whirlpool, sauna and outdoor swimming-pool, sealed when not in use by means of an ingenious, hydraulically-operated cover.

In the distance, Lake Geneva shimmers in the sunlight, while Mont Blanc, visible on a clear day, rises majestically on the horizon. With its pitched roof of red and grey 'fish-scale' tiles and ivy-covered turret – housing a semi-circular entrance hall – Au Clos du Château is an immensely appealing, yet unpretentious house, entirely befitting its equally unpretentious owner – Peter Ustinov.

Inside, the atmosphere is relaxed and welcoming. As I arrive, the only sounds to be heard are those of a tennis match received via satellite on a television in the ground-floor bedroom, a telephone ringing, and occasional noises from the kitchen where Amandio, the Ustinovs' Portuguese major-domo, is preparing lunch.

In the light and spacious living-room, where the walls are covered in a woven textile the colour of ripe corn, and silk curtains – very nearly the same shade – frame four sets of french windows, there is ample evidence of Peter Ustinov's compulsively busy life-style. On the day I visited him, he

1

had just spent the past two months in Britain, Germany, Czechoslovakia, Italy, Holland, Canada and the United States, had returned from Moscow only three days earlier and, with his wife Hélène, was about to leave for a month in Cancun, Mexico.

On almost every available surface – particularly on the occasional tables on either side of a pair of tan leather sofas, and on the glass-topped coffee-table – piles of papers, scripts, correspondence, books, magazines and classical records, vie with one another for supremacy. The records of course reflect Ustinov's great love of music, while an eclectic collection of *objets d'art* illustrates his keen appreciation of beautiful or unusual possessions.

In front of one wall, hidden by a long, white bookcase with cupboards beneath, is an old Chinese silk screen, which Peter came across in Paris. Hand-painted with typically stylised flowers on a rich, dark background, it stands near a pair of 'naïve' wooden figures representing Mexican soldiers, their uniforms painted a bright primary blue. Over on the piano – a Bösendorfer baby grand – are two sculptures by Ustinov's son, Igor, while in front of the open fireplace, a bronze Buddha's head – together with oriental companion – sits in harmony beside an intriguing religious artefact. Robed, enthroned, triple-tiara'd and looking like some long-forgotten pontiff, the figure, which Peter found in an antique shop in San Antonio, Texas, and which had once been worshipped in a Mexican cathedral, represents no less an entity than God the Father, Himself.

In this room, where the generous amount of window space admittedly imposes its own restrictions, the walls are hung with far fewer pictures than one might have expected of a man who not only has an impressive knowledge of art, but also a private collection of pictures and drawings that any self-respecting connoisseur would be proud to call his own.

Among Ustinov's paintings, for instance, are a very fine Renoir of a girl reading; a copy of Rubens's *Coronation of Catherine de Medici* so well done 'that it could be a Delacroix or an Isabey'; three studies by Alfred Stevens, a friend of Manet; and a large watercolour by Kokoschka. His collection of drawings includes works by Daumier, Forain, Sabattini,

Valotton and Steinlen. There is more than one Tiepolo and several drawings by Rowlandson.

None of these is to be found in the living-room at Au Clos du Château, however. Here, over the fireplace, hangs a painting by Cuyp – a *grisaille* of a horseman and pedestrian – in shades of brown and grey, while nearby hang two vibrantly modern Japanese canvasses. Most exciting of all – at least to my mind – is the large abstract by Rufino Tamayo, Mexico's leading contemporary artist, which was a gift to Peter from Elizabeth Taylor and Richard Burton.

Two more pictures, this time in ornate frames, are casually propped up on the floor. One is a portrait of Peter's father, apparently in pensive mood, the other a head-and-shoulders study of Peter himself, as a boy of thirteen. Both are the work of Ustinov's distinguished mother, the painter and designer Nadia Benois.

'I've left them there,' Peter tells me, 'because I've been trying to decide whether I should give them to the family museum in Russia.'

Throughout this surprisingly modest, albeit unusual, chalet-style house, which Ustinov bought in 1971, the ambience is one of comfort and informality; of understated sophistication. Unlike many 'star' residences in Britain and, particularly, in America, Au Clos du Château is first and foremost a home, devoid of any suggestion of vulgarity or ostentation. It is very much a house which reflects the personal style of its owner.

'I don't like rooms designed by interior decorators,' he says, 'because I always feel as though I am sitting on a stage, the curtain is about to go up and I don't know my lines.'

Gregarious and extrovert though Peter Ustinov is, he nevertheless enjoys the peace and quiet of home. 'Switzerland,' he once remarked, 'is the most congenial place to work or do any writing. They leave you alone. Stravinsky wrote his *Rite of Spring* near here and ever since the local people have been able to put up with almost any disturbance.'

Sitting chatting with Peter Ustinov, who is dressed in a bright blue sweat-shirt and light grey casual trousers, it is hard to imagine what sort of thing might be capable of disturbing the peace of this tranquil setting. In any event, Peter has a reputation for single-minded concentration wherever he is, even to the point of having once started to write a play in the midst of a party in full swing.

Here he works on the floor above, in a sparsely furnished study literally awash with paperwork, books and yet more records, at the top of a spiral staircase. On the edge of his desk sits a row of awards, most prominent among them the first Oscar he ever won, for his role as 'Batiatus' – 'a kind of crummy salesman of human flesh' – in the 1960 movie *Spartacus*; an Emmy – one of three – which he received for playing the eponymous role in the television production *The Life of Samuel Johnson*, and an *Evening Standard* Drama Award – designed by Henry Moore – for his play *Romanoff and Juliet*, which was first produced in London in 1956.

Among the papers on Ustinov's desk – deliberately positioned so that he looks into the room to avoid distractions – are all manner of letters, including invitations to write books, attend various functions or endorse new products. He shows me the world's first ecologically-inspired wrist-watch, ingeniously made entirely of 'unthreatened' wood. 'I was about to say, "Yes, I like it",' he says, 'when the company went out of business.'

Then there is the constant flow of fan mail, which Peter receives from all over the world. Most of it ends up in sacks in the busy Paris office run by Liliane Couturier, his secretary of more than twenty years. 'There is so much, that Peter isn't able to attend to it,' she says. 'It isn't that he doesn't want to, but simply that he *never* has enough time.'

Retracing our steps back to lower terrace level, Ustinov shows me the wine-cellar . . . vins de Bourgogne and Clos du Château. Each year, his vineyards produce some 4,000 bottles of light white wine, much of it sold locally. 'An unpretentious little wine,' is how he describes it in inimitable fashion, 'slightly nervous, ideal for marriages, divorces, baptisms, reunions and that type of thing.'

Once described as 'Britain's one-man beacon of Glasnost', Peter frequently plays host to a variety of visitors at Au Clos du Château. Hélène Ustinov says, 'Switzerland is very international and because we are so near Geneva, a lot of people come here to see Peter.' VIPs as well as journalists, film-makers and business delegates are among those who drive out to Au

Clos du Château when visiting Geneva, and I was recently reminded of one such visit when reading an interview Peter had given to the *Sunday Times* in September 1989. He told journalist Valerie Grove:

> Some very grand Swiss officials from the Red Cross came to see me about something very serious and they noticed my satellite dish. They said, we thought only public buildings could have these and I said, no, private houses too. Would you like to see something? They looked at their watches and said well, yes.
>
> And there, in the middle of Switzerland in the middle of the morning was Dr Ruth saying (perfect egregious Dr Ruth voice): 'And girls, go easy with your vibrators! Just remember one thing: nothing will ever replace a penis.' I have to tell you, adds Ustinov, there is no place for Dr Ruth in Switzerland.

In common with most of us, Ustinov finds television as much of an irritant as a source of entertainment. Michael O'Mara, one of his British publishers, told me, 'Peter likes lying on his enormous bed – like Nero or whoever – watching television. At home he picks up the American news which he finds very funny, and you'll constantly hear him talking back at this enormous screen. He gets completely taken over by whatever it is he's watching. Take Irangate, for example. That inquiry was the sort of thing Peter finds horrible and wonderful, horrible and funny. So whatever he's watching goes in through his ear and straight out of his mouth. Watching Irangate, he'll suddenly say to his housekeeper, who doesn't speak English, "Can you get me another glass of that goddam wine?" – crazy American accent, mood, tone and all. It's very funny.'

Peter Ustinov is a naturally entertaining man, who quite simply wants everyone around him to be happy. In November 1972, after he had acted as Master of Ceremonies at an exclusive evening's entertainment given by the Prince of Wales and Princess Anne at Buckingham Palace to celebrate the Queen and Prince Philip's silver wedding anniversary, Peter heard from Prince Charles, who opened his letter of thanks with the words, 'Your brilliance is unsurpassed'.

'Laughter,' says Ustinov, 'is a therapy. Sense of humour is the only thing that separates us from the animals. Being humorous is my form of being serious. I have always thought that a comedy is really a tragedy gone wrong and a tragedy is a comedy gone wrong. The roots are in human behaviour. The extremes of life are very close to each other. I can be easily moved, but I find that in my case humour is a stabilizing influence, because it can easily be turned to irony. There are many things I feel strongly about, but when I express myself on them they turn out as being ironical rather than flat dramatic statements.'

Until comparatively recently, this may well have been true. But over the past ten years or so, particularly since he has grown older and become a kind of 'Elder Statesman figure' – as Lady (Molly) Daubeny, widow of the impresario Sir Peter Daubeny, put it – the pungency of Ustinov's observations, whether they are connected with his work for Unicef or Unesco, his concern for the Third World or Russia, and so on, has become so implicitly 'dramatic' that, notwithstanding his stature as an entertainer and communicator, his voice is not only heard but listened to.

Indeed, quite apart from giving us an indication of the force which motivates Ustinov the man as much as Ustinov the public figure, one of the innumerable letters I received during my research, tells us something about the still deeper philanthropy of a man who is at once both a conundrum and an inspiration. Sir Yehudi Menuhin wrote:

> Too easily one's impression of Peter Ustinov could remain with the genial theatrical and witty man, with his unbelievable gift for mimicry and the caricaturing of every conversation and situation, be it speech or action – in short, with his overwhelming powers of entertainment.
>
> However, behind the façade is the heart of a most sensitive and compassionate soul, suffering with and for every deprived child on our abused earth, for

every injustice, for every agonizing stupidity and vanity.

No one knows better than he, no one sees more clearly than he, the absurdity and the paradoxes of life nor more clearly what seems to be the fatal flaw in *homo sapiens*, who would rather massacre in the name of hallowed grievances and then take refuge behind towering walls of prejudice and fear than collaborate in learning together.

I have sought to share with you the living Peter whose genius is his ability to identify himself through others.

By the time I left Au Clos du Château, it was already early evening. The shutters had been closed and table lamps suffused the living-room with a warm, subdued glow. Hélène, who had an appointment with the curtain-maker next morning, had left for Paris and the four-roomed apartment near the Trocadero which Peter has had for over twenty years. Ustinov himself was about to retreat to his 'den', there to work on his twelfth book, a novel about the first meeting on earth between God and the Devil, entitled *The Old Man and Mr Smith*.

As Amandio drove me back to my hotel in Geneva, I not only mulled over the day's events and conversation, but thought back on some of the previous meetings I had had with Peter Ustinov over the past two and a half years.

Sometimes I couldn't help wondering if the picture in my mind's eye was as clear as I wanted to believe. Did I know this man well enough to start writing about him with any degree of authority? What about the contrasts between light and shade? The faults? I hadn't got very far on that tack. Nobody really seemed to know, or if they did, they weren't telling. 'Peter,' I'd once said, 'there would appear to be very few skeletons in your cupboard.' He replied characteristically, 'It's not the skeletons I'm worried about. I can't remember where I left the cupboard.'

For a moment, I thought I understood what the late Geoffrey Willans, Ustinov's first biographer, meant when he said of Peter, 'There are so many parts to unravel [that] it makes the quest of looking for Ustinov one of despair'. That, to my mind, was perhaps a little too melodramatic to be taken literally. For while the 'quest' for Ustinov was – indeed *is* – a formidable undertaking, despair cannot be said to have come into it.

Of course, back in 1956 when he was working on his own book, Willans was writing of a man still only in his mid-thirties. When I first met Peter Ustinov he was already sixty-six, and the intervening years had produced infinitely more to 'unravel'. All the same, the one constant in Ustinov's life has always been his marked individuality. Questions of 'image', for example, have never concerned him.

'I'm not going to be influenced by what people think,' he once told writer and broadcaster Tony Thomas. 'I believe what I do is divorced from seeing myself in any context. The tendency today is to be more interested in the image than in the person – this is like Narcissus's image being more important than Narcissus – and we're all in trouble once the image resents the person who's looking at it.' More simply, Peter told me, 'Image is a word I hate. I don't think about myself or the abilities I am said to have. I do what I am capable of doing, but it is for others to say how well I do it.'

Actor, writer, novelist, dramatist, wit, mimic, raconteur, humorist, director, producer, goodwill ambassador, cartoonist and, above all, humanitarian: Ustinov's gifts and accomplishments are almost too many and too diverse to enumerate. However, add 'elusive' and 'enigmatic' to this list and the description of this very singular individual becomes rather more complete.

But who or what is the *essential* Peter Ustinov? 'The man is so amazingly complex,' said the actor Paul Rogers, 'that it would amount to impudence even to attempt to discover that.'

On the other hand, Lauren Bacall is of the opinion that while 'Peter is a very rare man, he always follows the needs of the moment. He is very sure of who he is and what he wants. He is always very focused on what he is doing, but he lets other people go only as far as he wants them to go.'

To Angela Fox, mother of the actors Edward and James,

Ustinov 'is an elusive gadfly; a genius life-enhancer. You could enjoy him for a little while and then he would be gone; on somewhere else to share and entertain.'

Another view, this time from the Austrian President, Kurt Waldheim, who was Secretary-General of the United Nations in New York when he and Ustinov first met, echoes some of the sentiments expressed by Sir Yehudi Menuhin. 'I have always had the highest regard for Peter Ustinov, both as an artiste and as an outstanding individual,' he says. 'His great artistic talent, combined with his wonderful humour have brought joy and happiness to innumerable people. It always seemed to be one of his main objectives to contribute to the alleviation of the suffering of the people in the world. His dedication to humanitarian issues merits great respect.'

Before I began looking into his life, I was aware of Peter Ustinov primarily as an actor and writer. I had little or no idea of the esteem in which he is held as an individual – quite literally from Moscow to Washington. His admirers include world leaders and statesmen, kings and princes, members of the international business community, relief agencies and, not least, people within the various denominations of that global fraternity we refer to collectively as 'the Arts'.

Respect for Peter Ustinov on the scale I encountered it, clearly stems from the recognition that he has not only been endowed with an especially fine mind – 'an intimidating intelligence' as one journalist put it – but that for much of his life he has found himself in a rare position to observe and comment on a wide range of socio-political issues, relevant not merely to any one nation, but to the world as a whole.

'There is a directness of vision in *his* view of the world,' says Frank Muir, distinguished British writer, television personality and no mean wit in his own right. 'It is an uncomplicated vision; not simplistic, but with all the rubbish pared away. He sees everything that ever happened and is going to happen in the world in the shape of an anecdote. He doesn't push it around too much, he doesn't pummel it into shape.

He just sort of picks it out, and that is a very, very rare gift.

'Of course, the problem with Peter – and it would be quite in order to say so – is that criticism of him just evaporates. I don't think you have got to try to drag him into line with other people. I don't think you have to make excuses for him. Here is an *extraordinary* man. It's as simple as that.'

If, as Frank Muir put it, criticism of Ustinov simply 'evaporates', it is for no other reason than that one's critical faculties are rarely ever engaged. This may be explained by the fact that Ustinov's personal 'angle' on the world is firmly rooted in a matrix of tolerance, common sense, generosity of spirit and, perhaps most important of all, a genuine respect for others. Couple with that a profound distaste for any form of bigotry, pettiness or prejudice, and it isn't difficult to appreciate why his observations contribute to what P. G. Wodehouse once called 'the Feast of Reason'.

'Everybody recognizes Peter Ustinov's integrity,' says the former British Prime Minister, Edward Heath. 'And, of course, somebody who has got a sense of humour is attractive and likeable, and there aren't all that many people in the world who have got his sense of humour. In addition, he brings a serious quality into his discussion of issues and events in which he takes part.

'I think what he is really saying is, "We are all human beings, we have all got that in common, so wouldn't it be rather more sensible if we recognized that and got on with each other." I think that is his "message" and it has been particularly valuable during the decade of the 80s, because while the super powers have been hurling abuse at each other, Ustinov has been pointing to the fact that there is such a thing as history and history explains a great deal. What we really ought to be doing is working on what we have got in common, rather than working on the differences.'

That there are no frontiers, whether cultural or geographical, to impede the frenetic nature of Peter Ustinov's life-style, is due as much to his own cosmopolitan inheritance as to his disinclination to recognize their existence. Before even attempting to understand the man, therefore, it is vital to become acquainted with his background. For while there is much about him to suggest a quintessentially English gentleman, Peter Ustinov is, in the strictest sense, English only by birth. Genetically he is anything but. In his own words, he is 'a mongrel whose pedigree is beyond repair'.

One

Peter Ustinov's genealogy is every bit as complex and bewildering as that of the Romanov tsars, whom certain of his forebears served – in offices both lowly and exalted – from the end of the eighteenth century to the start of the Bolshevik revolution in 1917. This was Imperial Russia at its zenith; a land of wild extremes, part western, part barbarian; rigidly structured and rampantly feudal.

Adrian Mikhailovich Ustinov, Peter's great-great-great-grandfather, had made his fortune from the salt mines of Siberia, at a time when, as Ustinov put it in his autobiography, *Dear Me*: 'It was quite in order for young Russians to scour Siberia in search of possibilities.

'This huge land,' he went on, 'was not merely a system of penal colonies as it appears in the western imagination, but a place of untold wealth, a place where fortunes could be made.' Chief beneficiary of Adrian Mikhailovich's own Siberian fortune was his son, Mikhail Adrianovich who, when he died in 1838, left 240,000 hectares of land on both sides of the Volga, in the province of Saratov, 6,000 serfs and sixteen churches, which he had built on an estate traversed by six miles of private railway.

Despite his evident rotundity – a legacy inherited by all his direct male descendants – this robust character, who was born in 1730, lived to the venerable age of 108. Widowed in his late seventies, Mikhail Adrianovich obviously regarded age as no barrier to marriage or procreation. At the age of seventy-eight, he took one Marfa Andreievna Vechniakova as his second wife and by her sired no fewer than five sons.

The youngest of them, Grigori Mikhailovich, who was Peter Ustinov's great-grandfather, died at the early age of fifty-four, having lived a life of 'rare dissipation and libertinage'. To quote Peter Ustinov further:

> [Grigori Mikhailovich] married a woman of exceptional beauty, Maria Ivanovna Panshina, who brought the village of Troitskoïe, near Moscow, as part of her dowry. By all accounts [Grigori] behaved disgracefully, setting her up in one [of his two St Petersburg] town houses while he caroused in the other with teenage peasant girls from his estate, only emerging occasionally from his bedroom to pick at a table covered with 'zakouski', pickled herrings, salted cucumbers, and the like, in order to renew his failing powers for further onslaughts on his victims, whom he preferred to enjoy two or three at a time.

Not altogether surprisingly, Grigori Mikhailovich's behaviour had a marked psychological effect on each of his three sons. One of them, Plato (otherwise Platon) Grigorievich – Peter Ustinov's grandfather – converted to the Protestant Lutheran faith, married a Fräulein Maria Metzler – daughter of the German pastor who had led him away from Russian Orthodoxy – and promptly had nothing more to do with his new bride when, on their wedding night, he discovered that she was not a virgin. Plato Grigorievich eventually divorced her, after she had had an affair with the gardener and had subsequently run away with a sea captain, but not before he himself had been banished from his homeland for an act of near treason.

Stubbornness – a trait of the Ustinovs – combined with the kind of fervour peculiar to many converts, religious or otherwise, had landed Plato Grigorievich in trouble with the state. As an officer in the Russian Imperial Army he swore his mandatory oath of allegiance to his sovereign, but refused to do the same to the Russian Orthodox Church or 'the true faith', as it was known. For his act of defiance – regarded as an outrage – the penalty was severe: exile to Siberia.

But for the timely intervention of one of his uncles, Plato Grigorievich would certainly have had his lands confiscated and his name erased from the memory of so-called polite society. His saviour was his late, unlamented father's elder brother, Mikhail Mikhailovich Ustinov. A diplomat, he had become Russian Ambassador to the Ottoman Court in what was then Constantinople. Returning to St Petersburg, probably on leave, Mikhail Mikhailovich engaged his friend and sovereign, Tsar Alexander II, in a tipsy evening at the card table. Choosing his moment well, he raised the subject of his erring nephew.

As a result of the Ambassador's appeal, Tsar Alexander commuted Plato Grigorievich's sentence. Instead of confiscation, he was to be allowed to sell off his estates in Saratov, and instead of permanent exile in Siberia, he was to spend the next forty years living abroad.

Heavily laden with a fortune in cash – none of which he ever deposited in a bank and all of which he washed in carbolic before handling, even then never touching it without first putting on gloves – Plato Grigorievich left Russia for the small teutonic realm of King Karl I of Württemberg. In Stuttgart, this musically inclined, highly-educated man, who could read and write several ancient languages, including Latin and Greek, Aramaic, Sanskrit, Arabic and Hebrew, was befriended by the King and his Russian-born consort, the former Grand Duchess Olga Nikolaievna, third daughter of Tsar Nicholas I and sister of Alexander II.

Adopting German nationality, Plato Grigorievich now became Baron Plato von Ustinov. Yet despite his ennoblement, his restoration to society and his friendship with King Karl and Queen Olga, Plato apparently decided that Württemberg wasn't for him and moved on; settling for a while in the South of France, in Switzerland and in Italy, where he built a house in Nervi, near Genoa. Some time later, religion inspired his nomadic spirit to move on yet again, this time to the Holy Land.

Palestine so appealed to him, historically as well as spiritually, that Plato bought a parcel of land in Jaffa. On it he built a house made entirely of white marble, complete with its own swimming-pool, around which he created a lush garden, full of exotic trees, palms, bushes, flowers and aromatic herbs, many of which he imported from botanical gardens in Europe. As this private oasis grew and flourished, so he introduced to it a variety of parrots and monkeys.

Locally Plato became known and respected by the Russian community, by the Benedictine monks, with whom he would argue theology or study ancient artefacts, inscriptions and medals, and by the large German contingent living in the port. Among them was the twenty-year-old Magdalena Hall, described as 'a handsome girl . . . with large almond-shaped, amber-brown eyes, beautifully chiselled features and a mass of healthy brown hair'.

So-named because she was born in a tent during the 1868 battle of Magdala – fought south of Tigré in Abyssinia, now Ethiopia, between a British expeditionary force and militia commanded by the lunatic King Theodore of Amhara – Magdalena was the daughter of a Swiss pastor from Rheinfelden near Basel, and his half-Portuguese, half-Abyssinian wife. In that part of Africa to spread 'The Word', Pastor Hall somehow found himself building a cannon for King Theodore. Once he had accomplished his task – and with the British at the door – the unfortunate man was chained to his own armament and, while he was being shaken senseless during the ensuing engagement, his poor wife was giving birth to their daughter in another corner of the battlefield.

Plato von Ustinov was already forty-eight when he befriended the Hall family in Turkish-ruled Jaffa in 1888. At some point that year, while they were visiting Venice together, Plato proposed to Magdalena on the roof of the Basilica di San Marco, overlooking the marble Piazza and Europe's most celebrated coffee house, Il Café Florian.

In December 1892, four years after she and Plato were married, and after Magdalena had had three or four miscarriages and was beginning to despair of ever having a child, she gave birth to a son, the eldest of their five children. He was christened Jonah, after the biblical character who spent three days inside a whale, until 'The Lord spake unto the fish, and it vomited out Jonah upon the dry land'. That land was Jaffa.

Jonah was born two-months prematurely, weighing little more than two pounds. As his young wife recovered, Plato kept their son alive by feeding him drops of milk from the inner tube of a fountain pen.

Jonah, who, not without reason, hated his one and only Christian name, was always a delicate child. After surviving the hazards of a premature birth, he nearly died of influenza not long afterwards and, in later years, suffered from severe attacks of malaria. Out of love and concern, Plato and Magdalena indulged the boy mercilessly. In their eyes he could do no wrong. Indeed, his mother once claimed to have suckled him on demand until he was over two years old.

At home in Jaffa – and in Jerusalem, where his parents had another house, their winter residence – Jonah, his brothers Peter (or 'Petja'), Platon and Gregory, and their only sister, Tabitha ('Bitha'), grew up in a cosmopolitan atmosphere, surrounded by Russian nannies, Arab servants and the French, English, German and Russian friends Plato and Magdalena often entertained. Life within the von Ustinov household, however, tended to be dominated at almost every level by 'der Baron'. In later life, perhaps as much from filial respect and affection as from his experience of others, Jonah once said that he was the most intelligent man he had ever known. Even so, there were aspects of Plato's personality and eccentric behaviour that he disliked or found embarrassing. His father's penchant for habitually dressing from head to toe in white, no matter the season, climate or geographical location, was one of them. So, too, was the sound of Plato's shrill, penetrating voice, and his apparent nonchalance and disregard for the sensibilities of others while strutting stark naked through the sand, whenever he took his family on picnics to the beach.

Yet if, as an adult, Jonah tried to avoid anything that reminded him of what he regarded as the worst in his father, he nevertheless followed Plato's example during his days as a student. Until he was old enough to be educated further afield, Jonah attended the local school for German children in Jaffa. Then, when he was about thirteen or so, he was sent to Düsseldorf, where his alert mind and academic achievements won him the accolade of best pupil. Later still, he went on to Grenoble University.

Not long after Jonah had completed his education the First World War broke out and, as German subjects, he and his brother Peter left for Germany. Their father, meanwhile, headed for London in the hope of selling his impressive collection of Roman, Greek and Egyptian antiquities, to replenish his dwindling finances. Having already sold his houses in Jaffa and Jerusalem, the latter to Emperor Haile Selassie, he had finally decided the time had come to make arrangements to return home to Russia. A German he might have become, if only on paper, but he had been born and would always remain a Russian. With the help of the Russian Ambassador in London, Plato Grigorievich petitioned Tsar Nicholas II, grandson of the Emperor who had sent him away more than half a century earlier.

In due course, the Tsar consented to the exile's return. Before sailing from England, however, Plato put his younger sons, Platon and Gregory, into a boarding school in Denmark Hill, south-east London. Having entrusted their well-being to a handful of very close friends, he and Magdalena and their daughter Tabitha were *en route* to St Petersburg, war and, ultimately, revolution.

At the start of the First World War, Jonah von Ustinov and his brother had enlisted in the German army, but soon transferred to the air force. This, to Jonah's mind, was much more as it should be. Instead of the rank trenches in the Ardennes, he and Peter, who both trained as officers, found themselves billeted in private houses, even châteaux, in towns where there always seemed to be enough pretty girls around to provide two confident young men with some of life's more earthly pleasures.

Jonah's enjoyment of the war, made exhilarating by both the dangers of combat in the air and the camaraderie of the officers' mess, was suddenly shattered one day in July 1917. On the morning of Friday the thirteenth, Jonah awoke to find his brother sitting by his bed. It was Peter's turn to fly over allied lines near Ypres to drop the mail-bag from British prisoners-of-war, and he had just looked in to say goodbye. Jonah wished him luck and urged him to hurry back. Peter replied that, since he felt very tired that day, he intended to fall back into bed once he returned and 'sleep and sleep and sleep'. With the words, 'I could sleep for ever', Peter left his brother's room. Later that morning, Jonah led the search party that found Peter's body lying on a wing of his aircraft in no man's land. He had been shot down.

In coping with his grief, Jonah presented a calm, detached face to the world. Already a popular figure in the officers' mess, Jonah's stoic handling of a bereavement which hit him harder than any he would experience subsequently, earned him yet greater support.

As an airman, he found himself mentioned in dispatches and decorated, though as he was to say many years later: 'I don't know why. I'm sure that I never killed anybody or bombed anything with success. Besides, my main job was to take photographs and report on anything unusual I noticed behind enemy lines.'

During the last year of the war, Jonah became a staff officer with special responsibility for interviewing prisoners-of-war. But when Germany got caught up in the ferment of revolution, he sought out influential friends in Berlin in the hope of finding a job. Several offers came his way, but the post he accepted took him to Amsterdam as a representative of the prestigious German news agency, the Wolff Büro. Part of his work involved reading all the Dutch and British newspapers, picking out the most important stories and telephoning them through to the head office in Berlin.

In April 1920 Jonah, who had lost touch with his parents and sister in St Petersburg with the start of the Russian Revolution three years earlier, now wanted to discover their whereabouts in person. With the help of Germany's Ambassador in the Hague and an official in the Foreign Office in Berlin, Jonah managed to travel to Russia aboard a boat full of prisoners-of-war who were about to be repatriated. His luck held when, upon his arrival in St Petersburg, by now renamed Petrograd, he found the house in which Plato, Magdalena and Bitha had shared a flat from the time of their return to Russia six years before.

Good news stopped at the threshold of that house near the Academy of Arts on the Vassilievsky Ostrov (Basil's Island), however, and any hope Jonah may have had of an immediate reunion with his family was dashed when he learned that his father had died of dysentery in 1919, and that his mother and sister were now living in Pskov, about 160 miles from Petrograd, where Tabitha had found work at the local post office.

Although the pandemonium caused by the disintegration of imperialism had subsided, fear and suspicion continued to stalk 'the land of terror'. As an outsider, Jonah, though cautious, remained largely unaffected by all that. Even at the *Tcheka*, headquarters of the dreaded secret police, from where he needed to obtain a travel permit if he was to get to Pskov, Jonah succeeded in charming one of the commissars, who not only kept guns and hand-grenades in his desk drawer, but bottles of French perfume to which he was rather partial. Questions were asked, endless forms were filled in and, as if on probation, Jonah was told that he would be expected to report back to the *Tcheka* from time to time. Despite all that, the commissar produced the required travel documents and rail tickets, allowing him to make a brief visit to his overwhelmed, if anxious, relations.

While in Petrograd (present-day Leningrad), Jonah stayed with a family friend, whose work for the Provisional Government allowed him the services of a secretary, a young woman called Valeria Poleschouk. Through her, Jonah met Nadezhda Benois, or 'Nadia', as she was better known. Described by *The Times* at the end of her life as an 'irresistibly attractive personality; handsome, impulsive, generous, witty and gay, with a deep voice and a great laugh that warmed the heart', Nadia was the seventh and youngest child of Professor Louis ('Leontij') Benois and his wife, Marie Alexandrovna Saponjnikov.

To begin with, Nadia and Jonah saw each other only in the company of friends such as Valeria Poleschouk or Nadia's cousin, Nicholas Benois. But in June 1920, as their whirlwind, fourteen-day courtship gathered momentum, they snatched every possible chance they could to be alone together. On the arm of her dark-haired suitor, whom she described as 'rather short but broad-shouldered . . . his head slightly too large for his height, with a very wide well-formed forehead . . . and almond-shaped slightly protruding large green eyes', Nadia strolled along the banks of the River Neva, flowing between the palaces and mansions of the now-vanished aristocracy. She took him to the homes of some of her friends, to concerts and dances at The House of Arts, introduced him to three of her uncles and, on one occasion, took him to the magnificent Hermitage Museum, so-named by Catherine the Great and once, since it formed part of the Winter Palace, official residence of the tsars, seen by none but the most privileged visitors.

Now, by order of the Council of People's Commissars – bearing in mind Lenin's philosophy that, 'the construction of a socialist society cannot be carried out without utilizing the cultural values accumulated by humanity throughout its history' – the Hermitage was open to all comers. Today the museum contains some 3 million treasures. Over half a century ago the collection would have been considerably smaller. But even then it contained one painting in particular that Nadia wanted Jonah to see – *The Benois Madonna* by Leonardo da Vinci.

This superb painting of a young and playful Madonna holding out a stem of small pink flowers – the petals of which symbolize the Crucifixion – to her well-rounded child, had been in Nadia's family from about the beginning of the nineteenth century, when it had been sold to one of her Saponjnikov forebears by an itinerant group of Italian tumblers and mountebanks who, it is thought, kept it in reserve as a kind of bargaining-counter, without realizing its identity or value.

Shortly after their visit to the Hermitage, Nadia and Jonah were invited by Valeria Poleschouk to a choral concert in a local church. That day, as they sat listening to the music, Jonah gave Nadia a heavy silver ring containing a flat black stone on which was engraved the head of an Egyptian princess. This was Nadia's engagement ring. In return she gave him a new name. At first she called him 'Klopik', which means 'Little Bug'. Later on he became 'Klop' – 'Big Bug' – the name by which he was known for the rest of his life.

TWO

Nadia Benois was a twenty-three-year-old art student when she and Klop first met. Of French and Italian descent, her ancestry – which still confuses members of her family to this day – is a convoluted network of humble peasant folk on the one hand and opera singers, composers, painters, sculptors, theatrical designers and any number of architects, on the other.

The family's earliest known ancestor, François Benois, who was born in about 1660, was a wine producer in Sezanne, a small town in the Champagne region of France. His son Denis, an ordinary labourer, married Marie Brochot, a washerwoman from Coulommiers in Brie, and had a son named Nicolas Denis who, by virtue of the fact that he became a schoolteacher in the small Brie village of St Ouen-sur-Morin, clearly aspired to better things. In turn his son Nicolas, who married a certain Marie Catherine Lorin, daughter of a locksmith from the town of Rebais, followed his father's example by becoming a schoolteacher, while *his* son Louis-Jules (1770–1822) – who would also appear to have been known as Jules-César – broke away into the mysteries of culinary art and, in the fullness of time, founded the Russian branch of the Benois family.

At the start of his career, Louis-Jules became pastrycook to Anne Léon, Duke of Montmorency, who – to escape the ravages of the French Revolution – fled first to the Netherlands and then to St Petersburg, taking Louis-Jules with him. Once the cries of the mob and the sound of the tumbrils carrying his kind to the guillotine had faded away, the duke returned to France. His pastrycook, however, having become *chef de cuisine* to the Dutch Legation, decided to stay put in the Russian capital and before long found himself engaged as *Maître de Bouche* to Tsar Paul I, son of Catherine the Great.

Of this particular ancestor's promotion, Peter Ustinov observed:

> In case it be thought that he was extremely fortunate to find such exalted employment so soon, it is only fair to point out that to be '*Maître de Bouche*' to Paul I was a little like being accredited food-taster to Nero. Both emperors spent their lives hovering on the edge of lunacy, yet were sane enough to be in constant fear of assassination, a fate which attended them both . . .
>
> Any native Russian would probably rather have walked to Vladivostok on foot than accept the job of teasing the palate of such a degenerate monarch, and it took an able and resourceful immigrant with no prior knowledge of the problems to make a success of such employment.

Louis-Jules not only made a success of his precarious situation, but survived the moods of his capricious employer to marry Fraülein Concordia Groppe, midwife to the Tsarina Marie Feodorovna. Of the seventeen children Concordia bore her husband, one son, Nicholas Benois (1813–99), found distinction as a court architect. Godson of Paul I's empress, protégé of Konstantin Ton, who built the Great Kremlin Palace in Moscow, friend of Tsar Nicholas I, and of such literary and artistic luminaries as Gogol and Sternberg, architect of two graceful pavilions in the grounds of the magnificent palace of Peterhof, now known as Petrodvorets, on the Gulf of Finland, and for some years head of the St Petersburg City Council's Technical Department, Nicholas Benois enhanced the standing of his family still further, when he married Camilla Cavos.

Daughter of the architect Albert Cavos – who not only won fame for building the Imperial Maryinsky Theatre, now the Kirov, in St Petersburg, but also for rebuilding the Bolshoi in Moscow after it had been destroyed by fire – Camilla was also the granddaughter of the Italian composer Catterino Cavos and his wife, the opera singer Camilla Baglioni. Born in Venice, Catterino Cavos was twenty-three when he left for St Petersburg in 1798. That year he became the latest – as well as the last – Italian Director of the Imperial Theatres. In Russia he threw himself energetically into every aspect of his work, so much so that it was he who played the dominant part in the development of Russian operatic life during the early decades of the nineteenth century. *Kapellmeister* of the Italian company between 1828 and 1831 and of the German and Russian companies from 1832 to 1840, Catterino's main influence on the musical life of his adopted country was undoubtedly as a composer.

After Tsar Paul I – whom we have already encountered as the employer of Louis-Jules Benois – banned Italian opera, Cavos turned his pen effortlessly to composing in Russian. *The Invisible Prince* (1805), *Ilya Bogatyr* (1807), *The Cossack Poet* (1812), *Dobrynya Nikitich* (1818) and *The Firebird* (1823), were all inspired by subjects close to the Russian heart. Yet of all his thematic works, *Ivan Susanin*, which he composed in 1815, is recognized as his most famous. When he died in May 1840, at the age of sixty-five, Cavos was buried in Russia's equivalent of Poets' Corner.

Well over a century later, his great-great-great-grandson, Peter Ustinov, was visiting Leningrad.

> I discovered Cavos' tomb in the Lavra . . . No member of my family had ever realized it was there, demure and undemonstrative among the tombstones of his peers, Tchaikovsky, Glinka, Borodin, Mussorgsky, to say nothing of the great writers and artists . . . In this quiet and damp place, Cavos is remembered by a simple black marble stone, setting off the restrained flamboyance of golden letters. Of all the epitaphs in this Slavonic Valhalla of the arts, that on Cavos' tomb is the only one defiantly written in the Roman alphabet; the language, Latin.

Catterino Cavos had been dead for ten years when his granddaughter Camilla presented Nicholas Benois with the first of their six children, five of whom survived into adulthood. The youngest surviving child, Alexandre (1870–1960), known to his friends as 'Shoura', was greatly beloved of both Peter Ustinov (his great-nephew) and his mother. He was indisputably the most famous member of the Benois dynasty. Friend and artistic mentor of Serge Diaghilev, designer for the Ballets Russes, art critic, painter, historian, author and one-time curator of the Hermitage, Alexandre, in the words of the noted writer and ballet critic, Richard Buckle, stood 'for romantic erudition, for the influence of the French eighteenth century on [Peter the Great's] capital, and for the Russian *fin de siècle* which was also a *renaissance*'.

With the financial backing of the Princess Tenisheva, Alexandre Benois, 'A gentle, studious, amusing man, devoted to all forms of art and applied art', was the animator of a journal called *Mir Isskustva* (The World of Art). In collaboration with Léon Bakst and Serge Diaghilev, whom he had met and befriended in 1890, Alexandre Benois produced *Mir Isskustva* as a showcase for the entire spectrum of Russian Art based on a belief that 'Russia was on the threshold of a Silver Age and that she had every right to be considered an equal partner in the European cultural mainstream'. *Mir Isskustva* was by no means the only vehicle of collaboration between Benois and Diaghilev.

For the Ballets Russes, of which he became Artistic Director, Alexandre designed five ballets. Among them he was responsible for the book, stage settings and costumes for *Le Pavillon d'Armide*, which Anna Pavlova and the young Nijinsky danced at the Maryinsky Theatre in 1907, and for the libretto, settings and costumes for *Petrouchka*. Together with the Muscovite painter, Golovin, Benois was also responsible for the sets and costumes for Diaghilev's production of Mussorgsky's *Boris Godunov*, which was presented at the Paris Opera in 1908.

Despite his overall gentleness, Benois' temperament was still that of an artist, which meant that he was not above fits of temper, sulks or even outbursts of passion. Indeed, Diaghilev himself was sometimes deliberately culpable for some of Alexandre's rages. On one occasion, for example, they are known to have argued furiously when Léon Bakst and not Benois was credited for the libretto of *The Firebird*, and another time Alexandre was so incensed when he discovered that Diaghilev had not included him in travel arrangements for visits by the Ballets Russes to Berlin and Paris, that he put his fist through a window pane and severed an artery.

Uncle of the composer Alexandre Tcherepnin, of the painter Eugène Lanceray, and of the Soviet film director, Andrei Frolov, Alexandre Benois was also a writer and art historian of considerable distinction. He catalogued the Alexander III Museum of Russian pictures in the Mikhailovsky Palace, for instance, wrote a book on *The Russian School of Painting* and, in 1902, prepared a lavishly illustrated volume about Tsarskoye Selo, now known as Pushkin, a favourite residence of the last of the Russian tsars.

In January 1960, three or four weeks before his death in Paris on 9 February at the age of ninety, and not so very long after he had visited London for Anton Dolin's Festival Ballet production of *The Nutcracker* – for which he had designed new sets and costumes – Benois' last book was published in Great Britain. Translated from the French by Baroness (Moura) Budberg, a family friend, this volume was the final part of Alexandre's own memoirs. In it he introduces his elder brothers Albert and Louis (Leontij), both of whom, like their father before them, became architects.

> Our father had bestowed upon all three of us . . . a gift for painting and a love for art, but Leontij, I believe, was the most talented of us. Albert [a leading member of the Russian watercolour school] was a great virtuoso as far as technique was concerned, but his nimbleness of hand was not the basic trait in his art, whereas with Leontij the dexterity was something inborn and fundamental. The fact that this virtuoso of pencil and brush chose architecture as his field was in a way the result of that characteristic.
>
> Leontij's career . . . started with an exceptional triumph. He finished at the Academy of Arts [in St Petersburg] one year before the appointed time, and received the large gold medal out of turn. The same distinction had been won by our father fifty years before, but these were rare occasions in the life of the Academy.

Prone to corpulence, which earned him the nickname 'Gros-gros', Professor Louis Benois – Peter Ustinov's maternal grand-father – began his public career as an architect with a faintly macabre commission – the result of one of the most chilling incidents in the history of the last years of the Romanovs. During his reign, there had been no fewer than seven attempts on the life of Tsar Alexander II, the monarch who had repealed the harsh sentence of Siberian exile originally imposed on Peter Ustinov's paternal grandfather, Plato Grigorievich. He had a reputation for being the most liberal of Russia's nineteenth-century autocrats, and was known to history as the 'Tsar-Liberator' for freeing the serfs.

Alexander II was driving through the streets of St Peters-burg on 13 March 1881, when a bomb was thrown beneath his carriage. In the blast, horses were maimed and the Tsar's equerries and members of his Cossack escort were wounded. Amazingly, Alexander II emerged from the wrecked equipage unharmed. But just as he was asking about the would-be assassin, who had been caught and was now under arrest, a second anarchist ran up and, with the words 'It is too early to thank God', hurled another bomb which landed directly between the Tsar's feet. In this explosion one of Alexander II's legs was blown off, his stomach torn open, one eye ripped out and the rest of his face hideously mutilated. *Still* conscious, the Tsar whispered that he wanted to be taken home to the Winter Palace nearby. There, in the presence of his son, who was about to become Tsar Alexander III, his daughter-in-law 'Minny' (otherwise Marie Feodorovna) and his grandson, who in turn became Russia's last emperor, Nicholas II, the dis-membered Tsar died.

It was on the site of that murderous attack that Louis Benois was asked to build a temporary wooden chapel, about which his brother Alexandre wrote:

> . . . modest though it was, [it] had an exception-ally graceful quality and earned general approval. A year later Leontij took part in the competition to design the church which was to be erected on the same spot. His plan, inspired by the work [of Bartolomeo Francesco Rastrelli, the Italian architect

who built a number of palaces in and around St Petersburg, among them the Winter Palace and the Great Catherine Palace at Tsarskoye Selo] was very beautiful and striking and was probably the best thing he ever produced.

In the event, Louis Benois' design for the permanent 'Church of Blood' was not chosen. The commission went instead to another architect who created a 'pathetic imitation of the Church of St Basil in Moscow . . . a real blot on the general Petersburg landscape'.

Though never one of Russia's 'great' architects – his designs, said his younger brother, suffered from 'a casual quality' – Leontij Benois went on to create several commercial buildings in St Petersburg itself, the Russian Church in Darmstadt, West Germany, and the 'majestic and luxurious' Cathedral in Warsaw, which was later demolished when Poland became independent.

Whatever his shortcomings in the field of architecture, Benois was always held in the highest esteem by all who knew him, not least by Nicholas II's uncle, the Grand Duke Vladimir, and his German-born wife, the Grand Duchess Marie Pavlovna who, from within the ranks of the imperial family, were undisputed champions of the Arts.

As a person, Louis Benois was an affectionate and warm-hearted man, and it is worth quoting his brother's description of him at some length, not only because it tells us about Leontij, but because Alexandre Benois might just as easily have been writing about Peter Ustinov, in whom so many of his grandfather's characteristics are quite clearly reflected.

Louis had a quiet, reasonable nature, neither violent not rebellious, yet at the same time ardent. He was a wonderfully humane person, kind and honest, a man of good will in the fullest sense, and he was loved and admired by everybody . . . . He was incapable of hypocrisy, guile or malice, and although he was sometimes impulsive and hot-tempered . . . his emotional outbursts were spontaneous and he would calm down as quickly as he had flared up . . . . He was fiercely opposed to any form of injustice and loathed any kind of falsehood, and throughout his whole life his capacity to feel indignation never diminished, whether over world events, specific aspects of Russian life which he considered disgraceful, or the idiocies of government.

During the last fifteen or sixteen years of his life, Louis Benois became closely associated with the Academy of Arts in St Petersburg when he was appointed its principal or rector. Even after the Bolsheviks abolished the actual office he held, Benois continued with his professorship, much to the satisfaction of his students, among whom his popularity never wavered despite the destruction of a social order with which he had been so closely identified. Indeed, no greater tribute could have been paid to Professor Benois – either by his students or, even more remarkably, by the new regime – than the state funeral he was accorded at his death in 1928. As his body lay in the Academy's round Conference Hall and Mozart's *Requiem* was sung, students mounted a vigil beside the coffin and, on the day of the funeral, carried it to the Novodievichy Cemetery for interment.

By the summer of 1920, Louis Benois and his wife, 'Masha', who had been married since about 1880 and had raised a family of seven children, one of whom, a son named Alexandre, had been killed during the revolution, were among the last to know that their youngest child, Nadia, planned to marry. She and Klop Ustinov had been introduced to one another on 1 June 1920 and had become engaged exactly two weeks later. Nadia's reticence at breaking the news to her parents was born out of concern that it should not upset them. After all, she wasn't only about to commit herself to a man she hardly knew, but by marrying him, she would also have to leave her family and her homeland behind in order to accompany her husband to a new and unfamiliar life in the West.

It seems unlikely that Louis and Masha had no idea of their daughter's intentions, but towards the end of June Nadia plucked up the courage to tell first her mother and then her father that she and Klop had become engaged. In her own memoirs, *Klop and the Ustinov Family*, Nadia recalled that her fiancé was captivated by her father 'and filled with respect for him'. She went on:

> Towards my mother he remained slightly on the defensive until she made a charming gesture. Nothing had been said about our engagement. After tea I took Klop to my room. A little later my mother joined us, carrying a pretty little samovar. 'There,' she said, placing it on a table, 'this samovar was given to me by my mother when Nadia's father and I got married . . . I give it to you now with my blessing and hope that you will be as happy as my husband and I have been'.

While Nadia and her family set about making arrangements for the wedding, Klop, who had heard that the new bureaucracy in Moscow had become suspicious of his presence in Petrograd, continued to pay regular visits to his acquaintances at the *Tcheka*, this time in the hope of obtaining an exit visa. To avoid alerting Nadia to all the potential dangers of his situation, Klop carried on just as he had when he first arrived in Russia in search of his family. But now his breezy, confident air belied his growing concern at trying to find some way out before Moscow caught up with him.

About a month after he and Nadia were married, on 17 July at St Catherine's Protestant Church on Basil's Island, an escape route presented itself and, with his wife beside him, Klop finally left Russia using the same guise that had originally gained him entry: that of a prisoner of war – this time a German one – on his way home.

For Klop and Nadia, as for the rest of their fellow travellers – genuine prisoners of war, some with Russian wives – the journey out of Russia was a long ordeal of uncomfortable trains, jam-packed with cargo, both animate and inanimate, transit camps and hotel rooms. At length, the newly-married Ustinovs arrived in Berlin, where they put up for a week or so, and from where they travelled on to Amsterdam. There, of course, Klop not only had his job at the Wolff Büro, but a small flatlet in which he and Nadia lived until Klop's transfer to the agency's London office was finalized and a slightly more settled future lay before them.

THREE

By the time Nadia Benois Ustinov arrived in smog-bound London three days before Christmas, she was already five months pregnant. Wrapped up in a heavy fur coat and feeling distinctly apprehensive about living in a city plagued by fog and 'unadulterated filth', Nadia managed to find her way through inhospitable streets to join Klop, who had travelled on ahead, at their temporary lodgings in Heathcote Street near Holborn. Situated off Gray's Inn Road, a bustling major thoroughfare, and only a few minutes away from not one but two railway stations, King's Cross and St Pancras, Nadia's arrival in so unprepossessing a part of the capital was scarcely the most auspicious of introductions to her new country – and she realized it.

Three months later, however, she and Klop deserted their grimy Victorian surroundings for a larger and sunnier flat on the top floor of a house in north London. It was from there that Nadia was admitted to the Adelaide Road Nursing Home in Swiss Cottage where, at about 11 a.m. on 16 April 1921, she gave birth to her only son.

Due to the unwelcomed administration of chloroform, Nadia remembered nothing about Peter's nativity, save for a feeling of resentment that she 'had been deprived from living through the moment I had been awaiting with so much longing'. Born under the sign of Aries, the premier sign of the Zodiac, with Cancer in the ascendant and the Moon in Leo – planetary aspects which I am told indicated the 'dynamic' path his life was to follow – Peter was every inch the prodigy his mother had expected him to be. In fact, so convinced was she of his distinguished future that, over thirty years later, she told the actor Robin Bailey, 'I knew before he was born that he was a genius'.

Peter Ustinov's earliest act, at no more than just a few hours old, tended to indicate physical strength rather than mental agility. For when the nurse who was bathing him turned him over to wash his back, an amazed Nadia watched her son 'lifting up his head, as though wanting to inspect the room'. This was, by all accounts, a regular occurrence, invariably accompanied by his nurse's trilling refrain: 'He is a very strong little chap, aren't you my precious? Yes, you are, my little Blessing.'

'In case of general incredulity,' Peter responded more than fifty years later, 'I must say that I have always benefited from an unusually powerful neck.' This was clearly just as well, especially from the point of view of everyone who looked after this spherically-shaped, almost twelve-pound baby, for only when he raised his head to look around was it possible – in his own words – 'to see whether I was the right way up or not'.

Three months later, on his parents' first wedding anniversary, Peter, who had been conceived in Leningrad and, in embryonic form, had arrived in England 'disguised as a piece of overweight luggage', was christened in Schwäbisch Gmünd, 'a beautiful old town a few kilometres east of Stuttgart', in what had been the tiny kingdom of Württemberg, until it became part of a united Germany in 1871.

The reason for travelling so far for so brief a ceremony was Klop's elderly mother, Magdalena von Ustinov, who had been allowed to leave Pskov after her son had managed to arrange the necessary documentation. She eventually wound up in Cairo, where she now lived. Daughter of the Swiss pastor who became almost fatally entangled with the mad king of Amhara, Magdalena had been raised on Bible stories, most of which, even in old age, seemed capable of touching her heart and reducing her quite effortlessly to tears. When she learned of her grandson's birth, Magdalena agitated for the christening to take place in Cairo. This was partly because she wanted him to embark on life in a suitably biblical manner, by being blessed with water from the Jordan, which she intended to provide.

On the grounds that he could not afford the journey, Klop dissuaded his mother from pursuing the idea of a christening in Cairo and instead suggested a somewhat unequal compromise. 'Since my grandmother's knowledge of geography was very hazy,' says Peter, 'Klop alleged that Schwäbisch Gmünd was half-way between London and Cairo.' The old lady believed him and it was therefore arranged that the family would rendezvous there.

In due course, Magdalena, accompanied by her daughter Bitha, her unmarried sisters, Christina and Augusta, and her two younger sons, Platon and Gregory, known as 'Tonchick' and 'Grisha', arrived at the Sanatorium Schönblick, which Nadia disdainfully described as a 'huge dull building on top of a mountain . . . surrounded by dark pine forests and filled with old women in retirement and Protestant parsons'. Be that as it may, the christening service was celebrated in the chapel of the sanatorium itself, where, as recently as 1989, Peter was shown a register in which the event has been recorded.

At the appointed hour on 17 July 1921, the Ustinov christening party duly gathered around the font, with Magdalena well to the fore. Determined that at least part of her original plan should be realized, she had brought with her an old earthenware hot-water bottle containing water from the River Jordan which, Peter says, 'she must have waded into with her skirts raised; though every time I have crossed the Jordan, it has been no bigger than an overflowed bath – a ridiculous little trickle'. Alas, even now the fates conspired against the hapless Magdalena for, as Peter describes, 'when she handed over her precious burden to the officiating minister – a geriatric parson with the shakes – 'he dropped the confounded hot-water bottle which burst into a million pieces and the water from the Jordan – and all its amoeba – flowed freely on to the floor and disappeared into the cracks of the mosaic. My grandmother, who was a very, very lachrymose person and wept at the slightest sign of trouble, would have wept a great deal at this and I could really have been christened in her tears.'

He was christened instead with local – albeit duly sanctified – water, receiving the names 'Petrus Alexandrus', or, more simply, Peter Alexander. During a visit to the Sanatorium Schönblick in September 1989, Peter not only saw his name inscribed in its register, but also discovered that at his christening he was watched over by no fewer than eight godmothers, though only one godfather – his uncle Tonchick.

'My father was a big flirt, as you know,' says Peter, 'and I understood why I had eight godmothers. I was used as some sort of pawn.' Klop's flirtations, not all of them entirely futile, were never concealed from his wife. Indeed, one of Peter's bevy of godmothers, who luxuriated in the name Trudl Weiffenbach, was mentioned in Nadia's memoirs. She wrote:

> Trudl was a girl Klop had met in Munich during the war. 'You see,' he explained to me, 'Trudl was very fond of me, but she was much too young at the time and I was more involved with her eldest sister. However, Trudl hoped that one day I would marry her. Well . . . it is too late now and as she can't be the mother of my child the least I can do is to ask her to be its godmother.'

Life in Britain at the start of the twenties was a distillation of pathos and hardship, optimism and pleasure-seeking. In January 1921 unemployment stood at almost 100,000. By the height of summer it had risen to 2.2 million, with roughly half that number claiming poor relief. In April the miners' strike had led to the imposition of a State of Emergency, coal-rationing and angry voices raised in protest against 'demoralization'.

The other side of the coin presented a very different picture. The rich indulged in pre-war extravagance, high-society's 'Bright Young Things' led syncopated lives amid bright lights, night-clubs and parties, while the *soi-disant* dabbled their toes in pools of opportunism. Somewhere in between fell those – neither rich nor desperately poor – who managed to live in reasonably comfortable circumstances. Nadia and Klop slotted into this category.

During their first three or four years in London, the Ustinovs – though not through choice – led insular lives; Klop attending to his work, much of it from home, and Nadia taking care of baby Peter. When they entertained, as Klop liked to do, their guests were invariably the handful of fellow Russians and Germans they had befriended since their arrival. This enforced isolation, which both Klop and Nadia felt very keenly, was due entirely to the xenophobic stance adopted by the nation Klop, in particular, so admired. To their English neighbours the Ustinovs were 'enemy aliens' and as such were regarded with suspicion. As time passed and attitudes began to thaw, so Klop and Nadia were gradually accepted into the community and made to feel at home. Their circle of friends became wider, more diverse and more colourful, their life-style became more bohemian and they began to entertain on a much larger scale – all of which appealed to Klop's hedonistic instincts. In short, life became infinitely more agreeable and attractive.

From furnished accommodation in north London which, because of their 'alien' status, had been difficult enough to find in 1921, Nadia and Klop were now able to move to a bigger, and this time empty, flat in Carlisle Mansions on the border between Pimlico and Chelsea, near Sloane Square. This they were able to arrange with furniture of their own choice, some of it bought on hire-purchase from Harrods, and a Bechstein grand piano which Klop, much to the delight of the entertainer in him, had been able to acquire from some friends of his brother-in-law. They also had a portable gramophone and it was probably from about this time that Peter can remember watching his parents dance to a recording of the popular song *Tea for Two*.

Having yielded to the blandishments of her forceful husband, Nadia had by now taken her first tentative steps towards what was to prove a successful career as a painter and theatrical designer. In the early days, though, Klop pushed her too hard and, despite protests that she was far from ready, bullied her into exhibiting paintings which she personally felt were unworthy of public display. She was right and the pictures were returned.

By 1929, Nadia's confidence had grown considerably and that year the first of her many one-woman shows was mounted at Tooth's Gallery. During one such exhibition, Augustus John viewed Nadia's paintings and afterwards sent her a note in which he expressed his admiration for her work. He signed it, 'Très belle artiste je vous salue!' The following year, the Manchester Art Gallery bought one of Nadia's pictures and, before long, so did both the Tate Gallery and the Carnegie Institute.

Like her famous uncle, Alexandre Benois, Nadia also received invitations to design for the ballet, as well as the theatre. For the Ballet Rambert her work included The Descent of Hebe, Bonnet Over the Windmill, Lady into Fox and Dark Elegies. But perhaps the most illustrious moment of her career came in March 1939 when, in honour of the state visit of President Lebrun of France, Nadia was invited to design the sets and costumes for Acts I and III of the Sadler's Wells' production of The Sleeping Princess. Presented at the Royal Opera House, Covent Garden, the interior of which had been decorated for the occasion by Rex Whistler, the sumptuous gala evening was held in the presence of President and Madame Lebrun, their hosts, King George VI and Queen Elizabeth, and the king's mother, Queen Mary.

Proud though he was of Nadia's paintings, her accomplishments and the praise she received through the years, Klop's Svengali-ish influence over her work was something that often irritated Peter. 'He had very definite ideas of how her paintings should look,' he says today. 'For instance, he would say something like, "Cézanne would have had that house blue", and she would say, "I'm not Cézanne". "Well," he would reply, "if you don't want to learn . . . " It was that sort of thing. Once she destroyed a picture that I thought was wonderful and when I asked "Why did you do that?" she said, "Well, he didn't like it".'

Klop's dogmatic influence extended well beyond his attempts to dominate Nadia's art. Like his father, he was an autocrat who not only wanted to rule his household, but to control the lives of his wife and son as well. In a tiny family unit of only three, this not unnaturally created enormous difficulties and added immeasurably to Nadia's burden. For while she worked quietly but assiduously to maintain her own identity she had, perforce, to tread the precarious path of wife and mother; coping with Klop's volatility, his mercurial and sometimes wicked temper, listening with admirable forbearance to his tales of amorous adventures and, as their son grew up, trying to keep what Peter called 'a fragile peace in the household'.

'The family rows were far too frequent,' he once wrote, 'and were obviously exacerbated as I grew older and developed a mind of my own, and a kind of recklessness in expressing it.'

For Peter, the turning point in his relationship with his father came with Nadia's destruction of the painting he had so much admired.

> My fury knew no bounds. I surprised both my parents by the violence of my sentiments, and for the only time in my life had them both shouting at me. I banged the door of my room and locked myself in . . . Once inside, I felt a new strength I had never experienced before. It was the premature rage of an adult . . . . For the first time, or so it seemed to me, I had spoken from a platform of my own . . . . From then on, I became calculatedly cold, deliberately impervious to my father's sarcasms and even to my mother's appeals for good sense. The atmosphere at home was no longer changeable, but glowering and intense. . . . That awful day was a date in my calendar. I had become myself, to myself.

At that moment of self-discovery, Peter was in his very early teens, a point at which a child's independence first begins to awaken. Yet, in his fury, the schoolboy Ustinov's awakening went further than most, for he was suddenly and unexpectedly introduced to his inner-self, to the individual who would become the individualist we know today. At that moment, Peter began to grow up, his father's omnipotence to recede.

To the outside world, as to his wide and often brilliant circle of friends and acquaintances, Klop was perceived in a different, rather more superficial light. In a television interview during the late 1950s, for example, Dame Rebecca West said that Harold Macmillan was 'a most wonderful and brilliant raconteur, the best I've ever met, except Peter Ustinov's father'. As a host, conversationalist, wit and entertainer, Klop was in his element. 'He always said it's a great gift to make people laugh, and that should be enough,' Peter once told me. 'As a matter of fact, he thought superficiality was one of the blessings of life. He was absolutely hedonistic in that respect. In ancient Greece he'd have been a philosopher of some kind. He lived a slightly preposterous life, but lived it well.'

In his every day guise as a journalist and subsequently press attaché at the German Embassy in London, a post he accepted in the mid-1920s, Klop was no less intelligent, urbane, amusing or quick-witted. It was only behind closed doors that the flaws were revealed or, as Peter himself put it, ' . . . only as a father that he was sometimes difficult to stomach, and, by the same token, as a husband'.

There can be little doubt that Nadia Benois put up with a great deal of unnecessary pain in her frequently difficult marriage to a man who was once described in print as 'a bigot and a snob'. Equally, there can be little doubt that, despite everything, she never stopped loving him. In the introduction to his mother's memoirs, published in 1973 two years before her death, Peter Ustinov wrote:

> From my position of vantage, which was also frequently a position of disadvantage, I cannot imagine any other woman as a life partner for my father. She learned neither to take him too seriously, nor too lightly. She bent with the wind, but never broke. She never seemed anywhere near breaking. She [was] basically of a much tougher fibre than he ever was, and in her heart I think she knew it, and so perhaps did he.

Peter enjoyed an especially happy relationship with his mother. To him, Nadia was: 'a remarkable woman, a sister, an aunt, sometimes a daughter, always a mother, and yet without a trace of that saccharine possessiveness which traditionally marks a certain aspect of maternity.'

As a child, and an only child at that, Peter was what his mother called 'an old soul . . . far wiser than many an adult'. Early on it was clear that he possessed a finely tuned ear for accents, languages and sounds of all kinds, most of which he reproduced with an accuracy that surprised and amused his parents. Nadia, for instance, enjoyed telling the story of a visit she, Klop and their three-year-old son, paid to Scheveningen on the North-Sea coast of Holland, not far from the Hague. Peter was playing in the sand when a little Dutch boy ran up to him and started talking very quickly in Dutch.

> Peter looked a bit bewildered at first and then, possibly thinking it was a kind of new game . . . answered in a perfectly Dutch-sounding cascade of words. The boy was perplexed. It was Dutch all right but he could not understand it. Nonplussed, he turned on his heels and ran away as fast as he could. Peter followed him with a surprised gaze, then hearing us laughing, came running towards us to join in the fun.

On another occasion, over tea at the German Embassy, Peter asked the ambassador's wife if she was from Hamburg, where his parents' cook came from. When she said that that was so, he asked if they could talk in German, 'because, you know, you speak rotten English'.

At home, mimicry and impersonations were evidently not the sole preserve of Klop Ustinov himself. Peter's entertainment value was clearly highly prized, though not by his nanny when guests were invited to inspect Peter at bathtime, on the premise that the naked child then resembled 'a young Bacchus of the Etruscan school'.

Peter's precocious talent to amuse first surfaced when he was no more than two years old, as Klop put his trilby hat on his infant's head and encouraged him to declare: 'I am Lloyd George and you are rascals.' Later on, when he was four-and-a-half, both Klop and Nadia realized that their son absorbed rather more than they might have imagined. One morning at the breakfast table Peter asked his father, 'What is Conservative, Liberal and Labour?' Klop, according to his wife, explained that Conservatives 'are people who don't want any change at all, Labour are people who want a very quick change, and the Liberals are those who also want a change, but a slow and gradual one.'

'Then I am Liberal,' Peter replied unhesitatingly. When asked by his astonished parents why, he explained, 'If you make a quick change it will be a mess, but if you have no change at all you will have no history'.

Although Peter has never been in any sense politically active – beyond an awareness far sharper and more pungent than that of many who actually attain political office – it is interesting to note that neither his stance nor his philosophy have ever wavered since then.

Despite, or perhaps because of, the constant presence of adults in his life – from his parents and their cosmopolitan circle of friends to his various nannies – Peter was always a solitary, though highly imaginative and self-sufficient child. In the absence of any brothers or sisters and any real playmates, he created his own kind of universe. In it, motor cars played a very large part, not only because he could recognize and imitate the individual sounds of a whole range of makes, but because he once lived as an Amilcar (one of the most famous of French sports cars, or *voiturettes*, built between 1921 and 1939), producing all the appropriate sounds of acceleration, changing gears, braking, screeching round corners and, above all, the startling hoot of a klaxon horn, to perfection.

> Why I chose this spindly little vehicle, with its look of an angry insect, I do not know, but I suspect it was a wish-dream for a tubby little fellow . . . to transmogrify himself into a svelte and insubstantial *'bolide'* . . . I switched on in the morning, and only stopped . . . at night when I reversed into bed, and cut the ignition. It was an admirable escape. I avoided answering questions, and every other contact, rational or unreasonable. It was a luxury I could afford in a safe and immobile world.

Peter Ustinov – or von Ustinov as he still was – started school in 1927 at the age of six. To be able to afford the fees at Mr Gibbs' Preparatory School at 134 Sloane Street,

Klop and Nadia moved from Carlisle Mansions to a cheaper flat in Lexham Gardens, a square of tall Victorian houses in the less fashionable part of Kensington.

Now party to the English educational system, Peter was dressed in the red cap and red sweater of Mr Gibbs' place of learning and trundled off to Sloane Street. Only those who have forgotten the nightmare of their first day at school could possibly fail to recognize and pity the image of the young Peter, clinging in awful apprehension to his mother, and being taken into a classroom full of staring, potentially hostile, strangers, all of whom were already vaguely familiar with one another – term having begun a week earlier.

For a boy whose mother was half-French and half-Russian, whose father was, to all intents and purposes, German, and whose bohemian home life was delightfully free of the British preoccupation with class and background, attending day school with the English well-to-do was both alien and confusing. Even 'Old Gibby' himself had neither the tact nor the sensitivity to realize that audibly acknowledging a boy's weaker points did nothing for either his confidence or his morale. At that time, for example, Peter had still to master the intricacies of bows, knots and laces. 'Oh, Oosty-Boosty, can't tie his shoe laces,' the headmaster would sing out. 'Come over here . . . Mr Gibbs will help him, won't he . . . sit down fatty.'

Cricket was, and still is, a tradition inflicted on boys as part of the school curriculum. It was when introduced to this most soporific of English sporting activities that Peter says he felt his 'inherent foreignness for the first time'. Picturesque though the game may appear when glimpsed on some attractive village green on a warm summer's afternoon, it isn't everybody's idea of heaven and it certainly wasn't Ustinov's. Nor for that matter was football, a game supervised at Gibbs' by a Miss Dacie, who also taught music and who used to keep something of an affectionate eye on Peter.

Geoffrey Willans, Ustinov's first biographer, tells us that 'Oosti' was:

> . . . not good with his hands and he was described
> as being impractical as well. Nearly always he
> donned the wrong jersey – red when picked for

whites and vice-versa. Sometimes he wore both, with the wrong one uppermost. He confessed later that this was due to a desire to be on the winning side at all costs. He cannot have been much of an asset to any [football] team. Bewildered by this barbarous British sport he was usually running in the wrong direction, away from the ball. Miss Dacie recollects that he did kick the ball once – bang in the direction of his own goal.

Peter himself records:

I learned at Mr Gibbs' how to survive by emphasizing the clumsy and comic aspects of my character and to hide my secret ambitions for fear of challenging those better equipped by nature too openly. For instance, I was often encouraged to play in goal during football matches, partly because I was not the fastest of runners with the ball, and partly because I was large, and therefore occupied more of the goal-mouth than a slender boy, the theory being that there would a greater chance for me to deflect the ball unwittingly simply by being hit by it.

If Peter's prowess as a sportsman left virtually everything to be desired, his earliest appearances as an actor on the school stage seem to have fared no better. As a pig in a dramatized nursery rhyme he was considered to be no more than 'adequate', while his appearance as one of a trio of sirens attempting to lure Ulysses to his doom seems not to have been remarked upon at all – save for Peter's own wry comment many years later that, despite his blonde tresses and his then piercing coloratura-soprano voice, 'Ulysses wisely passed on by'.

Academically, however, the news was a good deal more promising. For while subjects such as mathematics, algebra and, to some extent, Latin, tended to defeat him, Peter always came top in geography and not far short of top in history, French and English.

After seven years the time finally came for Peter, who was

by then thirteen, to leave preparatory school. His headmaster wrote: 'We know that he has unusual ability and his slowness in the more "cut and dried" subjects e.g. L. Gram. only emphasizes his brilliance in more original work. He has a gentle and charming nature and I shall always value the fine example he has set in the school during all his time here.'

FOUR

After what he called the 'sheltered charm' of his preparatory school, Peter Ustinov went on to complete his formal education in the 'unreal atmosphere' of one of England's leading public schools. Given the choice of attending St Paul's or Westminster, neither of which his parents could really afford, Peter chose the latter. His decision rested chiefly on the fact that, like Harold Lloyd, the famous American film actor, the boys at St Paul's wore straw boaters, whereas those at Westminster, like Fred Astaire or, more sombrely, like juvenile undertakers, wore top hats and tailcoats. 'I thought that once I was to look ridiculous, I might as well look utterly ridiculous and opted for Westminster,' is how Peter explained his choice many years later.

Westminster School was originally founded as a grammar school in the first half of the fourteenth century, and refounded in 1560 by Queen Elizabeth I, for whom the earliest Latin plays were performed in the medieval College Hall – where to this day students still take luncheon at rows of well-scrubbed refectory tables, laid out beneath the original hammer-beam roof. It is situated quite literally within the shadow of Westminster Abbey – referred to, somewhat patronisingly, as the school's 'chapel'.

It also lies no more than a few minutes' walk from the Houses of Parliament at the Palace of Westminster, outside which boys from the school have traditionally acted as 'cheerleaders' whenever the sovereign rides in state to open the new

47

session of Parliament, and inside which 'Old Westminsters' dominated proceedings for much of the eighteenth century.

The catalogue of former pupils includes such illustrious names as: Ben Jonson, the sixteenth-century poet and dramatist; Sir Christopher Wren; Lord Byron; Benjamin Hall, after whom 'Big Ben' was named; Sir Adrian Boult; and Sir John Gielgud. Together with other familiar names: Kim Philby, the double agent who defected to Russia in 1963; the radical politician, Tony Benn; the modern playwright, Stephen Poliakoff; and the philosopher, Richard Wollheim.

When Peter Ustinov entered the ancient portals of Westminster School for the first time as a pupil, on 20 September 1934, it was, unlike today, a single-sex establishment – strictly boys only. Peter, who regards the whole business of single-sex education as 'a sort of apartheid, just as far reaching as the other', was a boarder at Busby's, to begin with. The house was named after Dr Richard Busby who, during the seventeenth century, was headmaster of Westminster for fifty-seven years.

Later on, as his parents had originally planned, Peter became a day boy in the graceful surroundings of Ashburnham House, named in honour of William Ashburnham, a companion of King Charles II and a friend of Samuel Pepys.

As a pupil at Westminster, where 'there are arches galore on which to hit your head, steps of time-worn irregularity on which to break your neck [and] portraits of dead clerics before which to lose your faith', Peter achieved no greater celebrity than he had at Mr Gibbs'. Indeed, the record books for the two years and ten months he attended the school mention him by name only twice, and even then merely *en passant*.

Through the centuries Westminster has produced its fair share of eminent scholars, clergymen, politicians and the like. It has even set certain notable individuals on the road to subversion. But that even the smallest percentage of those educated at a school where originality was frowned upon – and a boy's unchannelled potential left more or less to chance – should achieve distinction within the arts, seems somehow quite remarkable. At one point during his time there, for instance, it was said of Peter: 'He shows great originality, which must be curbed at all cost.'

On another occasion, his English master, Mr Carleton, who had 'a slight grievance against him for having such a name ... was it spelt with a "w" or a "v"?', claimed to have commented on one of Peter's end-of-term reports: 'This boy will never be able to write English.'

Westminster failed to curb Ustinov's originality and, despite Mr Carleton's caustic observation, his English was sufficiently intelligible to earn him the princely sum of £1 from the London *Evening Standard* for his very first newspaper article.

For nine months, from October 1936 to July 1937, one of Peter's classmates was Rudolf, son of Joachim von Ribbentrop, then German Ambassador to the Court of St James's and later Hitler's Foreign Minister, who was hanged as a war criminal in October 1946. Having been refused at Eton, von Ribbentrop junior was accepted at Westminster, even though, as the *Standard* told its readers, 'the London German colony most emphatically take the view that Germans abroad are under a special obligation to see that their children get a specifically German education'.

Seated at a desk between the new boy and the son of an oil-rich Arab, Peter had ample opportunity to observe his freckle-faced contemporary with the badge of the Nazi Youth Party pinned to his lapel. It was that proximity, combined perhaps with youthful intrigue, that led Peter – who was once overheard debating the Brest-Litovsk treaty with Rudolf – to set pen to paper on the subject of the young German's 'artistic efforts'. Innocuous though it was, the news story caused a furore at the school, and although Peter was never identified as the author, his housemaster, Mr Bonhote, clearly had his suspicions. 'I can't help feeling that whoever was responsible will go far in life,' he said. 'Damned clever.' Peter solemnly agreed, but suggested, 'Still, one doesn't want to encourage that kind of thing, does one, sir?'

'No,' Bonhote replied, then added with a twinkle, 'of course, some people don't need encouragement.'

Early in 1936, the fifteen-year-old Ustinov became a founder member of 'The United Front of Progressive Forces', described as 'a radical pacifist society' and which, in the words of its motto, stood for 'Peace, Liberty and Social Justice'. Better known as the 'Uff-Puffs', the scope of political thought amongst its seventy-three members ranged from 'Reactionary Tory and Independent Conservative' to 'Christian Socialist, Liberal-Pacifist, Labour, and Communist'. Number 29 on the membership roll-call and sandwiched between 'B. Turner Samuels, Labour' and 'M. W. West, Labour', was the Liberal 'P. A. von Ustinov' himself. Like the rest of their compatriots, each boy was dedicated to mounting 'a concerted attack on militarism and reaction' under a fourteen-point manifesto which, among other things, called for: 'Uncompromising resistance to Fascism, Conservatism and War; Unswerving support for the League of Nations or Complete Pacifism; Opposition to the rearmament programme; Nationalization of the armament and coal industries; Abolition of the Family Means Test; Drastic reform of the House of Lords; Slum clearance, and Penal Reform.'

Despite its noble ideals, there is little evidence that the society achieved anything of consequence, over and above producing a weekly 'newspaper' entitled *Yours*, establishing branches at Oxford and Cambridge, staging peace rallies, and frightening 'Old Westminsters' into attacking what they regarded to be a 'Bolshevist scandal'.

The Uffs-Puffs existed for a year but then, in the words of John Field, who has been a teacher as well as Librarian and Archivist at Westminster since 1964, collapsed because the society was 'stricken by internal divisions, about the Abdication [of Edward VIII in December 1936] and between Marxists and moderate Leftists, and also perhaps having expended the enthusiasm that had fuelled its idealism for a few exciting months'.

On the Ustinov home front, any attempt at 'pacifism' on the part of a strong-willed son and his fastidious father also collapsed – over Peter's dishevelled appearance. Nadia Benois recalled that:

> [Klop] could not stand Peter's untidiness and scruffiness as a Westminster boy. It was hard on poor Peter, because to keep tidy and clean in that most unpractical of uniforms was hardly possible, unless helped by a regiment of valets. The white collars were always grey and the black coat covered with

dust. Klop was disgusted and showed his feelings uncompromisingly by being aggressive and abusive. Peter, from a defensive attitude, soon became defiant and rude. Violent scenes developed. Naturally I tried to protect Peter, whose shortcomings did not seem to me to deserve such harsh treatment. This infuriated Klop and he accused me of siding with Peter and even of 'conspiring' with Peter against him. It was all very unfortunate and unnecessary and made me very unhappy at times.

It was at about that time, however, that Klop had problems of his own. Peter's appearance, like a red rag to a bull, combined with their on-going war of attrition, and concern over meeting Peter's school fees, merely served to exacerbate Klop's anxieties still further. He had left his job at the London office of the Wolff Büro to take up the post of press attaché at the German Embassy in Belgrave Square during the mid-1920s. Now, increasing fanaticism under Adolf Hitler, whom President von Hindenburg had appointed Chancellor in January 1933, the meteoric rise of the Nazi Party, the persecution of the Jews, and all manner of nefarious decrees, all contributed to Klop's mounting disaffection with Germany and consequently with his own job at the Embassy, causing him to engage in a little subversive activity of his own.

To begin with he consistently disobeyed instructions to distort news from England in favour of Hitler's regime and later, as Peter Wright mentioned in his controversial book *Spycatcher*, went on to prove himself of very considerable benefit to British intelligence through his knowledge of the German hierarchy and how it functioned, and as an 'agent runner'. Before long Nazi suspicions were aroused and Klop found himself ordered to complete a questionnaire to prove that he was of 'pure Aryan descent'. Not only did he flatly refuse to do that, but he also ignored an order to go to Berlin for 'consultations'.

The outcome was that Klop was dismissed from the Embassy and, with the help of Sir Robert (later Lord) Vansittart, then Permanent Under-Secretary of State for Foreign Affairs, took British nationality. His 'notice of intent' was first published in

the columns of a Welsh language newspaper, the object being
to foil the Gestapo, whose interpreting skills evidently stopped
short at Celtic.

From then on, the exact chronology of Klop's working life
becomes a little blurred, though one fact is abundantly clear:
he was forced to live by his wits. At one point, for instance,
he had a brief, but ignoble, career as the art critic of the
News Chronicle. With a zero-rated appreciation of ultra-modern
art one of his reviews – of a Henry Moore sculpture – resulted
in a large number of prominent artists lobbying the newspaper's editor with angry demands for Klop's dismissal. They
got their way and Klop was fired without really understanding why. 'I only made a joke about the holes,' he protested
innocently.

Not long afterwards, he fared no better as the account-
ant at the Vaudeville Theatre. 'That job didn't last,' Peter
says today, 'because he didn't understand the rudiments of
accountancy . . . which figure went into which column, that
sort of thing.' Unabashed, Klop turned his hand – often with
spectacular success – to finding old masters and various other
works of art hidden among the bric-a-brac of the antique shops
he visited at random up and down the country. 'Sometimes he
got it all wrong,' says Peter. 'I mean, he left me some bronzes
which turned out not to be terribly good, though he thought
they were all sorts of rare things. But on one occasion he
found some of Rembrandt's sketches for the *Farnese Bull*,
which he sold to the Rijksmuseum in Amsterdam for £1,000.
In those days that was quite a lot, but today their value
would be astronomic. Once he'd made a killing, my father
was very happy, but he didn't want to advance it. He waited
for the meter to go back down to zero before plunging a pin
into a map of England and taking himself off to Tewkesbury
or wherever the pin had landed.'

The rest of Klop's activities remain shrouded in mystery.
That he worked for British Intelligence from about the end of
the 1930s until he retired in 1957 is a well established fact. But
quite how and in precisely what capacity is still not clear. In
her memoirs, for example, Nadia Benois teased her readers by
referring to Klop's 'hush-hush' job. But then, having got them
leaning forward in keen anticipation, she coyly retreated, only

to tempt again by revealing that she had been told, 'by a highly placed person', that Klop had 'served the cause of freedom with devotion and courage and that [Britain] owes him a considerable debt of gratitude'.

From the knowledge that Klop was often mysteriously sent abroad, and that he was an influential witness at the denazification court, which exonerated the German conductor, Wilhelm Furtwängler after he had been accused of being a Nazi collaborator, it is not unreasonable to suppose that Klop was a spy. Peter Ustinov remains uncertain that this was so, though he freely admits that he is still learning things about his father who, he says with a hint of pride, ended the war with the rank of Colonel.

While Klop was reaching the end of his days at the German Embassy, his son was on the point of emerging both from school and from childhood, which he says 'wasn't unhappy, but was impatient. I was dying to be responsible . . . and very impatient to be grown-up.'

After Westminster Peter would probably have liked to have gone on to university, but realizing that his parents had found it difficult enough to put him through public school, he pretended it was time to look the real world in the eye. Forty years later Peter would not only find himself showered with honorary doctorates in Music, Fine Arts, Letters and Law, from universities as widespread as Dundee and Lancaster in Great Britain, Georgetown and La Salle in the United States, and Toronto and Lethbridge in Canada, but would indeed be 'admitted' to a British university.

At sixteen, however, Ustinov dreaded even the thought of sitting a series of important examinations, which at that time came under the general heading of the School Certificate. 'There was little or no hope of my passing them, at least on the modern side,' he said in *Dear Me*. 'I was absolutely without a vestige of hope in the general field of science and mathematics, and that was going to ruin my chances of advancement.' Fortunately, Peter's future may be said to have been decided for him, long before it became necessary to take any conscious decisions. His sense of humour, together

with his ability to impersonate anyone or anything, from film
stars to school teachers, or from animals to radio or wireless
transmissions as they were then known, or from musical instruments to cars and goodness knows what else, so obviously
pointed to a career as a professional entertainer.

It was here that his mother, who recognized that Peter 'had
to have a career free and flexible enough to give scope to all
his gifts', was able to help. One of her contacts was the French
producer, Michel St Denis, who had brought the avant-garde
Compagnie des Quinze to London. A couple of years later he
returned to found a drama school in Islington. Known as the
London Theatre Studio, it was located in a converted chapel
containing its own small theatre with properly equipped
dressing-rooms and workshops.

In July 1937, Peter Ustinov was finally free of the ultra-
conservative and, on the whole, unimaginative influence of
Westminster and, though Klop felt that his son might have
made a better barrister or diplomat than he would an actor,
he joined Monsieur St Denis' new intake of drama students.
Another of them was Peter Daubeny, who shared much in
common with the young Ustinov, not least his depth of vision
and the contribution he was to make to the history of the British
theatre. The loss of an arm while serving with the Coldstream
Guards at Salerno during the Second World War put paid to
Daubeny's own career as an actor, but persuaded him to turn
his sights instead towards theatrical management. This was
the friend with whom Ustinov took the bus each morning
to the London Theatre Studio, their journey enlivened, as
Daubeny put it, by Peter's 'graphic anticipations of whatever
new fantasies the day might hold in store for us'.

Of the two years he spent at the drama school, Peter
Ustinov told me: 'I disagreed with so much that it did me a lot
of good. As a student you have to find out why you disagree
and what you would put in its place. And there's a stimulus
for thought. By the same token, I think that sometimes an
indifferent education is better than a good one if a person has
the kind of character that will use an indifferent education to
his own ends and not be intimidated by it. But in any case,
I was very ambitious, in the sense that I was impatient to be
my own master, and I don't think I would have enjoyed [the

school] even if it had been terribly good. I had a kind of affection for St Denis and for the people like George Devine, who was in charge of improvisations, that were around him, but I didn't think [the system] was quite fair and I quarrelled with it a great deal.'

One of Ustinov's greatest 'quarrels' with Michel St Denis centred around his method of teaching.

> Deriving from Stanislavsky, it was much given to analysis, making the smallest gesture the pretext for lengthy discussions. My instinctive quarrel with the so-called method, valid to this day, is that so much of what is said, done and more importantly, thought, during rehearsal is untranslatable into dramatic terms. This leads to the all-too-frequent phenomenon of actors who have reached devious and impractical conclusions about their roles, doing incomprehensible things with an aura of self-satisfaction and even authority, which, not unnaturally, tends to alienate an audience.

Echoing Ustinov's grievances, Peter Daubeny, who confessed to hating every moment he spent at the school, always maintained that the London Theatre Studio and its curriculum seemed 'more suitable for a seminary of psychiatric therapists than students of drama'. He went on:

> [Day after day] we would improvise solemnly on what seemed to me extravagantly bizarre themes. 'Now you're a dinosaur in labour'; 'Now you're a bush in a snowstorm'; 'Now you come home to find there's no tea and your mother has been raped'. I suppose it stretched and tested our imagination, but at the time I found it only incomprehensible, boring and grotesque. . . . I failed to see what significance these studio exercises could have in the English theatre.

In spite of his irritation at the process of learning an art to which he 'was not irresistibly drawn', and in spite of reports which criticized both his technical and physical capabilities, none of which did much to convince his father that he would ever be any good, Peter Ustinov found great encouragement in a letter he received from his great-uncle, Alexandre Benois. 'For two centuries,' he wrote, 'our family has been sniffing around the theatre. We have designed for it, we have composed for it, we have conducted in it, we have applauded and we have slept. At last one of us has had the incredible audacity to clamber upon the boards himself.'

Spurred on by his great-uncle's delighted interest, Peter became a little more tolerant of St Denis, even when instructed, during rehearsals of a French play, to contract his buttocks as a means of conveying fear.

> I didn't understand how such a muscular change could be conveyed to the public, especially to those seated far away. A little later [St Denis] stopped the rehearsal to ask me why I was waddling instead of walking. I explained that, according to the text, I was still very frightened, but that it was extremely difficult for someone with my lack of experience to walk while contracting his buttocks. He nodded dangerously, savouring my semi-conscious sarcasm as though it were pâté de foie gras . . . and for a little while longer I was allowed to express fear by more personal methods.

As a drama student, Peter took part in three end-of-term productions. Dressed in nothing more than a tiger skin, he appeared as Herakles in *Alcestis* by Euripides; as Bramwell Brontë in Clemence Dane's *Wild Decembers*; and as Sir John Moneytrap in *The Plain Dealer* by William Wycherley. Acting also occupied much of his time during the summer holidays, when he was to be found at the Barn Theatre in Shere, Surrey. It was there, as 'Waffles' in *The Wood Demon* – the first version of *Uncle Vanya*, by Chekhov – that he appeared 'before a paying and anonymous audience' for the very first time. In the next production, the British première of *Mariana Pineda* by Federico García Lorca, Peter played the part of 'a lecherous Spanish Chief of Police'. His interpretation of the role caught the attention of *The Times*' theatre critic who, in the first notice Peter ever received in a national newspaper, said Ustinov had given 'the part of Pedrosa a sinister restraint'.

Not long afterwards, during the summer of 1939, Peter not only took part in, but also produced, *The Rose and the Cross*, a Russian play by Alexander Blok, which he and his mother translated from the Russian. Among those attending a performance at the Barn Theatre one night was another young, aspiring actor, Dirk Bogarde. 'I knew somebody who was in the play,' he told me, 'and so I went to see it and met Peter Ustinov, a rough-haired, scatty boy in wrinkled tights covered with grass. We were sitting on a bank watching the audience arrive at this very, very ramshackle theatre, which actually was a barn. Ustinov and I were exactly the same age . . . and I said that I wanted to be an actor. He said, "All that counts is dedication, total dedication," and went lumbering off to do his play. I remember him as being a very impatient young man, desperately anxious to get on, with blinding ambition and this all-consuming passion for his work at the theatre, and for writing, and for music. Peter was streets ahead of anything I'd ever come across.'

Much to the chagrin of Michel St Denis, who felt that he was not yet ready to branch out alone and ought to have stayed on for another year, Peter had by now left the London Theatre Studio. According to Peter Daubeny, St Denis considered Ustinov 'to possess "a dangerous facility" which would need counteracting with discipline'. It is a criticism that is still heard on occasion to this day. However, disappointment did not prevent St Denis offering Peter the role of understudy to George Devine in *The Cherry Orchard*, which he was about to produce in the West End and which was to feature an all-star cast, including Edith Evans as Madame Ranevskaya. War, or the declaration of war, on Sunday 3 September, squashed St Denis's plan for his new production. It also curtailed Peter's plans to leave home on the salary he anticipated earning as Devine's shadow.

During the subsequent period, known as the 'Phoney War', Klop suggested that Peter might join military intelligence, rather than sit waiting for his call-up papers to be posted through the letter-box. Klop arranged a meeting which ultimately came to nothing, but which might well have been taken straight from an old black and white celluloid Ealing comedy. Peter was to meet a man who would be waiting for him outside Sloane Square underground station, reading a copy of the *News Chronicle*. Spotting him, Peter was to ask for directions to Eaton Square, whereupon the two of them would casually set off for a stroll.

All of this was duly effected and, as they walked, Peter was asked why he considered himself to be a suitable candidate for military intelligence. He replied, 'Good memory. Language.' Did he speak Dutch? 'Ja.' French? 'Oui, monsieur.' At that point, the mysterious man in the homburg hat looked at his watch, excused himself and disappeared. 'I took care not to follow him. I don't know why,' Ustinov recalled, tongue-in-cheek, 'but I had an idea people like him simply hated being followed.' Peter's 'interview' was not a success. His face, he learned, was not one that could 'be lost easily in a crowd'.

King and Country summoned Ustinov soon enough but, in the meantime, the theatre beckoned.

FIVE

Through a friend of his mother, Peter was given an introduction to the actor Leonard Sachs, who for a long time compèred a Victorian 'cabaret' or 'music hall' at the Players' Theatre. Originally known as 'Playroom Six', the Players' had started life in 1927 as a membership club on the first floor of 6 New Compton Street. Nine years later, the Players' moved to premises in King Street, Covent Garden, and in 1940 moved again, this time to 13 Albemarle Street, just off Piccadilly.

For his audition, Peter wrote a monologue inspired by a talk an ancient cleric had given in Westminster Abbey to some of the boys from the school next door. The original lecture was about 'the onward march of Christian soldiers in the heart of darkest Africa'. It was undoubtedly the kind of thing that was guaranteed to induce sleep in all but the most eager of budding missionaries. For Ustinov, however, the old bishop's talk was made memorable by the fact that 'the climax of every moral example' was delivered in Swahili.

'He had evidently been in Africa for so long,' Peter once said, 'that he could no longer conceive of anybody being unable to make himself understood in native dialects.' Out of the genuine divine's laborious sermon, Peter, who was then still only nineteen, created 'the Bishop of Limpopoland'. Unctuous and drooling and prematurely aged by the deft application of heavy stage make-up, Ustinov's bishop began his monologue:

Bo-o-o-ys, I remember when I was a boy – or rather when I was *not* a boy, but when one is ninety years of age – twenty-one seems very near boyhood . . . I remember embarking on a ship flying the Portuguese Jack, which set me off at the small native village of *Ki-ik hech*, built on stilts on the bank of the river *Ll-ptt*. Three years' journey up-country on the . . . three years' journey up-country on the back of a pigmy – whom I later succeeded in converting . . . heh . . . brought me to my living in a clearing in a great virgin forest near the confluence of the *Siglich* and of the *Gau-kau*.

The bishop bumbled happily on with guttural sounds emphasizing fantastic place names, all conjured from Ustinov's imagination, until he reached the point at which a frightened native boy ran up to him on his veranda.

Well now, what was I to do? Well, I had two courses left open to me and, naturally, I chose the second. I looked him straight in the eye and I said to him: '*Ou ng au knk eek*?' Well, not unnaturally, he got more excited, (he was very young and his background was not particularly happy) and he expostulated: '*Ng pau, poy, ngh nf k-k-h? Heh tr ou gau kk*!' Of course, this was the big decision I had to make. I took him firmly by the arm and addressed him on equal terms, and said to him with as much calm and simplicity as I could muster: '*Aug ng k nh, rk p tttt kdrt tau*!' So from that you can see that the Christian Church is a very live force in the jungle of Central Africa.

Leonard Sachs was captivated and Peter was immediately engaged to play the Bishop of Limpopoland as and when contracted. Peter couldn't have been more delighted, not least because he would earn £5 a week, but his father's stinging verdict was scarcely encouraging. 'Not even drama,' Klop declared uncharitably, 'vaudeville!' His opinion was soon to change, however, when the much-respected Herbert ('Bertie') Farjeon, 'genial writer of revue material' and then theatre critic of the *Tatler*, wrote glowingly of Peter's nonagenarian ecclesiastic. 'Here were the authentic tones, the English of Oxford overlaying the faint original cockney,' he wrote, 'the slight, clerical turns of phrase, never over-exaggerated; the interpolations, at every critical point in the story, of most convincing native dialect.'

Encouraged to work on another monologue for the Players', Peter created the outrageous Madame Liselotte Beethoven-Fink, remembered today by certain elderly, but distinguished thespians as Madame 'Schumann-Heink', a singer who did in fact exist. To quote 'her' creator, Liselotte Beethoven-Fink was: 'an ageing Austro-German lieder singer, who sang bits of unknown Schubert – that is, unknown even to Schubert . . . . She was a sort of blowzy Malaprop – in order to clarify Schubert's tangled family relationships, she cannily half-closed her mascara'd lids and cattily proclaimed there to be "a little bit of insect in that family".'

So great a success was this garishly berouged, bewigged and begowned apparition, that the leading theatre critics of the day – James Agate, Ivor Brown and Bertie Farjeon – again reached for their pens to praise Ustinov's brilliance. Farjeon, for instance, was of the opinion that:

> It is difficult to write temperately of Mr Ustinov, who, though only nineteen years of age, leaves such a deep impression that – well, if it had been Edmund Kean doing a stunt at a party, I should have thought it well worthy of the man who could play Richard III so superbly. Mr Ustinov's character was that of an old Austrian prima donna in the last stages of her farewell performances, grimly mustering the remains of a charm that never existed and then amazingly giving us a taste of her quality. This is an immense piece of acting, too macabre and too true to be merely funny, though funny it undeniably is.

Robert Eddison and Bernard (now Lord) Miles, who also performed a variety of sketches in a number of guises in the revue, are no less generous in their praise of Peter Ustinov's work at the Players' Theatre. Eddison, for example, spoke to me of the newcomer's 'enormous brilliance'. 'He was so very witty and adroit,' he says. 'Nothing fazed him at all, and of course his original creations were very funny. His jokes were erudite, he knew all about music, and he really got inside the skin of all his characters . . . intuitively, I suppose. In a peculiar way, I think Peter was a little bit aloof amongst us . . . but he was a good deal younger than we were. It might have been modesty; but he was still very much his own master.'

Bernard Miles also remarked on Peter's backstage reticence, but attributed it to a 'retiring nature'. What neither he nor Robert Eddison recognized was that, behind Peter's apparent extroversion and *bonhomie*, lay a deep shyness. Like so many sensitive people who, because of insecurity or lack of confidence, feel vulnerable or exposed, Peter realized early on that his strongest means of self-defence lay in projecting his sense of humour – in his ability to entertain and amuse. Nowadays, of course, it has become a way of life. Yet while his greatest strength undoubtedly lies in his ability to communicate – not merely through the measurable potential of *comedy*, but the immeasurable medium of *humour* – Peter remains, perhaps unexpectedly, a fundamentally shy person.

Equally unexpected, given her wish to see Peter follow a career in the arts, was his mother's own need for reassurance. Bernard Miles recalled: 'Nadia asked me one day, "Peter is very self-willed. Do you think he is doing the right thing?" I remember saying, "He undoubtedly has more things in his head than he has time for – but, yes, he has made the right choice."'

Two months' experience with the Aylesbury Repertory Theatre, appearing in productions such as *French Without Tears*, *Pygmalion* and *White Cargo*, preceded an offer which took Peter into a new revue. *Swinging the Gate*, which marked his West End début, was produced at the Ambassadors Theatre in May 1940. Its leading lady was Hermione Gingold. In her autobiography, *How to Grow Old Disgracefully*, she wrote: 'The cast . . . included Bobby [Robert] Helpmann . . . and Peter Ustinov, whom I'd seen doing an act at the Players' Club. I was enchanted by him and insisted on his being in the revue. We gave him two spots that were supposed to last a maximum of three minutes each, but Peter ended up making each of them last for ten.'

After the decrepit bishop and the jaded diva, Peter now created an elderly Russian playwright who delivered lines such as: 'First there was Ivan the Terrible. He was followed by Ivan the Good, but he was only good at being terrible'; and 'My father drank, my mother ran away with a grave-digger, and all my brothers and sisters shot themselves for a bet – which they won.' Yet again the critics were on Ustinov's side. The Russian, they said, may not have been as 'tremendous' as his predecessors, but Peter Ustinov 'gives a glorious picture of a frosty-bearded virtuoso who, dur-ing months in the country, had discovered, if nothing so crudely English as bats in the belfry, at least sea-gulls in the samovar'.

In Britain that summer of 1940, the effects of war were rammed home by the first air raids on the Channel ports and the east coast of England, then by the Blitz and the Battle of Britain. Theatres opened and closed unpredictably, but there were always audiences; always people in need of momentary escape from all that was happening outside.

Peter Ustinov – the 'von' had now been irrevocably dropped from the family name – had still to be called up and, with at least some money in his pocket, and enough flats for let at reasonable rates, he meant to enjoy what was left of his freedom. He found a small penthouse with blood-red walls and a highly impractical glass roof in Dover Street, Piccadilly – 'one of the centres of traditional British hypocrisy, high-class commercial addresses by day, low-class commercial addresses by night'. Indeed, the accuracy of his description was borne out by the very fact that his next-door neighbour was a distinguished prostitute.

During the run of *Swinging the Gate*, Ustinov took on yet another role, but this time a real-life one. That of husband. At the Marloes Road Registry Office in Kensington, on 8 August, Peter married Isolde Denham, daughter of the actor, author and playwright Reginald Denham, and of his first wife, the actress Moyna McGill. At nineteen, Isolde – whom Peter had first met when they were both students at the London Theatre Studio – was six months older than her husband.

After the unrelieved monotony of male faces at Westminster, Peter was grateful to find himself in female company at Michel St Denis' school. Though she was neither pretty nor beautiful in a conventional sense, Peter was attracted to Isolde from his very first day at Islington. 'She held mystery for me,' he recalled, 'and that was enough to cause indescribable confusion in my thoughts and feelings. I found myself planning to sit close to her, or in her eyeline, or behind her. Eventually we just drifted into one another's company.'

Although she had made her first stage appearance as a dancer at the King's Theatre, Hammersmith, in the pantomime *Jack and the Beanstalk* in December 1935, Isolde's acting career didn't really start until the summer of 1939. Then she was cast in Peter and Nadia Ustinov's translation of *The Rose and the Cross* at the Barn Theatre. At the end of that year she appeared at Richmond and the following April opened at the Queen's Theatre, Shaftesbury Avenue, in the role of 'Snippet' in *The Best of Triangles*. Throughout the 1940s Isolde rarely found herself without work. Seven months after she and Peter were married she took over from Celia Johnson as Mrs de Winter in the revival of Daphne du Maurier's *Rebecca* at the Queen's; she appeared in *A Month in the Country*, which Michael Redgrave directed at the St James's; and she then became a member of the Old Vic company at the Liverpool Playhouse. Later she returned to the West End in Peter's own play, *The Banbury Nose*, and in 1946 was cast in the role of 'Bolette' in *The Lady from the Sea*, at the Arts Theatre, Leicester Square.

Although Isolde was known to a somewhat wider audience than her young husband, still neither earned a very great deal and in Peter's own words, they began married life 'on peanuts'. For that reason, the tiny blood-red penthouse in Dover Street was given up for a much cheaper, but damp, orange-and-brown basement in Redcliffe Road, where the peeling stucco of insalubrious Fulham met the no more appealing façades of peripheral Chelsea.

At a time when sex was still an embarrassingly difficult, if not strictly taboo, subject; when babies were either found beneath gooseberry bushes or arbitrarily dropped by storks,

winging their way to and from who knew where, the fundamental realities of married life came as a stark revelation, as
much to Peter as to his bride.

'Had I but realized for a moment how little I knew,' Peter
was to write, 'I would doubtless have been more cautious
about plunging into marriage . . . .' As a boy, Peter had sometimes been embarrassed to the point of youthful outrage when
his father cast a lascivious eye at any passing female and
then expected him, a mere child, to respond to his ribald
observations. Small wonder that Peter was later to remark, 'the
antics of men assessing women I found annoying, whereas the
response of women went as far as sickening me'.

Though Klop, who always fancied himself as Casanova
reincarnate, had no inhibitions about sharing private thoughts
with his son, he remained uncharacteristically mute at a time
when a proper man-to-man 'chat' would have been in order.
When, at last, Nadia herself took the initiative to explain the
facts of life to her sheltered teenaged offspring, Peter was
thunderstruck and, by his own admission, experienced a
moment of horrified claustrophobia. Thus, in a state of awk-
ward and self-conscious ignorance, coupled, perhaps, with
other deeper insecurities, Ustinov embarked on a marriage
that ended in divorce ten years later.

That it foundered was undoubtedly due as much to the war
and the amount of time Peter and Isolde spent apart, as to their
youth and dewy-eyed innocence. Of course, had they been
older, more experienced in the ways of the world, and a little
less in love with the idea of being in love, then they might have
had a clearer understanding of their parallel needs. As it was,
neither was properly prepared for so great a commitment, or
for what Peter referred to as 'choppier seas and fresher winds'
later on. To him, at this time, marriage was part and parcel of
being 'grown-up'. To Isolde, it represented anchorage in the
midst of change and uncertainty. Her parents had divorced
when she was a child and had both remarried not long
afterwards; her father to a Lilian Odland, her mother to Edgar
Lansbury, son of the socialist politician George Lansbury, who
had been leader of the British Labour Party from 1932 to 1935.

By Edgar, Moyna McGill had twin sons and a daughter,
the actress Angela Lansbury. If, as seems likely, Isolde felt as

isolated by these events as Peter always had at being an only child in an adult world, her sense of solitude can only have been heightened when her step-father died of cancer, and her mother decided that America was the place to give her three younger children a fresh start in life. They sailed for the New World shortly before Peter and Isolde were married.

With the closure of *Swinging the Gate*, Peter began a flirtation with films. The first was a semi-documentary called *Mein Kampf – My Crimes*, in which he played Marinus van der Lubbe, the simple-minded Dutchman who was put on trial for setting the Reichstag ablaze in February 1933. Then came what Peter called 'a preposterous short film' entitled *Hello, Fame!* In it he performed one of his monologues before joining Jean Kent and others on one of a series of decorative rope-ladders. The scene was, of course, blatantly symbolic; the British entertainment industry's new young stars climbing the proverbial ladder to success.

After that, Peter was again cast as a Dutchman, this time as a priest as opposed to an arsonist, in Michael Powell's *One of Our Aircraft is Missing*. Considered to be a minor classic of its genre, the film – which served the dual purpose of entertainment and propaganda – told the story of the crew of a Wellington bomber forced to bail out over Holland. The crew members were Bernard Miles, Eric Portman, Godfrey Tearle, Hugh Williams, Emrys Jones and Hugh Burden.

Peter recalls the film with satisfaction and, inevitably, a good deal of humour. Since he was playing a priest – who was involved with the Resistance and helped the Wellington's crew to get back home to England – two special advisers were brought in to assist Ustinov with the role; both of them genuine men of the cloth. 'One of them was always having coffee when the other one was on the set,' he recalled. 'One would always be horrified when I had played a scene without a cross around my neck, then the other one would come back and say, "What are you doing with that cross around you?" So we shot all my scenes twice in order to pacify these gentlemen.'

A film adaptation of J. B. Priestley's novel, *Let the People Sing*, then followed. Peter's involvement as dialogue director also led to him being cast as a ninety-year-old Czechoslovak professor. Then came *The Goose Steps Out*, a film Peter would rather forget. Its star was the comedian Will Hay, who was often likened to Hollywood's W. C. Fields, but, according to film writer Tony Thomas, 'with nowhere near the wit or comic inventiveness'.

About a year after Peter Ustinov had delighted theatre critics and audiences alike with his presentation of Madame Liselotte Beethoven-Fink at the Players', Herbert Farjeon requested 'her' resurrection when he engaged Peter for a new revue he had devised. Called *Diversion*, it opened at Wyndham's Theatre – for matinées only – in October 1940, and starred an incongruous troupe of artistes, including Edith Evans, Dorothy Dickson, the young Joyce Grenfell and Dirk Bogarde, with whom Peter shared a dressing-room.

'We were really glorified chorus-boys,' Bogarde recalls, 'though Peter had more to do because he performed Liselotte Beethoven-Fink. It was his party piece. It *was* brilliant, though I got awfully bored with it after I'd seen it fifty or sixty times. Still, it made people laugh and his impersonations were *very* funny. He did some of various theatre directors, including Michel St Denis. His humour was always on an intellectual level, but he still made it funny.

'I didn't know Peter very well. When we shared a dressing-room, he was always playing Bach or Beethoven, Mozart or whoever on a portable gramophone. He was far ahead intellectually, whereas I was so abysmally unintellectual. He scared the shit out of me. While I was whistling things from *Babes in Arms*, he would be whistling Vivaldi.

'I think you come from the womb as an intellectual. You are born with a particular knowledge or awareness of what you are. Whether your genes come from your grandparents or great-grandparents, doesn't matter. But you have them, and that comes from birth. I think Peter was born an intellectual. Up in the dressing-room between numbers in the show, he would sit writing a play. I think it was his first. And there was Joyce Grenfell, who was his acolyte, lying on the floor in blue velvet, taking the pages from him while he was playing Russian music on the gramophone. He used to hand her the sheets and she'd take them, saying, "Oh, they're divine . . . too wonderful", and nurse them as if they were the Holy Grail or the Turin Shroud. And Peter would put another record on . . . .

'I was such a clodhopper that I didn't know what the hell they were up to. I'd just think, "Oh, Christ, there they go again". Peter must have thought me terribly boring. I know he hated my whistling. It was very shrill and it went against the intellectual grain.'

In due course, *Diversion 1* gave way to *Diversion 2*, which Herbert Farjeon devised for much the same cast as before. During its run Peter completed his play, entitled *House of Regrets*, which he had worked on both at home during the nightly air raids, and in his dressing-room in the presence of the bemused Dirk Bogarde. He then gave it to Herbert Farjeon, who had agreed to read it. Several weeks passed during which nothing more was said and, despite Peter's hints, the script consistently failed to reappear. In the end, he reluctantly came to the conclusion that Farjeon either thought it unworthy of comment or had lost it.

In the meantime, while Peter was appearing in the West End by day and writing to the drone of the Luftwaffe by night, his mother had been persuaded to leave London for the safer surroundings of Gloucestershire. In the spring of 1941, Klop and Nadia had spent a weekend with Sir Thomas Bazley at Hatherop Castle, and it was he who offered Nadia the use of part of Barrow Elm, a large, late-Victorian farmhouse on his estate.

In June, Nadia accepted Bazley's invitation and in no time at all was sufficiently well organized to receive her first weekend guests – Peter and his father. At dawn on Sunday 22 June, Hitler broke his non-aggression pact with Stalin and, with the back-up of Germany's Finnish and Romanian allies, sent 100 army divisions over the 1,800-mile border from the Arctic Circle to the Black Sea.

At Barrow Elm that day, while his parents anxiously discussed the wider implications of this latest atrocity, Peter toyed with an old radio, 'capturing garbled voices in a hail of static which we imagined was both Russian and hysterical'. Later on, after the initial excitement had abated somewhat, Peter settled down to look at the arts page of the

Sunday Times. At the top of James Agate's column he noticed a headline hailing 'A New Dramatist', and 'felt a pang of envy. The foremost dramatic critic of the day had seen fit to bestow his accolade on some fortunate soul'. As he read on, Ustinov realized with utter astonishment that it was he who was the recipient of Agate's praise.

Far from being uninterested, Herbert Farjeon, who had been an avowed admirer of Peter Ustinov's work since the appearance of the 'Bishop of Limpopoland' at the Players' two years earlier, had had *House of Regrets* typed up at his own expense, and had sent it on to his fellow drama critic. Agate's response was as enthusiastic as Farjeon might have expected, and in his piece for the *Sunday Times* that fateful weekend, he wrote: 'When peace permits the English theatre to return to the art of drama as opposed to the business of war entertainment, this play will be produced. Let not the ordinary playgoer be dismayed at the prospect before him. This tragi-comedy is funny to read and will be funnier to see ... Yes, a new dramatist has arrived, and his play will be seen.'

Six months later, Peter, who was then almost twenty-one, finally received his call-up papers and, on 16 January 1942, started to play the longest part of his entire career; the one in which he was 'least suited and least appreciated' – the part of 6411623, Private Ustinov, 10th Royal Sussex Regiment.

SIX

Peter Ustinov has always regarded war, in all its guises and for all its historical consequences, with profound abhorrence. Nor has he ever found it easy to tolerate the posturing of military personnel, caricatured with such subtle irony in so many of his plays. Schuyler Chapin, Dean Emeritus of Columbia University's School of Arts, and a close friend of Ustinov's for more than thirty years, believes that Peter's undisguised loathing of warfare stems 'from what it has brought on mankind since day one. It is one of the areas of human behaviour that he would like to obliterate.'

Putting that to him, Peter says his response is more practical. In the case of the Second World War, he points not simply to the years it snatched from the lives of him and others of his generation, but to the terrible waste in terms of fatalities, of potential, of resources. He told me: 'I think I can sum it up more succinctly, by saying that I hate it for the same reason that I could never be a conscientious objector. It draws too much attention to one's own plight at a time of general chaos. I hate waste of any kind, and here it was the death of education, of perception, all those things. It is beneath human dignity.

'But I can tell you here and now, that I would never have shot anybody during the last war. I wouldn't have been capable of doing it and, quite frankly, if I'd been selected as a member of a firing squad, I would have aimed away from the victim. I hate war for the same reason that I hate the death penalty. You are not condemning a man to death, but to spending the last days of his life as unpleasantly as they can possibly be made. It is uncivilized.'

In January 1942, Peter travelled down to Canterbury, where he had been instructed to report to a kind of sorting camp. From there he was sent on to another at Cliftonville, for preliminary training. 'My military career was like some diabolical return to school,' he says. 'I imagine the only other place where you could get such a complicated and disturbing impression of life would be in prison.'

Even in times of peace, the average 'squaddie' is hardly likely to be drawn from the apex of society. But in wartime, the lower ranks of the army comprised an assemblage of 'toughs' and 'toffs'. Among the former there were inevitably some rather unsavoury characters, who in Civvy Street would probably never have amounted to much. Put in uniform, however, especially with a stripe or two on their sleeve, they became tyrants, intoxicated by a sense of power.

'One of the saving graces of life in the army,' Peter told a recent television audience, 'was the proximity of humour all the time, because we had some of the last sergeants who, I think, came in a direct line from Waterloo by way of the Crimean War. Nothing much had altered and they spoke with this extraordinary accent, which suggested they had fairly humble origins but had been close enough to the officers' mess to hear certain pronunciations, and they came out with a language which was absolutely bizarre and baroque.

'We had a particular sergeant-major who was punch-drunk and who spent all his time avoiding imaginary blows. The nearest he could get to my name was "U'nov". When we were first called into the army, we spent a horrifying five or six weeks in billets which were dreadfully overcrowded. There were six of us in a room the size of a toilet. Later on we were moved to more commodious billets . . . and I met this sergeant-major in the street and he said, "Mornin' U'nov. How's your new billet?" I said it was much less congested, "sir", and he said, "I know. More room, too, i'n there?" It was always full of that kind of thing.'

Another story Peter enjoys telling concerns a sergeant who, at the age of only twenty-eight, was completely toothless. A set of false teeth had been ordered for him from the Army

Dental Corps in 1937, but five years later he was still waiting for them to arrive. In the meantime, he was the scourge of all new recruits. The moment they received parcels from home, he would pounce, enquiring, 'Any cake?' 'Once you got wise to this,' says Peter, 'you'd say, "No, but I've got some excellent toffee". At this his face would begin to twitch with irritation. "You fuckin' well knows I can't fuckin' eat fuckin' toffee".'

The sergeant's new teeth finally arrived in the spring of 1942 and, almost immediately, Private Ustinov and company were spared any more profane onslaughts from that particular quarter. Out on parade the next day, the sergeant yelled, 'Squad . . . hrrr!' and collapsed to the ground, bleeding from the mouth. 'He had bitten right through his tongue.'

With the threat of invasion, first planned by Hitler in July 1940, hanging in the air, coastal defences around the island he was determined to break were on constant alert. Early in his military career, when 'Writer's cramp gave way to saluter's elbow', Peter Ustinov was detailed to St Margaret's Bay, near Dover, to help forestall just such an eventuality.

Charged with guarding the beaches beneath the famous white cliffs, Peter and his comrades-in-arms were stationed in an earthwork pillbox, from where they kept watch and waited. At night the sky over Calais burned scarlet, tracer bullets drew diagonal lines across the Channel itself, the RAF bombed the French coastline and the Artillery rattled out its response. On the clifftops there was the occasional alarm; Ustinov kept a wary eye on the box of phosphorus grenades in his 'dug-out' and an even more cautious hand on the four grenades suspended from the belt around his waist; but otherwise not much happened.

In time, Peter's regiment was relieved of cliff-top duty and marched off towards Maidstone, the county town of Kent, some fifty miles inland. The object of that particular exercise was to test the defences and efficiency of the local Home Guard. Made up of old soldiers and younger recruits who, for whatever reason, were disqualified from serving in the regular army, Maidstone's Home Guard was commanded by a crusty old general who, though now retired, had known greater glory in a previous war.

As part of the manoeuvre, the men of Ustinov's battalion had to pretend to be German in order to 'simulate actual conditions of warfare'. Peter succeeded in capturing the 'enemy' single-handedly. Having devised his own stratagem for the early morning 'raid', he dropped down from the Bren-gun carrier in which he and his comrades were being transported, and approached the centre of Maidstone alone. By the novel expedient of waking, up local residents and explaining his mission, he asked to be allowed to run through their houses and out across their back gardens. By darting in and out of people's front and back doors and negotiating any number of garden fences, Peter avoided using the main streets. Shortly after dawn, he found himself standing in front of the head-quarters of the Home Guard. At that point, who should put in an appearance, but the irascible general himself.

Peter raised his rifle, shouted 'Bang!' and told him, with respect, that he was now dead. British generals appear not to want to die in quite so unspectacular a fashion, and certainly not on the steps of their own HQ. At all events, this particular general wasn't having any of it and flatly refused to play the game. Peter, who had by now launched into German, was taken 'prisoner', marched inside and locked up in, of all places, the armoury. Seizing a sten gun, he kicked open the door, overturned the staff table and splashed red ink over all the plans and maps in sight.

This so infuriated his 'captors' that he was locked up again. This time in a disused scullery, where he remained until his own colonel arrived several hours later. Asked to explain what he had been doing, Ustinov replied, 'Simulating actual conditions of warfare'. The colonel nodded approvingly, but asked why he needed to harangue the Home Guard in German. To this latest idiocy, Peter replied pragmatically that, in the event of a genuine attack, the invaders were unlikely to speak English!

It was initiative such as this which doubtless caused Private Ustinov's superior officers to issue an official decree, to the effect that he was at no time to be considered for a commission. Here were shades of Westminster School and Michel St Denis all over again. And here, lest Peter needed to be reminded, was further confirmation that the military was the seat of stupidity and confusion.

Throughout this period, Peter sometimes gave vent to his unhappiness and sheer frustration in letters he wrote home to his parents. Klop, who was of course engaged in special assignments of his own, far removed from the unremitting stupefaction of fatigues, sentry duty, exercises that not even senior officers fully comprehended and bellowing sergeants, with or without teeth, was less than sympathetic. Ignoring the fact that the war in which he had participated over twenty years earlier afforded him all manner of luxuries denied his son, Klop found it impossible to conceive why Peter wasn't enjoying himself as he once had.

'My heart was aching for him,' Nadia recalled. 'Peter was different. He was by no means a born soldier and . . . his attitude to demonstrations of patriotism and unimaginative daring was a critical one.'

In August 1942, the tedium of Peter's day-to-day existence was relieved by news that his application for secondment to the Army Kinematograph Service had been approved. This specialized unit was largely responsible for helping to maintain troop morale by supplying and screening films. Another of its responsibilities was rather more incongruous: to produce films under the aegis of the Directorate of Army Psychiatry.

Peter Ustinov's initial introduction to the unit took him, if only briefly, to Troon in Scotland. There, as the only private among a battalion of officers, he met the eminent film director Carol Reed, the thriller-writer Eric Ambler, and Reed's assistant-director, Michael Anderson. At that time the unit was preparing to make a film about amphibious attacks, which was to be called *How to Land on an Enemy Beach*. However, on 19 August the disastrous allied assault on Dieppe took place, with such severe losses that the film was abandoned and Major Reed, Captain Ambler, Sergeant Anderson and Private Ustinov found themselves ordered to return to London.

But for an inspired thought on Ustinov's part, all four would have been put back on 'regular' duty far sooner than any one of them might have expected. Thus, in order to avoid the unthinkable, Peter came up with the idea for a film about the problems experienced by new recruits. The proposal was soon given the go-ahead and his team was attached to the Army Kinematograph Service at Wembley Park. *The New Lot*, on which Peter

worked as a scriptwriter, proved so successful that the Army
Council suggested another film, this time for general release.

Propaganda films such as *The Way to the Stars*, with Trevor
Howard, and Noël Coward's *In Which We Serve*, had already
done much to burnish the ever-popular images of the RAF
and the Royal Navy respectively. Now it was time for the
army to receive a long overdue lick of fresh paint. Carol Reed
was assigned to direct *The Way Ahead* and he engaged both
Eric Ambler and Peter Ustinov as scriptwriters. Its star was
yet another actor in khaki, Lieutenant-Colonel David Niven.

While all this was set in motion, Peter's morale received its
biggest boost since James Agate had paraded him across the
arts page of the *Sunday Times*. On 6 October 1942, far earlier
than either Agate or Ustinov could ever have foreseen, *House
of Regrets* was produced by Alec Clunes at the Arts Theatre.
'It wasn't on for very long, four weeks extended to six,' says
Peter, 'but it had a terrific political success.'

To quote Geoffrey Willans, *House of Regrets* was, 'By any
standard . . . a remarkable play for a young man to have
written. It depicted, as might have been expected, an exiled
community of Russians, living in London amid dreams of
Tsarist restoration. It also depicted the revolt of youth against
the conditions imposed upon them by their elders . . . '

As for the drama critics, their response couldn't have
been more ecstatic. 'Mr Ustinov's first play is one of brilliant
promise', proclaimed *The Times*; while the *Daily Telegraph* said,
'For some time past Peter Ustinov has been making himself felt
in the London theatre, both as an actor and as a writer of revue.
His full-length play, *House of Regrets*, showed quite clearly that
he is going to be a serious dramatist of importance.'

In years to come that view would be challenged many
times. When, for example, Peter's next play, ironically called
Blow Your Own Trumpet, fell with a resounding crash after only
thirteen performances at the Playhouse Theatre the following
year, it did so not because of adverse audience reaction but
because of the critics. Even James Agate came down heavily
on his protégé when he wrote that Ustinov had 'every quality of
a first-class playwright except one – he cannot think of a story'.

Still more vitriolic was Ivor Brown of the *Observer*, who
wrote:

If, as was publicly stated [this] new piece was really written . . . in three days, then [Ustinov] was a dilatory young man. Someone of his nimble brains should have knocked off such a trifle of sonorous nonsense in three hours. Mr Peter Ustinov must really start to grow up. At present he unwisely retains two juvenile notions: one, that any kind of shapeless scribble may pass off as a play so it be full of character parts all in full voice; his other (and very dangerous) belief is that old bores are extremely diverting. They are not. They are just old bores . . . .

Peter's response to the news of his play's collapse was brave, but indignant. Writing to theatre manager Bronson Albery, he said: 'I think the critics on the whole have been fantastically heartening in their condemnation . . . I am not nearly as disappointed now as I am defiant and rather angry.'

Michael Redgrave, the play's director, was also angry. So much so that he openly rebuked the drama critics in a piece he wrote for the *New Statesman*, part of which read: 'It is sadly amusing to notice how frivolously the critics will condemn a new play, and in almost the same breath cry out for new, original writers. We are not asking for the milk and water criticism of the parish or school magazines; rather that professional work be judged professionally.'

Though 'angry' and 'defiant' at having his latest work demolished so unanimously, Peter must also have been hurt and not a little irritated at being told to grow up. After all, he was still only twenty-two. However, *House of Regrets* had been an unmitigated triumph, and there could be no doubt that his personal star was still very much in the ascendant.

Richard Attenborough, then a young actor who had appeared in *Awake and Sing* at the Arts Theatre just before Peter's first play opened there, retains warm memories of that time. 'There was no doubt in our minds that the genius of our generation was Ustinov,' he says today. 'We regarded his potential to be as great as Chekhov or Shaw, but he hasn't yet written what he is capable of writing; largely due to his diversity of talents.'

After the excitement of his début as a playwright, Peter went back to work on the film script of *The Way Ahead*. However, while a London base certainly had its advantages (one of them being that he could return home at night to Kensington Close and the flat he and Isolde had taken on after America bought an option on *House of Regrets*); it also had its disadvantages. Chief among them was Peter's lowly – if anomalous – station.

No private soldier in normal circumstances would have been allowed to consort with senior officers. Yet Peter Ustinov was working on more or less equal terms with a lieutenant-colonel, a major, a captain and a sergeant. Then there was the non-stop business of saluting. Walking across London, as he did twice a day, Ustinov's right arm was never by his side for long as, like some mechanical toy, he continuously acknowledged military personnel of superior rank. He decided to fix this problem by wearing his almost ground-length greatcoat in all weathers and all but hiding the badge on his beret by folding the surrounding material around it; and by smoking through a long, amber cigarette holder and carrying an empty, but official-looking, briefcase. Now he could have been almost anybody and, indeed, there were occasions on which *he* was the recipient of a respectful salute.

In order to overcome the dilemma posed by his hob-nobbing with the exalted, it was agreed that Peter should be appointed batman to David Niven. To complete the arrangement, he was given a special pass which 'announced to the prying eye of the Military Police that, "This man may go anywhere, and do anything at his discretion in the course of his duty".'

On one occasion, as Peter recalled so vividly in his autobiography:

> An MP . . . stopped me in front of the Hippodrome Theatre, and demanded to see my pass . . . His cruel mouth dropped open, and he asked me, "Ow d'you wangle that?" I told him that such passes were extremely rare, but that they came with "David Niven's autograph, an' all". He sent me on my way with an obscenity of such surpassing vulgarity that even the permissiveness of the day does not allow me

to quote it, but it did adequately dramatize the degree
of his envy.

In due course, Lieutenant-Colonel Niven, together with his
ostensible batman and the remaining members of their team,
left their office in the Ritz Hotel for Denham Studios in
Buckinghamshire. Shooting began there but, since the film
told the story of a group of soldiers sent into action in North
Africa, filming was wound-up in Algiers.

The Way Ahead, which also starred William Hartnell, Stanley
Holloway, John Laurie, Renée Asherson and Tessie O'Shea,
and in which Ustinov himself was cast in the role of 'Rispoli',
the irate French-speaking owner of a down-at-heel hotel, was
released in 1944. It was not only a huge and immediate success
with cinema-goers and film critics – to say nothing of the Army
Council itself – but has often been referred to as 'the Second
World War's best film tribute to the British Army'.

For two years Peter Ustinov had lived the life of a private
soldier, a playwright, scriptwriter and actor. He had been
shunted from the cliff tops at Dover to Troon in Ayrshire;
from Wembley Park to the Ritz, Piccadilly; from a film-set in
Buckinghamshire to the capital of Algeria. He had been yelled
at by self-important sergeant-majors, acclaimed – and berated
– by the national press, cheered by audiences at a brace of
London theatres, and treated as an equal by fellow artistes,
who also happened to be officers in his Majesty's Armed
Forces. Emotionally he had swung from intense frustration
to elation and back again; one minute square-bashing, the
next fulfilling the role of propagandist, helping to maintain
the nation's morale.

It was a heady cocktail for any twenty-three-year-old to
swallow, and its effect resulted in Peter being admitted to
the military hospital at Shenley, after complaining of stomach
cramps. In the event, his condition was attributed to nothing
more alarming than nerves, and a short period of rest was
prescribed; albeit in a room which overlooked the recreation
ground of a neighbouring mental institution.

It was also at this time that Peter clashed angrily with
a pedantic Personnel Selection Officer who, from spite,
incompetence or blatant stupidity, considered him to be

'psychologically unsuited to film writing'. Peter listened with mounting fury as he was told that he would be transferred to the Royal Army Ordnance depot at Donington Park. There, as a clerk-storeman, he would be responsible for sorting underwear into corresponding sizes. At that, Peter's temper exploded, the frightened officer called for help, and two Military Policemen marched Private Ustinov into the office of the resident psychiatrist, who was not only a colonel, but a woman with a keen appreciation of the absurd. At her recommendation, Peter left hospital to join the army entertainment unit, based in Grosvenor Square.

In the meantime, another of his plays, written when he was working with Eric Ambler on *The Way Ahead*, opened at Wyndham's Theatre. Including a short one-acter called *Beyond* – which had put in a brief, but successful, appearance as part of a double-bill at the Arts Theatre in 1942 – *The Banbury Nose* was Ustinov's fourth West End play in only two years. Starring Roger Livesey and Peter's wife, Isolde, this new work was inspired by the Danish philosopher Kierkegaard's belief that 'Life can only be understood backwards, but it must be lived forwards'. Tracing the lives, traditions and self-deceptive practices of four generations of 'Hume-Banburys', a gentrified English family, the play opened in the present – that is, in the 1940s. It then moved steadily backwards in time, so that by the fourth and last act the mood reflected Victorian England in the early 1880s.

Though mocking the rigidity of a certain class, Peter did admit that his characters tended to be a little larger than life. To him, however, the most important thing was not always how accurately the past is portrayed, but what its events tell us about human nature. The originality of *The Banbury Nose*, which ran for over 100 performances, restored Peter to favour. The same critics who had so effectively crushed his last play, were again euphoric. The author of one notice, for instance, compared him with George Bernard Shaw, while James Agate called him 'the greatest master of stagecraft now writing in this country. He has as much wit as Mr Coward . . . a much greater sense of the theatre than Mr Priestley . . . .'

Revitalized, Peter now undertook what was to be his only assignment for the army entertainment unit. At the Garrison

Theatre in Salisbury, he directed a part-civilian, part-military
production of Sheridan's Restoration comedy, *The Rivals*. Edith
Evans appeared as 'Mrs Malaprop', while Peter himself played
the part of 'Sir Anthony Absolute'. No sooner had he returned
to London at the end of the play's short, but diverting, run,
however, than Peter's heart sank when he learned that he was
to join the cast of another comedy; this time a farce, that was
about to be despatched to the Far East.

Fortunately his dismay at such a dismal project was short-
lived. For with the dawning of D-Day, 6 June 1944, and
the start of the allied invasion of Europe, Peter became
part of the British, American and French team responsible
for producing *The True Glory*. Directed by Carol Reed and
Garson Kanin, under the aegis of SHAEF, the Allied Supreme
Headquarters, the film was made for the United States Office
of War Information and Britain's Ministry of Information.

Released in 1945, *The True Glory* represented a visual
record of how, as General Eisenhower put it in his introduc-
tory sequence, enlisted soldiers, sailors and airmen, 'fought
through every obstacle to victory against Germany on Europe's
Western Front'. Opening with dramatic footage of the moment
troops landed in France, on sections of beach code-named
Utah, Omaha, Gold, Juno and Sword, the documentary was
assembled from film shot by over 1,400 combat cameramen.
As the reels of film were received in London it was part of
Peter's job to select material for inclusion in the final version
of what, even in 1990, was described by one magazine as a
'breathtakingly good wartime documentary'.

Peter's next – and, as it turned out, last – assignment in
uniform, was to write and direct a film for the Air Ministry.
With a cast led by Ralph Richardson, David Tomlinson,
Michael Hordern and Richard Attenborough, *The School for
Secrets* told of the invention, and subsequent vital role, of
radar during the course of the war. Peter had landed the job
through the recommendation of an Italian friend, Filippo del
Giudice, whom he had first met while working on *The New Lot*,
and whom he describes as 'a kind of Diaghilev of the English
cinema'.

Sir Robert Renwick, the brisk and enthusiastic spokesman
for the Air Ministry, arranged for Ustinov to work with the

full co-operation of the scientific research establishment at Malvern in Worcestershire. There, to Peter's immense surprise and the sheer incredulity of RAF personnel, he had not only been allocated a staff car with driver, but also a suite of rooms normally reserved for the use of none but the most senior-ranking officers. To add insult to injury, two members of the Women's Auxiliary Air Force had been detailed to act as his attendants: waking him with tea each morning, pressing his uniform, cleaning his boots and dusting his rifle. Of course, Peter had tried to explain to Sir Robert that he was only a humble private, but it was all to no avail. He simply laid on everything that could possibly be needed and told Ustinov to make himself at home.

It was a preposterous scenario, but so far as Peter could see, it was just one more in a war that had been full of them. Amusing in retrospect, embarrassing at the time, Peter's first duty at Malvern was a tour of inspection or, to put it another way, he had to tag along on a tour of inspection carried out by Air Chief Marshal Sir Charles Portal (later 1st Viscount Portal of Hungerford) and Air Vice-Marshal Sir Victor Tait.

In *Dear Me* Peter recalled:

> I was not introduced to the two high-ranking officers until the whole ghastly joke was over. Whenever they stopped to ask questions, I stopped also. After all, I couldn't very well overtake them. Thus I frequently found myself standing . . . before some colonel or group-captain, staring at his buttons, and glancing down at his shoes . . . Whenever some expert explained technicalities . . . I leaned forward and nodded sagely, and whenever the air marshals glanced nervously back at me, I seemed to be digesting this knowledge while making rapid mental calculations.

At one point, Portal was overheard to remark that the trailing private was 'quite the scruffiest brown job I have ever seen', but made no move to enquire who he was or, more to the point, what he was even doing there. It was only afterwards that Sir Robert Renwick, who was highly amused by the whole business, asked, 'Why didn't you tell me you were only a Private?' 'He characteristically gave me no time to reply.'

In due course, *The School for Secrets* took its place among the handful of films regarded as the best of all wartime pictures. But during its production, the Second World War finally came to an end, and something that had been started by Private Ustinov of the 10th Royal Sussex Regiment was completed by Mr Peter Ustinov, *civilian* – to his intense relief.

SEVEN

Peter Ustinov has a wealth of amusing stories to tell about the four-and-a-half years he spent in the army. He also admits that there were things he learned from the experience. Nevertheless, Ustinov and militarism were – and still are – diametrically opposed to one another.

Raising the subject with him today, Peter says, 'What gives me great pleasure is that the military career as such is, I think, at the end of its tether. There is no country proud of its military past which will resist the temptation to be jealous of its military future. But now it has become like a casino, in which we can't win. What is the point of gambling if you know you are going to lose? Nobody is tempted, not even an inveterate gambler. There is always the temptation to hit a jackpot but, nowadays, your jackpot is going to destroy you as well, so what is the point of it?

'Even the generals today are no longer in control of what they are doing. They are led by the hand by science. But nobody knows what sort of battleships to build. You can't build big ones because if they are hit, the disaster is too great. Too many people get killed. So they try to lodge them in smaller things like submarines, which go under water and send rockets. But the whole thing is technically so absurd because it is so expensive. Now consider that in Unicef they have the capacity for innoculating every child in the world against the six killer diseases which afflict children in babyhood. This would cost the price of three sophisticated military aircraft.

'Frequently these days, there are crashes of demonstration squads and trick fliers, in which at least three aeroplanes vanish from the radar screens and disappear into the crowds of onlookers. It is all very tragic because one's lament on those occasions is not only the loss of life, which is tragic in itself, but the fact that all the serum needed for the children in the world is splashed – symbolically – over the landscape. The whole thing seems to me so repellent, so wasteful, so stupid.'

Peter's concern for humanity, his advocacy of understanding and tolerance, even of harmony among nations, has always been an intrinsic part of his character. Indeed, even as a small boy, he created an imaginary state over which he presided and from which cruelty and discord were exiled. In later life, his concern for children, especially those in underprivileged countries, became manifest in his active commitment both to Unicef and Unesco. However, his first contact with children, in any real sense, hand-in-hand with a gradual awareness of their needs, came with parenthood. Children, he says, 'are a confirmation of life, the only form of immortality that we can be sure of'.

In 1945, Ustinov's delight at the cessation of war was heightened by the birth, on 25 July, of his eldest daughter, Tamara. Only one member of the Ustinov family was less than jubilant at Tammy's nativity, and that was Klop. Although only fifty-three at the time, he hated the idea of being a grandfather, just as much as he hated the prospect of old age. 'It seemed to me that it had come as a shock to him,' Nadia later recalled, 'like a calamity . . . he had never expected to happen . . . .'

During his last days in the army Peter, the dramatist, looked away from the present and, for the theme of his fifth play, turned to the long-distant past. For inspiration he anchored his thoughts on the Crusades, the epic medieval battles waged between Christians and Moslems for supremacy in the Holy Lands. *The Tragedy of Good Intentions* was produced by the Old Vic at the Liverpool Playhouse in 1945, but was never destined to reach the West End.

It was about now that Peter's life became set on the frenetic course it has followed ever since. By his own admission, he was determined to make up for lost time, and to that end set himself an initial target of undertaking one film, one play and a certain amount of acting each year. Thus, in 1946, he wrote a play entitled *High Balcony*, which was eventually produced at the Embassy Theatre in 1952; he co-wrote the screenplay of a film called *Carnival*, and, although he was only twenty-five, he was cast as the sixty-year old detective 'Porfiry Petrovich' in Rodney Ackland's adaptation of Dostoevsky's *Crime and Punishment* at the New Theatre. Directed by Anthony Quayle, it starred Edith Evans and John Gielgud, the 'idol' of all Michel St Denis' students – including Ustinov – at the London Theatre Studio not quite a decade earlier.

Recalling their first professional encounter, Gielgud says, 'Peter played the detective brilliantly, of course, but was inclined to embroider and over-elaborate. His Russian background was naturally very useful to his interpretation. He was charming to act with, though I was somewhat dismayed by overhearing him say, as I passed his dressing-room, "Oh, well, I shan't act in the theatre again unless I get £100 a week".'

Intrigued by what struck me as being an uncharacteristic remark, I mentioned it to Peter just in case some entertaining story lay behind it. He was unable to recall the incident and, with a quizzical look, asked, 'A hundred pounds? *A week?*' I was about to drop the story altogether when Peter stopped me by saying, 'No, no, do put it in. You can say that I didn't know what John was referring to, but replied, "It was never my ambition to be overheard in the corridor".' With that he burst into laughter and we moved on to other things.

In 1947, Ustinov, acting as writer, director and co-producer, brought F. Anstey's comic novel, *Vice-Versa*, to the wide screen. Roger Livesey, who had appeared with Isolde Ustinov in *The Banbury Nose* five years before – and whom Peter and his wife had invited to stand as godfather to Tamara – was now cast in the leading role of 'Paul Bultitude'. In the film, his son 'Dick' was played by a young, unknown south-Londoner, Anthony Newley; while the bearded, bear-like, James Robertson Justice – with whom Peter was occasionally confused – was recruited to play the part of the irascible headmaster of the school young 'Dick' attended. In the kind of absurd situation that is only possible in the world of fiction, father and son suddenly swap places when Bultitude senior reprimands Bultitude junior for being a poor student and says wistfully that he wishes he were a boy again. Tony Thomas wrote of it:

> Vice-Versa is pure Ustinov, highly stylized, somewhat surrealistic and piquantly whimsical . . . . This is Victorian England, and the military, the class structure, the public school system, female opportunism and the law all take a Ustinovian drubbing . . . Vice-Versa, like most Ustinov stories, is a possible reflection on his own experiences, always with amused detachment and artistic licence for exaggeration.

For all its merits and its brief cult-following, the film was not a great success. Peter's treatment of the story was considered to be far ahead of its time; something that would often be said of his work.

If Vice–Versa made no real impression on cinema audiences, Peter's next play fared little better. Among certain theatre critics there tended to exist a feeling that Ustinov's sense of irony led him to create 'brilliant vignettes' rather than plays with 'conventionally unified and carefully developed' story-lines. Even James Agate, writing not long before his death in 1947, said, 'I have a feeling that Ustinov is whipped by something which must be Genius since it can't be Talent, for the reason that the first characteristic of Talent is the taking of trouble, and I suspect Ustinov never takes any.'

In writing The Indifferent Shepherd, Peter heeded his critics – at least to some extent – and, for once, attempted to confine himself to a more conventional framework. In so doing, he took as his theme that most conventional, most established of institutions, the Church. This in itself was not without a trace of irony, particularly when seen in retrospect. For Peter is a man who, as he puts it today, has 'no need of popes, archbishops or ayatollahs', and whose deeper personal convictions are not up for discussion, on the grounds that, 'You are only asked about your beliefs so that others can attempt to demolish them'.

Though not a tremendous success, *The Indifferent Shepherd*, which starred Gladys Cooper, Francis Lister, Arthur Cruickshank and Anna Turner, still enjoyed a decent enough run at the Criterion Theatre, where it opened early in 1948.

Peter's next theatrical venture was also one of his most ambitious. For the only time in his career, he chose to adapt a play by a contemporary writer. Ingmar Bergman's *Frenzy*, which had already been made into a film in Sweden, told the story of a well-to-do adolescent who, during his last year at school, finds himself terrorized by a sadistic teacher. Partly as a means of escape, the youth becomes involved with a young prostitute, only to discover that she, too, is being terrorized by a man she refuses to name. As the plot unfolds, it transpires that both the boy and the girl are the victims of the same man – the schoolmaster, played by Ustinov.

Co-starring Denholm Elliott and Joan Greenwood, *Frenzy* succeeded in riveting the attention of its audiences at the St Martin's Theatre, even though Peter himself felt that the play had lost much in translation. 'In removing the exoticism from the text by making it understandable,' he said afterwards, 'we had also dispensed with a certain mystery which gave the work its quality, or illusion of quality, there was no way of knowing which'.

As the forties drew to a close so, too, did Peter and Isolde's marriage. From the end of the war it had become clear that, while Peter was set on broadening his professional horizons, Isolde was in search of a much more settled way of life. Almost inevitably, the tension which grew between them not only served to highlight their differences, but sharpened Peter's unhappiness at the prospect of parting from their four-year-old daughter. Writing of this period in *Dear Me*, Ustinov said, 'If there is anything I detest in life, it is irresponsibility. I have a puritanical revulsion for the kind of self-indulgence which creates life and then abandons it to fend for itself.' Although his message is perfectly clear, neither he nor Isolde was about to 'abandon' Tammy to her fate. If anything, the reverse was true.

At some point, Isolde had met a former pilot turned journalist, with whom she had fallen in love and whom she wanted to marry. His name was Derek Dempster. Before Isolde formally introduced them to one another, Peter had seen Dempster on a number of occasions, though only as a stranger who visited his home. Vaguely surprised that nothing was ever said, Peter, who is a great believer in personal liberty, asked no questions. To most people, this would seem an inconceivable, if not untenable, situation. Yet it is one that serves to remind us of Peter Ustinov's very singular nature. By his own admission, he is not a naturally jealous man, even though he is not above feeling the occasional pang. Nor is he a man who likes the idea of confrontation. It is, in fact, something he will always do his best to avoid, no matter how provocative the circumstances.

The Ustinovs' marriage finally ended in an amicable divorce in January 1950 and, almost immediately, Isolde became Mrs Derek Dempster. That marriage was to last for seventeen years. (When it ended Isolde went to live near Brighton where, nursed by Tammy, she died in April 1987 of the same tragically debilitating motor neurone disease that had claimed the life of Peter's old friend, David Niven, four years earlier.)

Today, Tammy Ustinov – who became an actress after being educated at Farlington School in Sussex, where her love of drama was first awakened, and at St Hilda's College, Oxford – has very fond memories of her early years. Of her father, whom she calls by his Christian name, Tammy says: 'He was like a fairy-godfather. I didn't spend much time with him when I was growing up ... but I used to see him occasionally. He would turn up with lovely presents and we'd go off to stay somewhere. It would be like holiday time; lots of fun and treats. He's always been a very good dad.'

When Peter remarried a few years later, however, Tammy's relationship with her stepmother, whom she diplomatically referred to as 'a difficult lady', was never particularly warm or comfortable. Conversely, she and her stepfather, Derek Dempster, always shared a mutual affection; so much so that when she married fellow actor Malcolm Rennie, in the autumn of 1989, Dempster was high on the list of people Tammy wanted her new husband to meet.

During the last year of his marriage to Isolde, Peter became involved in three almost simultaneous enterprises. *The Man in the Raincoat*, his seventh and latest play, which he also directed, was presented at the Edinburgh Festival; while Eric Linklater's *Private Angelo* and *Love in Albania* brought him back to the West End, both on screen and on stage.

Filmed on location in Italy – in the Tuscan village of Trequanda, and in Rome – *Private Angelo* told the story of a young and rather cowardly conscript searching for the gift of courage in the midst of a war he wants to escape. Acting as producer, director, scriptwriter and eponymous hero, Peter turned *Private Angelo* into something of a family affair. For not only did he engage his mother, Nadia Benois, as designer and costume supervisor, but he invited his mother-in-law, Moyna McGill, to play the part of 'the Marchesa Dolce'.

After *Vice-Versa*, for which, incidentally, Nadia had designed the costumes, Peter teamed up with James Robertson Justice, who was cast in the role of 'Fest'. He was also directly responsible for furthering the career of one of Britain's best – but most modest – actors, Robin Bailey. Recalling that time today, Robin says: 'I'd met Peter when I was with the Worthing Rep in late '45 or '46, when I thought I was being particularly terrible in some awful farce. I don't know what he saw in me, but he asked if I'd like to be in a film he was going to make . . . *School for Secrets*. And then I saw him just by chance from time to time, and he was being wonderfully kind. I couldn't understand his continuing interest and enthusiasm, but I know he was spreading the word and talking to other people about me.

'I then came to London with the Birmingham Rep Company in 1948,' Robin continued, 'but come the end of the season, the years stretched ahead and they were absolutely empty. Within two or three weeks, there was Peter – with a gift. He asked if I'd like to be in *Private Angelo*. The part would involve my being in Rome for a fortnight. I was to play an Intelligence Officer with no name. So off I went to the costumiers for a fitting of my uniform . . . and explained who I was and what I wanted. They looked on their list and said, "You're playing Captain Simon Telfer." I knew the novel and that's a leading, *leading*, character. So I said, "No, I'm playing an Intelligence Officer." "Well, we've got you down here for Simon Telfer," they said, "so we'd better fit you out for that."

'Without telling me, *there* was the gift. It is typical Peter. He had arranged it with the casting directors. It was a charming way of doing it, and I went to Italy, not for a fortnight but for three months, which was wonderful; Tuscany, Rome, and God knows where. When I came back, again wondering what I was going to do, there was Peter saying, "What about this play, *Love in Albania*"? So he started me off with a career in London, both in the theatre and in films.'

After pre-West-End runs at the Bath Festival and the Lyric, Hammersmith, *Love in Albania*, which Ustinov produced, opened at the St James's Theatre. Set in a London flat during the summer of 1944, the plot revolved around 'Sergeant Dohda', an American military policeman shipped over from the East Side of New York. Descended from Albanian bandits and described as part-panda, part-gorilla, 'Dohda' is in search of his daughter who, while engaged in mountain warfare with the Albanian resistance, had become involved with an English partisan-poet. It was a zany production which the critics adored.

'Peter Ustinov has not only magnificently produced this glorious absurdity,' wrote Cecil Wilson for the *Daily Mail*, 'he magnificently plays the sergeant – a lumbering, bullying, blubbering great baby, combining all the roaring villainy and all the pathetic helplessness of the gangster breed.'

Robin Bailey as the 'magnificently circumspect' 'Robert Lawn', whose flat Dohda invades, together with Brenda Bruce as his wife 'Susan', Peter Jones as the poet 'Will Ramillies' and Molly Urquhart as 'Flora', the Lawns' maid, supported Ustinov in what the majority of drama critics regarded as an 'extravaganza' not to be missed. Looking back to that production Ustinov himself has said, 'It was far-fetched and preposterous, but the situations were such as to keep the audience in stitches.'

There were even times when the same was more than true of

the cast themselves. On one occasion, as Peter recalled, 'the pause imposed by the audience was just too long, and Peter Jones and I were off. We turned our backs to the audience, but it was to no avail. The audience that night had the same dangerous characteristics, and now they began to laugh as heartily as we for as little reason. . . . To make matters worse, we had an excellent stage-manager . . . His head suddenly appeared in the fireplace, upside down behind the false logs, the fire reflected in his glasses. "Pull yourselves together!" he snarled. Thanks to him, we were both now well beyond the point of no return. Only exhaustion enabled us to continue to the end of the play when the worst was over.'

Brenda Bruce has her own fond memories of 'dear Usti'. 'Peter and I lived quite near one another in Kensington and he sometimes gave me a lift to the theatre,' she says. 'There were days in the theatre when we weren't allowed to speak, we had to sing. And if we forgot and said something, we had to pay a fine.'

As a man who enjoys driving, not simply as an effective means of getting from one place to another but as a leisure interest, cars have always been a feature of Ustinov's life. Over the years, he has admired and test-driven, as well as owned, a fleet of cars, from which the little Amilcar of his boyhood imagination cannot be excluded. Later on, when dreams became reality, Peter invested in everything from saloon cars to high-powered models such as a Maserati Quattroporte, an Aston Martin, a BMW and so on. The most majestic of all, however, is his tank-like, 1934 twelve-cylinder Hispano Suiza, which he calls 'le Monstre'. Stolen from its garage in Nice early in 1989, it was eventually located by a private detective several months later, still in France and still in one piece.

While discussing cars, Peter told me that 'le Monstre' had been given to him as a birthday present in 1962. 'I had just opened in *Photo Finish* in Leeds, and it was driven up there,' he said. 'There is no room in it for the driver. He is squashed against the steering-wheel. All the rest is passenger room, so the children, when they were small, were playing hide-and-seek, hopscotch, leap-frog and all those sorts of things in the back.'

While appearing in Leeds Peter was invited to lunch with the late Princess Royal at Harewood House, and naturally he drove himself in the Hispano Suiza. 'I managed to get it through the gates by some miracle,' he says, 'and I parked in front of the house.' Over lunch, Peter noticed that the princess's eye kept wandering and it was clear that something was annoying her. At last, in a manner worthy of her regal mother, Queen Mary, 'She suddenly said, "What *is* it that's blocking the view?" and, of course, it was the car, which was much higher than anything else around.'

Even funnier is Peter's account of his very first driving experience. He says: 'I bought a car for the first time in 1942. I had never driven one before and I'd never had a lesson. I'd been told how it worked and I drove it – with Dickie Attenborough in the passenger seat – in to Hammersmith Broadway. There the gear-lever broke in my hand, and I was stuck in top gear in a Fiat Topolino. I must say, I've never laughed so much in my life. This was much funnier than any film we could have appeared in.'

Another of Peter's cars, which he owned until the very early 70s, was a two-seater 1927 Mercedes Benz 'S'-wagen. With neither doors nor running-boards, and its white-painted bodywork visibly riveted together, it tended to resemble something that might have been assembled by a collector of model cars. Today, magnificently rebuilt and restored by Lord Montagu of Beaulieu, it is one of more than 200 historic vehicles on permanent display at the splendid National Motor Museum at Beaulieu, in Hampshire.

Throughout his life, Peter Ustinov has, of course, made a host of distinguished friends. One of them was Sir Alec Issigonis, perhaps the best known of all British car designers. When Issigonis died in 1988, Peter was asked to write a tribute to him, which was read at Sir Alec's funeral.

There is no more fitting memorial to Alec Issigonis than his greatest creation, the Mini; not only because it places him comfortably among the greatest innovators of automotive history, but because it so faithfully reflects his own twinkling personality. His eyes, of a surprisingly intense blue, were recollected in the wide-eyed innocence of the Mini's headlights, an innocence which is at once childish and highly sophisticated . . . .

The Mini appeared during an unhappy period in the design of motor cars. Small ones were usually mere painful reductions of large ones, in which all sense of proportion had been lost, coachwork bulging as fat over the rim of a corset. As for the large cars, they were uniformly as pompous as organ lofts . . . .

Into this ponderous, inefficient traffic came the Mini, as transparent as a fugue . . . Like the Tin Lizzie, the Deux Chevaux, the Beetle, it marks a high point of brilliance in the history of horseless travel . . . But perhaps the real reason for the success of both the magician and the trick was their mutual capacity for dispensing charm. The Mini is still with us today because it is not only a triumph of engineering, but because not even Walt Disney at his height could have invested it with a more endearing personality . . .

One admires people for their virtues, but one often loves them as much for their faults. When I was allowed to drive a car before its appearance on the market, I was besotted with admiration as I stepped out of it on to that windswept aerodrome near Oxford. But to qualify my enjoyment of it, I did say that the gear-lever felt like a brush which had been left for too long in a pot of glue. Alec laughed until the tears dislodged themselves from the blue eyes and ran down the craggy cheeks. 'I can't wait to tell them,' he said.

No man and no car is perfect. The distance which separates them from perfection renders the one human, and the other one of man's best friends.

EIGHT

There is a certain amusing irony in the fact that, despite his well-reasoned attitudes towards war and militarism, Peter Ustinov has often appeared in uniform, on both stage and screen. In 1950, after *Private Angelo* and the triumphant *Love in Albania*, he was signed up for the role of 'Arnaud', a radio operator, in yet another war story – Herbert Wilcox's *Odette*.

This time, however, comic fiction gave way to dramatic fact, as Anna Neagle portrayed the outstandingly courageous Odette Churchill. One of the most famous of all secret agents, she joined the French Resistance in 1942, only to be captured by the Gestapo a year later. Despite being subjected to brutal torture, including having her flesh seared by burning pokers and her toenails torn out, the Gestapo obtained nothing from her and she ended the war incarcerated in Ravensbrück concentration camp, from where she was freed in April 1945.

In the film, Trevor Howard played Captain Peter Churchill, Odette's boss and the man she married, while Ustinov played his assistant. Herbert Wilcox, Anna Neagle's real-life husband, cast Peter as 'Arnaud' out of sheer admiration for his work. Tony Thomas wrote:

> Wilcox first saw Ustinov on stage in *Crime and Punishment*. 'I thought he overshadowed Gielgud, my favourite actor. His film *Private Angelo* was a gem, at the time way ahead of the critics and beyond the vision of the distributors and the cinema

owners. My only experience of directing Peter was in Odette. What a joy and inspiration he was! As soon as the camera turned, he would disappear and Arnaud would come to life . . . I've had many opportunities of studying the genius of Ustinov, that enables him, with a chuckle, to slip slyly inside the skin and mind of the personality he is describing. And he does not let go until he slips out again and rejoins you as himself, having had as much fun as his audience.

'I enjoy acting because it is exciting,' Peter has frequently said, 'but for the benefit of the soul, I am compelled by nature to attempt the impossible, and write. I act for my living; I write because I must.' After Odette, the fusion of excitement and compulsion led to two of Ustinov's greatest successes: Quo Vadis, which Variety called 'a box-office blockbuster' – and for which Peter won his first Oscar nomination for his role as 'Nero' – and The Love of Four Colonels.

The history of first-century Rome, under the influence of her Julio-Claudian emperors, of which there were five, swung from colossal glorification under Caesar Augustus to utter disaster under Nero. It was his depressing reign that Mervyn LeRoy recreated for MGM, in the $10 million spectacular Quo Vadis, based on Henry Sienkiewicz's novel of the same name. Co-starring Robert Taylor, Deborah Kerr, Leo Genn and Finlay Currie, Ustinov had been chosen to play Nero after a successful screen test sometime in 1949.

The producer, Sam Zimbalist, had announced that Peter fitted his and LeRoy's idea of the 'strutting, vain, weak and treacherous' emperor who, in AD 54, at just seventeen, succeeded his stepfather, Claudius. Given to a life of unashamed pleasure, Nero was infinitely more interested in singing, acting and watching chariot races than he was in affairs of state. Even so, his fourteen-year reign is noted more for its barbarism than for anything that might have helped gild the Roman lily still further. For instance, he not only had his mother, Agrippina the Younger, and two wives, Poppaea and Octavia, murdered, but after the burning of Rome had the Christians, whom he used as scapegoats, fed to the lions.

Though filmed entirely in Rome, Quo Vadis represented

Peter's début as a 'Hollywood' star. In an article he wrote for a film magazine not long afterwards, he said:

> Acting in the movies is a battle with no holds barred . . . But however diverting are the films and however exhilarating the excitements of acting . . . it is writing for the theatre that provides the greatest challenge.
>
> The history of the drama has shown clearly that to be a dramatist is to essay one of the most difficult art-forms evolved by man. There are fewer great plays than there are great novels; there are far, far fewer good plays than there are good novels; there are quite as many bad plays as there are bad novels.

On 23 May 1951, *The Love of Four Colonels* opened at Wyndham's Theatre to the sort of reception that instantly put it among the contemporary 'greats'. Even today, J. C. Trewin, doyen of British theatre critics, says that he regards this pageant of Ustinovian burlesque as 'a small masterpiece of its period'. Set in post-war Germany, four colonels – British, Russian, French and American – are charged with administering the territory of Herzogenberg, which contains the fairy-tale castle of none other than the Sleeping Beauty herself.

While the officers discuss the problems of occupying this impenetrable fortress, two 'Miserable Immortals' enter the fray. The Bad Fairy, embodying 'a touch of Mephistopheles, a hint of Puck, a pair of searching eyes and a weary pout', was played by Ustinov, while the Good Fairy, otherwise Gwen Cherrell, appeared as a trim young figure in a khaki uniform, full of love and beneficence. Transported to the castle by their unlikely visitors, each of the four colonels is invited to woo the sleeping princess 'according to the hidden longings of their hearts' and in a manner and period of their own choosing.

Thus, the British officer undertakes his labour of love in the time of Shakespeare; the Russian against a setting that is inescapably Chekhovian; the Frenchman in eighteenth-century France; and the American in a 1940's 'honky-tonk' café. However, while none of the colonels manages to win the heart of the beautiful princess, played by Moira Lister, two of them elect not to return to reality. The American stays on because he has found an escape from life, and the Frenchman because only the unattainable holds any allure.

'Mr Ustinov is an author touched with the magic wand of genius, who spares neither himself nor his audience,' wrote the drama critic of *Queen* magazine. 'This search of man for the satisfaction of his soul is witty, stimulating and excellent entertainment.' Anthony Cookman, writing for the *Tatler*, praised the play as 'a deliciously impertinent fantasy'. *The Times* called it 'highly theatrical and richly rewarding', while Harold Conway of the *Evening Standard* was of the opinion that it afforded 'more laughs and stimulation than a dozen comfortably-conventional "drawing-room" successes'.

Yet for all the praise lavished on both play and playwright, *The Love of Four Colonels* did not escape a certain amount of criticism. For example, Beverley Baxter opened his own review in the *Evening Standard* by saying:

> Mr Peter Ustinov is a young man of genius, but he is not always the best adviser to Mr Peter Ustinov. He finds material for satire wherever his eye roams, but forgets that brevity is its first law . . . Having said all he has to say he insists upon saying some more. We began to have the feeling . . . that the play would never end and that we might all become sleeping beauties. Audiences are notoriously ungrateful. Ten minutes of tedium towards the end of a play can obliterate the happy memories of two hours of enjoyment.

Although Baxter's opinion was shared by one or two of his colleagues on other newspapers, the playwright himself remained unmoved. *The Love of Four Colonels* was never to lose its 'ten minutes of tedium', any more than Ustinov would personally prune future plays which tended to be too long. That task was left to others who, though not without some trepidation, snipped away here and there in order to save time as well as tighten the production as a whole.

If, however, there was sometimes a danger that Ustinov's

verbosity would get the better of his audiences, a play's lengthy run could also get the better of him. The danger Peter faced was boredom through repetition. Cyril Luckham, who took over from Colin Gordon in the role of the English colonel, 'Desmond De S. Rinder-Sparrow', told me not long before his death in February 1989: 'The play had been running for about a year when I took over and Peter had started to get a bit bored, to the point of interpolating and trying to make the others in the cast laugh while on stage. He'd already finished off the American 'colonel' and creased one or two of the others. Then he tried working on Moira Lister. But no, she wouldn't give in.

'Anyway, there was a Shakespearean inlet scene, in which Peter, acting as the "Bad Fairy", played a clown. I was the English gentleman and when I came on I had to give him a little push and say something like, "Out of the way, varlet". First night I came on and huge, immovable Peter just stood there with a rather pained expression on his face. I couldn't move him and I couldn't get by. So I gave him a hell of a jab and he gave in half a step. He hoped it would make me laugh. Actually it made me a little bit angry. So I thought, "Oh, he's going to start on me now, is he? Right, I'll be ready." The following night I came on, said "Out of the way, varlet", gave him a gentle push and he fell flat on his face. Well, I must admit I did have to fight for control there. On the third night, I was prepared for him either not to make a move or for him to fall. But after I pushed him, I was not prepared for him to push me back, sending me right off into the wings. I then had to go back on, quite as though nothing had happened. But you see, Peter was getting bored with playing the same part and saying the same thing. He isn't really a straightforward "actor". His brain is too agile. He is a brilliant genius of an *entertainer*.'

Boredom or not, *The Love of Four Colonels* was Ustinov's first great success as a playwright and, in his own words, he had come of age. 'From now on I might be *terrible*, but the *enfant* was gone for ever.' In London the play ran for over 800 performances. On Broadway, where it opened in 1953, it earned him the New York Critics' Award for Best Foreign Play, while in Paris it ran for six years at the Théâtre Fontaine and was revived twice thereafter.

Buoyant with success, Ustinov now took a lease from the Church Commissioners on a handsome, red-brick, Queen Anne house at 215 King's Road, Chelsea. In most people's imaginations it is linked, even to this day, with the legendary actress Ellen Terry, who once lived there. In response to that, Peter has been known to say, 'England has had many fine actresses. She's precious short of composers – and Dr Arne, who wrote *Rule Britannia,* lived there.'

At around this time Peter made two more films, *Hotel Sahara* with Yvonne de Carlo, and *The Magic Box* with Laurence Olivier, Richard Attenborough, Bernard Miles, Michael Redgrave and a host of others. He directed *A Fiddle at the Wedding* at the Savoy Theatre; wrote the screenplay for *The Secret Flight,* and saw his latest play, *The Moment of Truth,* live but briefly at the Adelphi. In stark contrast to the fantasies of Ustinov's four colonels, this was straight drama, inspired by recent French history and the parts played in it by Pierre Laval, head of the Vichy government, and Marshal Philippe Pétain.

In a contemporary essay, the writer Frances Stephens suggested that *The Moment of Truth* 'might easily have succeeded at some other time', but added, 'perhaps this piece of history is still too painfully recent and controversial for the theatre'. J. C. Trewin also remembers it as 'an admirable play', but recalled that, after the curtain came down on the first night, 'People were standing around in the foyer, talking about it. That in itself was unusual, because as a rule, they were too anxious to get off home. But that night, they were all talking about the play, not so much with enthusiasm as analytical interest. I don't think that is a good sign. You ought to throw your hat in the air, especially for a Ustinov play.'

Radio, which Ustinov had sometimes mimicked as a boy, if hidden from view by a screen or from behind the folds of a cloth draping the tea-table, now became an adjunct to Peter's professional activities. In 1952, Frank Muir and Denis Norden, who had seen Peter in revue, approached the BBC producer Pat Dixon with a proposal that Ustinov be engaged for a radio series that had yet to be devised, but which they suggested would need to be unscripted to allow his humour free rein.

Recalling that time, Denis Norden says, 'Up to then, everything on the BBC had to be in script form – even interviews

– in case somebody said something injudicious . . . and in those days [so far as the BBC was concerned] practically everything was indiscreet. So Pat Dixon, Frank Muir and I took Peter out to lunch to discuss the idea. Afterwards, we presented the BBC Light Entertainment department with the biggest expense chit for a lunch it had ever received. That was because we were determined to impress Peter and because it got so enjoyable that we just stayed on and on. That afternoon, Peter was at his most Ustinov, most impish, and he changed accents throughout the lunch. At one point he became a big American executive – "I will take the idea under advisement and I will check with my West Coast office" – and then an East End garment manufacturer, and so on.'

The outcome of that meeting was that Pat Dixon not only pioneered the first unscripted radio comedy series in the history of broadcasting, but one of the most outstandingly successful. Precursor of the legendary Goon shows, the first series, entitled *In All Directions*, was transmitted in September 1952. A second series, *Some Diversions on a Projected Trans-Atlantic Expedition*, began in May 1953, while a third, *Some Further Diversions*, followed in January 1955.

Aided and abetted by Frank Muir and Denis Norden, Ustinov and fellow comic-actor, Peter Jones, created a couple of East End 'spivs', Morris and Dudley Grosvenor, who were, to quote Ustinov, 'low characters with high ambitions'. Though improvised, the shows always followed one particular theme. Denis Norden explained that, as the shady Grosvenor brothers, 'the two Peters would be in a car trying to find Copthorne Avenue, and things *en route* would then suggest various situations. For example, they might stop a flag-seller to ask for directions and she would turn out to be a "deb" who had never been in that part of the world before; "Daddy just dropped me here in the Rolls". Then they'd become "Daddy" pulling off a deal in the car on his way to the office. Peter [Ustinov] not only played "Morris", but most of the people they stopped on the way. He also played the car, providing all the sound effects. It was pure gold!'

In spite of his undoubted success and rapidly spreading fame, or perhaps because of them, Peter had become increasingly lonely. Since his divorce from Isolde two or three years earlier, he certainly hadn't wanted for either girlfriends or congenial company. Yet even so, transient relationships, the company of friends, even success itself, could never hope to take the place of an emotionally-fulfilling partnership. Indeed, all too frequently, they merely served to remind him of that cold inner void.

Peter's feelings about this period in his life were eloquently summarized in his autobiography, when he wrote: 'You look around you at the growing edifice of your life, and admit to yourself that it is beautiful, but beautiful to what purpose? What and who is it for? Solitude is a necessary ingredient in the act of creation, but loneliness is very different – not loneliness while alone, but loneliness in public places, in the midst of gaiety and joy.'

During my research, a lone voice volunteered the opinion that Ustinov is 'unemotional'. 'A man who resists becoming emotionally involved.' It was an intriguing thought. But since it ran contrary to everything I had seen and heard, I concluded that as a single, uncorroborated impression, it had to be placed in a particular context; one that had more to do with Ustinov the public figure than with Peter as a person. Since my informant belonged to a peripheral branch of an industry that is rife with artifice and affectation, to say nothing of rampant egotism, it wasn't so difficult to appreciate why Ustinov might be seen in a more remote light.

Unlike many in his profession, he is not an overtly demonstrative man. In fact, he sometimes appears to have a vaguely detached air about him, as though he has taken a few steps back in order to gain a wider perspective. And unlike a great many minor celebrities who seem all too willing to sell their 'sensational' souls to the popular press, Ustinov has always been intent on safeguarding his privacy. Nor, indeed, should it be overlooked that Peter had learned the art of self-preservation early in life, so that while he is capable of externalizing his emotions through his craft, he nevertheless remains in total control of himself.

'I have come to the conclusion that the only *real* vice

is excess,' he says. 'That in point of fact, practically everything is normal in small doses. Cruelty, courtship . . . embody all the elements which, if pushed to excess, become vices and can lead to murder, even. And so I think that you must not do things in life, the consequences of which suddenly come back to you later on. That goes for everything from overeating to the risk of AIDS, or whatever it may be.'

In 1953, Peter's thoughts were partially occupied by bringing the Prince Regent – a man of undoubted excess – back to life. Though made in England at Elstree Studios, *Beau Brummel* was Peter's second film for MGM. Chosen for the Royal Film Performance the following year, it starred Stewart Granger as the dandy who befriended and influenced the future King George IV and co-starred Elizabeth Taylor, Rosemary Harris, Paul Rogers, and Robert Morley – as the Regent's much-afflicted father, George III.

Throughout his career as an actor and especially as a playwright, success and failure have visited Ustinov in almost equal measure. It was acknowledged, for instance, that much of *Beau Brummel*'s success was due to Peter's participation. Yet that December his newest play, *No Sign of the Dove*, all but collapsed at the first hurdle. 'I remember the first night,' J.C. Trewin told me. 'I felt from the first that something had gone wrong, but couldn't put my finger on it at all. So much was good in it and yet the audience was getting decidedly restive by the second act.'

Looking back, Robin Bailey, who appeared in the play, said: 'There was a theory that gallery first-nighters, who were quite powerful then, were determined to get Peter because of his success. I don't know. But, anyway, they did on the first night, and we really got the bird in the middle of the second act. When the catcalls started, they went on to the end of the play. Disaster! Next night, the audience rallied, but it still closed after only ten days.'

Peter's immediate reaction was one of disgust, followed by something not far short of contempt. He said at the time: 'The first thing to realize as the witless cries come tumbling from the gallery, is that you are being initiated into the magnificent company of men who have gone through it in the past and who have survived with grace and humour.'

But whatever the slings and arrows, Peter could at last take refuge from his critics in the arms of someone who was more than just a passing fancy.

In a West End newspaper shop a while before he had been captivated by a face on the cover of a women's magazine and had bought a copy. A day or two later, he was visited by his French agent, André Bernheim. By sheer coincidence, Bernheim had with him another of his clients – the girl on the magazine cover. Daughter of a government official in Ottawa and part of a long-established French-Canadian family, Suzanne Cloutier was in her late teens when, in 1945, she ran away from home to become an actress. With the equivalent of about £30 in her pocket, she bought a one-way ticket to New York. There, as a result of a chance conversation with a fashion model in a restaurant at Grand Central Station, she found herself introduced to the world of catwalks and *haute couture*. Within three months, Suzanne appeared for the first time on the front cover of *Vogue*.

Early the following year she was offered a contract by George Stevens, the Hollywood film director, and left immediately for California to become part of the firmament of attractive starlets, all clamouring for stardom. Hollywood was not all that it may have seemed to the young and impressionable, but Suzanne at least fared better than many. For even if her contract did not guarantee overnight success in films, it did lead to a meeting with Charles Laughton and six months' experience as a player in his Shakespearean repertory company.

When at last she and the Bard finally parted at the end of the season, Laughton advised Suzanne to spend some time on the European stage and 'learn to become a good actress'. With that aim she left for Paris, taking with her a letter of introduction to the famous French actor and director, Louis Jouvet, through whom she joined la Comédie Française. In time, she attracted the attention of another director, Jacques Duvivier, who cast her in his film *The Sinners*. Although still relatively unknown, Suzanne's greatest opportunity presented itself during the late summer of 1949 when Orson Welles, who was to play the Moor, was casting his own film version of *Othello*.

From January 1949 to March 1950, the Irish actor Micheál
Mac Liammóir, who played 'Iago', kept a diary of the making of
the film, which was later published under the title *Put Money
in Thy Purse*. From the outset, Welles had unsuccessfully
screen-tested several actresses for the role of 'Desdemona'.
Eight months later the right candidate arrived in Venice,
where the film was shot against such magnificent settings as
the Doge's Palace on the Piazzetta, and Ca' d'Oro, the 'House
of Gold', one of the most famous fifteenth-century palaces on
the Grand Canal.

In his diary, Mac Liammóir described 'Desdemona' as:

> French-Canadian, bi-lingual . . . voice warm, flex-
> ible and soft; her face a Bellini with large grey
> eyes that bestow lingering and slightly *reproachful*
> glances, perfect nose and mouth, chin a little too
> broadly modelled . . . figure good; a gentle dignity
> is her authentic hallmark; name Suzanne Cloutier.
> Manner rather *fin de siècle*, the childish, vague inten-
> sity of Mélissande [but] feel sure that somewhere
> in her There is Steel. Interesting; I smell Ham,
> Character, Individuality, and above all Indestruct-
> ible Will . . . prophesy that Orson will have trouble
> with her (as she no doubt with him), but somehow
> a Desdemona will emerge.

As the months slipped past and the film gradually evolved,
'Schnucks', as Welles had nicknamed Suzanne, 'in a moment
of desperation' was summed up by other members of the cast
– which also included Fay Compton – in a variety of ways.
Mac Liammóir himself came to the conclusion that she was
'a peculiar girl'; others that she was 'An Iron-clad mass of
egocentricity', 'A fascinating little baggage' and 'A mental
ju-jitsuist'.

'She will, with or without the attention of an audience,
interrupt, declaim, misquote, advise, question, beg for advice,
recount, flatter, boast, invent, be amusing and embarrassing,
but never stagnant; even when she is silent you know that, like
a cat, an immense activity is in progress.'

By the time she met Peter, for whom she played a one-word

part in the ill-fated *No Sign of the Dove*, Suzanne had appeared in Orson Welles' first Paris play, *The Unthinking Lobster*, had completed her second film, this time for another French director, Marcel Carné, was about to appear in *Derby Day* for Herbert Wilcox, and would shortly find herself working alongside Dirk Bogarde, Kenneth More, Donald Sinden and Muriel Pavlow in the comedy *Doctor in the House*.

After that her career as a professional actress came to a halt. Some time towards the end of 1953, Peter proposed and Suzanne accepted, though the wedding itself had to wait. The reason for the delay was that Suzanne was already married – albeit in name only. Suzanne's first marriage, to Dr François Richer la Flèche – which had been celebrated in great style seven years before – began and ended, quite literally, on the same day. Suzanne had apparently married only to please her parents and then, without so much as a thought for them or, even more importantly, for her wretched bridegroom, had calmly walked away from the wedding reception and returned to Hollywood.

Not long afterwards, the Cloutiers themselves petitioned the Catholic Church for an annulment of their daughter's unconsummated marriage. But it was not until 1956, by which time the Ustinovs had been married for two years and already had two children, that the Vatican finally approved the application. While Rome went its own sweet way, however, Suzanne had sought to end her marriage by swifter, more practical methods and, on 8 February 1954, the London Divorce Court granted her a decree nisi on the grounds of *la Flèche's* 'adultery and desertion'. The decree was made absolute two days later, and at 9.30 on the morning of 15 February, Peter and Suzanne were married at Chelsea Registry Office, a few minutes' walk from Ustinov's house on the King's Road.

Despite the hour, what had been planned as a private, unceremonious occasion, witnessed only by three friends, was turned into something of a media event as news leaked out and a posse of journalists descended on the Registry Office. Bernard Hall of the *Daily Express* reported:

> Ustinov – playwright, actor, writer and spare-time comic – had begun to dress in a dark suit and

grey tie, and then he had thought of improvements. He wore a kind of sawn-off British warm and suede shoes. He was hatless and his hair was tousled. . . . Suzanne was a little informal too. She wore a black astrakhan coat and no hat.

For the benefit of reporters [Ustinov] stiffened into Prussian rigidity, raised his hand peremptorily, goose-stepped across the landing, and declared: 'Gentlemens, ze conference is over. There is nozzings more to say.'

It was only as the news was published in the lunch-time editions and surprised friends began to telephone their congratulations, that Peter and Suzanne decided some sort of reception was called for. Some hours later, a typically informal party was in full swing and Bollinger and Casanove champagne flowed like water. Among the guests were Peter's parents, Klop and Nadia, Baroness Budberg, Sir Carol and Lady Reed – the Ustinovs' next-door neighbours – the publisher Hamish Hamilton, Hollywood film producer Sam Zimbalist, André Bernheim, Igor Markevitch, the conductor and composer, and his wife, and Baron, the society photographer.

Of her new husband, Suzanne told one journalist:

I have never met anyone who makes me laugh so much. He is always making light of things . . . life is happy all the time. There is nothing sad or depressing when he is about . . . I love him, red socks, long hair, sawn-off overcoats and all. I'd never try to change him, I couldn't! He's not like other men. He doesn't get excited by trifles like missing buttons . . . nor does he need to shut himself away to work. He writes in the bathroom or lying on the floor. . . . The only thing he insists on is loud music. He says you can't be irritated by a little noise if there is a big one going on.

Two days after they married, the Ustinovs left London for America and the first of Peter's 'Hollywood' films actually to have been made in Hollywood. This was *The Egyptian*, based on the novel by the Finnish writer, Mika Waltari, and produced by Darryl F. Zanuck for 20th-Century Fox. When Peter agreed to play the part of 'Kaptah', a one-eyed servant, Marlon Brando had been engaged to play his lord and master, a young and adventurous doctor called 'Sinuhe'. But by the time Peter and Suzanne arrived in California, Brando 'was no longer part of the cast. He had taken one look at the final script, and become victim of a rare illness, from which he made a miraculous recovery once shooting had begun on his replacement.'

Peter was afforded no such luxury. 'Egyptian art is the most fragile of all,' he said afterwards, 'and this was a kind of Victorian concept of surpassing absurdity. I didn't enjoy the film one little bit'.

NINE

In Los Angeles, Peter was joined on·the set of *The Egyptian* by the British actor Edmund Purdom, who had risen to fame a year or two before when he replaced Mario Lanza in *The Student Prince*. He now succeeded Marlon Brando in the film Ustinov later declined to see, on the grounds that he found it all too ridiculous while making it.

Directing this picture was the Hungarian Michael Curtiz, about whom Peter has a fund of amusing stories to tell. A tall man with pupil-less blue eyes, Curtiz had been in America long enough to have forgotten most of his Hungarian, but evidently not quite long enough to become fully acquainted with the American language, much less the English. Communication was consequently perilous. 'He seemed to understand absolutely nothing I said,' Peter recalled, 'while agreeing with it all and doing just the opposite.'

In 'How to Manage Directors', an article he wrote during the mid-1950s, Peter devoted a large part to his experience of working with Michael Curtiz:

> On one occasion he told an actor that he was not achieving that certain quality of goodness which he described as 'Love Thy Neighbourhood' and on another he looked blankly into the five yards that were at the moment separating Edmund Purdom from myself, and said 'Purdinov'. He was pained when no one responded to his call.

Ever open to new ideas as ... to new words, he embraced the idea of CinemaScope with relish. 'Ustom,' he said to me one day, looking past me at Purdom, 'In dee nex' shot, you come from house visper in dee ear otter actor secrett.' This was the most lucid sentence I ever knew him to pronounce, and I did what I was told. Running from the house in my highly uncomfortable costume, which looked like a tea-gown for an outsize dowager, I approached Purdom, and whispered a discreet message in his ear. 'Koot!' screamed Curtiz, the great technician. 'No goot. Dis is Zinemaskop – Vide Shkreen – ven you visper, muss be four foot apart!'

Another memorable incident involved a burly young film extra, who clearly suffered the same frustrations with Curtiz as the stars of the film. Peter recalled:

I was supposed to run through a public place ... and from somewhere a soldier would come and arrest me. This soldier was a vast American of immense physical power, dressed only in a loin cloth and a helmet which sat on his head in the General Patton manner, concealing the eyes and thereby emphasizing the dimensions and the grimness of the jaw. Mentally, however, this fellow was a tender child, who had theatrical ambitions, and had been studying the methods of Stanislavsky without profit to himself or Stanislavsky. He had conceived a theory that an actor should not make any gesture without a deep subconscious motivation. This devotion to his own brand of dramatic integrity meant that, by the time he had set in motion the laborious mechanism which would culminate in the stretching forth of his arresting hand, I was well past him and running at a steady canter in the general direction of Los Angeles.

I have always believed that a respect for other points of view is an essential for the maintenance of a spontaneous personal humility, and so I did my best to help him during rehearsal by either slowing down as much as I dared, or by trying to leave one arm behind for him to grab, but Stanislavsky frustrated my designs, and the soldier consistently seized the air a full ten seconds after I had passed.

Curtiz arrived full of fury and censorable Transylvanian vocabulary, and told this fellow that he stank, that he'd never been a soldier, that he knew nothing of the fury of battle and the vagaries of revolution. The gentle artist suddenly forgot all about Stanislavsky and the inner motivations, rose a couple of feet in height, and proceeded to undo his period bikini in order to show Curtiz a wound which had been suffered in the cause of democracy. So terrifying did he become that Curtiz walked away prudently, muttering, 'Maybe haf been soldier, but nefer Cavalry officer.' To hear Hungarians talk, you'd think Hungary never had any infantry at all.

As a committed European – and with his type of background and cultural heritage, how could it be otherwise? – America is not a country Peter Ustinov has ever enjoyed unreservedly or felt particularly at home in. There is, nevertheless, much about the American way of life that he admires and, inevitably, much that he does not. His UK publisher, Michael O'Mara, himself an American, says: 'Peter has very strong likes and dislikes and he dislikes what America has become. He doesn't like that kind of pushy, "We're the best, do what we say, we're running the show" attitude. He doesn't like the ignorance of Americans . . . and especially the ignorance of American politicians, towards the rest of the world. That drives Peter crazy. He doesn't like the "us and them" [mentality]; 'We have all that's good . . . We have democracy here, nobody else has it" – that kind of thing. And a lot of Americans do think like that.'

Of his experiences of specific American cities, Peter talks candidly of his likes and dislikes. Of New York, for example, he says, 'It's just not for me. I don't feel well there; I don't like their values, and I don't think they understand what I'm doing.' On the other hand, he considers Palm Beach to be worse. A few years ago, when on tour in *Beethoven's Tenth*, which currently stands as his most recent play, Peter said, 'I came out of the theatre after a matinée and an old lady with blue hair, it's almost a cliché now, came up to me very affectionately and very charmingly, patted me on the arm and said, "Your Mozart was darling". Palm Beach is the place where I found myself saying on local television: "I don't think anybody here has ever heard of Beethoven; that is unless they knew him personally." It all made me realize that I am much too European.'

During his first working visit in 1954, Peter absorbed the atmosphere of Los Angeles with interest and amusement, storing away impressions that would be useful to him as story-teller and raconteur, and for when he added the role of novelist to his list of accomplishments. More immediately, he observed the local scene for some of the articles he was asked to write for newspapers and magazines at home. On one occasion, he wrote:

> Geographically, Los Angeles is a huge town – and it is not a pretty town. Its development has been violent and drastic, so that there is no civic personality whatever in these suburbs devoted to the art of the moving picture. . . . The houses, in a variety of styles from mock-Moorish to mock-Tudor, are interspersed with enormous used-car lots which are so deeply involved in cut-throat competition that the gentlemen with that habitually sour smile of welcome practically pay you to take a new car away. . . . I must be careful not to give the impression that life is unpleasant. On the contrary, it is very, very pleasant indeed, and to anyone from England it even satisfies a certain nostalgia. There are many mornings when vision is restricted by a deep, lifeless fog, and it is on these mornings that one forgets all about the sunny California of the travel posters, and believes oneself to be in Uxbridge or Slough. Any trace of homesickness vanishes with the first conscious inhalation of the bitter air in the morning, and with the sight of a landscape which looks like a watercolour picture left out in the rain.

A little later on, he reported sardonically:

> Hollywood is as great a leveller as death. Those
> who hoped for much, have rather less than they
> wished. It is the true democracy of art, in which
> the ignoramus with the gift of instinct argues it out
> with the Professor, late of Vienna, crammed with
> knowledge and rancid ideals. And in the corner of
> the room, the great oracle of television blurts on
> unheeded, like a pianist in a crowded bar. For those
> who come there with a knowledge of human frailty
> and with eyes wide open, it can be heaven. For those
> who expect miracles it can be just the opposite.
> The legend of Hollywood is like some endless
> teaser campaign, manufactured by publicity depart-
> ments and columnists, but reality has entered its
> portals to stay. I dare swear that nowhere in the
> world is there such a concentration of artistic tal-
> ent although the methods of setting that talent to
> work have deservedly met with criticism – some of
> it very amusing. But there is nothing which separates
> Hollywood off-duty from the rest of America. It is
> just a section of a town devoted in some measure to
> the moving pictures, just as Harley Street is, in the
> main, dominated by doctors. The people who work
> here are people who think as hard as any others,
> speak as much as many others, eat and drink no
> more than any others. And they laugh at us and
> civilize us quite as much as we laugh at them, which
> is an excellent tonic for us all.

When he and Suzanne arrived in Los Angeles, Peter rented
an apartment on Wilshire Boulevard from Loretta Young's
mother, Gladys Belzer. Frank Sinatra lived in the same building and, after a while, the sound of his voice began to
penetrate even Peter's fabled concentration. When at last
he said something about it to Suzanne, she delivered a
lecture on Sinatra's dedication to perfecting his art. But
hardly had she finished speaking, than providence intervened
to demolish her argument when the stylus of the singer's hi-fi

suddenly got stuck in the well-worn groove of one of his own records!

Although Hollywood afforded the Ustinovs almost limitless social opportunities – there were times, for instance, when they were invited to as many as three or four parties a night – Peter's fees were still sufficiently modest for him to have to keep a tight rein on expenditure. Income from his role in *The Egyptian*, however, was about to be supplemented. Michael Curtiz invited him to appear in his next film venture *We're No Angels*, a comedy based on Albert Husson's play, *La Cuisine des Anges*, which was to be made for Paramount and would also star Humphrey Bogart, Basil Rathbone, Aldo Ray and Joan Bennett. Not only was it a successful picture, and one that Peter enjoyed making, but it led to friendship with 'Bogie' and his wife, Lauren Bacall, who were near neighbours on Wilshire Boulevard.

In fact, it was at a drinks party at their house on the evening of 2 June 1954, that Peter received congratulations at having become a father again. That afternoon at St John's Hospital, Santa Monica, Suzanne had given birth to her first child, and Peter's second daughter, Pavla. It was also with the Bogarts that Peter sometimes indulged his favourite sport, an interest developed far away from the enforced schoolroom periods of football in winter and cricket in summer. Despite having inherited the build of his Ustinov grandfathers, something about which he is infinitely more conscious than others, incidentally, Peter has always been a devoted tennis buff.

As a player his partners, perhaps even more surprisingly, have included friends such as Australian champions Fred Stolle, Roy Emerson, John Newcombe and Lew Hoad (with whom he would not only exchange tales of fatherhood but, says Peter, 'swap baby clothes'); Prince Rainier of Monaco; Gene Kelly; and even Soviet diplomats. Robin Bailey and Denis Norden have also played him on occasion. Norden recalled that when their children were young, 'we used to go to a place called "Climping" in Sussex. It wasn't a specifically "show-biz" place, but Jack Hawkins would sometimes be there with his kids, and Frank Muir with his. It was like a country house, a great rambling place. The tennis court was surrounded by trees and sound was therefore amplified.

If you happened to be walking along the drive and heard certain kinds of footsteps running, you'd say, "Ah, Peter's playing". Over a couple of years or so, if we were all there for the weekend, I'd sometimes play him. He was *ferocious* to play against and he *looked* ferocious. He played "Californian", not the English game of patball, and he played to win!'

At much the same time, Peter had astounded 'Bunny' Austin with his 'extraordinary knowledge' of the game, its history and of the individual careers of scores of players. Austin, who was the No. 1 British player from 1926–32 and who had represented Britain in tournaments all over the world during the 1920s and 30s, had several conversations with Ustinov when they lived in London. 'Peter actually knew more about my career than I did,' he recalls. 'He reminded me of matches I'd long forgotten playing and, through talking with him on one occasion, I found a challenge cup I had even forgotten winning!'

Before he and Suzanne returned to London with their three-month-old daughter, Peter had been asked by the BBC to make a recording about the notorious anti-Communist witch-hunt then terrorizing America.

On 9 February 1950, Joseph McCarthy, the Republican senator for Wisconsin, announced at a meeting of the Ohio County Women's Republican Club that he had in his possession a list of 205 members of the Communist Party, 'working and shaping the policy of the State Department', but offered no proof and refused to reveal any of the names on the list. Three years later, McCarthy accused former president, Harry Truman, of aiding many suspected Communists, and in February 1954, having pursued his televised one-man investigation from the State Department to the army, found himself in direct conflict with the White House when, during the course of making enquiries into an army dentist accused of Communist sympathies, he told one much-decorated brigadier-general that he was a disgrace to his uniform. At the beginning of June, McCarthy went still further by alleging serious Communist infiltration of the CIA and nuclear weapons plants. At that point, President Eisenhower stepped in to announce that he would prevent the senator from investigating the CIA. At the

end of the year, McCarthy was finally condemned by the US
Senate for 'conduct unbecoming a Senator', but by then
the damage had been done, panic was widespread, and
'McCarthyism', as it had become known, had already reached
its peak.

Though outraged by what he called McCarthy's 'prolonged
drum-head court-martial', Ustinov followed the television inter-
rogations and news reports with rapt attention. At one point he
reported:

> The quest for Communists, or, as they are now
> called, 'Commies', goes on apace. This quest has
> created its own confusions, at least in this mind, for
> whereas I knew when I left home more or less exactly
> what a Communist was, I must admit now to certain
> doubts. [In America] the word has almost qualified as
> a regular adjective meaning anything from criminal
> to disobedient. Another, and infinitely sadder dis-
> crepancy in the language is the different meaning
> for that noble word 'liberal' which in America has
> become dissociated from its essential humanism and
> sense of equity, and now apparently means a kind
> of embryonic commie, a nuisance who asks embar-
> rassing and subversive questions . . . A third word
> which crops up almost anywhere the other two are
> mentioned is 'smear', which was, I believe, fathered
> by that eminent parent of the gold-plated phrase,
> Senator McCarthy, in order to show what the vast
> army of huge subversive Davids were supposed to
> be doing to the poor small, fearless Goliaths from
> Wisconsin.

Later, in his fifteen-minute appraisal of this grotesque episode
for the BBC, he said:

> To the outside observer there is nothing particu-
> larly striking about the Senator. . . . Words come
> more easily to him than sentences . . . but even
> words fall grudgingly from his lips – his eyes,
> meanwhile, having all the dispassionate intensity

of a lion who is having his own private troubles gnaw-
ing a juiceless knuckle. . . . It is as though he had
cheated the physical restrictions imposed on him by
nature, and had turned the very shortcomings of his
equipment into weapons . . .

If, therefore, Europeans have had the audacity to express fears with regard to the Senator,
it is because they share with the United States
that machinery of state which makes freedom of
opinion sacrosanct, and because they have learned
to mistrust fanaticism in all its many forms. When
anti-communism becomes a creed, it fights with the
arms of its enemy, and, like its enemy, it breeds
injustice, fear, corruption. It cuts away the true
platform of democracy, and destroys the sense of
moral superiority without which no ethical struggle
is ever won.

On that note Peter, his work completed, left Los Angeles
with his wife and daughter, for London, travelling by a slow
and circuitous route, which brought them home via Mexico,
Cuba and the West Indies.

Lola Montès, which was made in France in 1955, was Peter
Ustinov's eighth film in five years. It was also his strangest
and, in some ways, most sinister. Directed by Max Ophüls,
it was based on Cecil St Laurent's novel, *La Vie Extraordinaire
de Lola Montès*, which in turn was based on the life of
a nineteenth-century dancer, adventuress and courtesan,
whose real name was Maria Dolores Eliza Gilbert. Born in
Montrose in about 1820, the exact year isn't known, 'Lola'
proved herself to be quite a character. As a girl barely into
her teens, she deliberately turned to high-class prostitution as
a means of making a living, and on one occasion is known
to have refused to sleep with the Viceroy of Poland, on the
grounds that he had false teeth.

Although she was married three times in her comparatively
brief life, Lola continued with her 'career' and took a host of
lovers, including the father of Alexandre Dumas and Franz

Liszt; also King Louis I of Bavaria, who is said to have told
a friend that she could 'perform miracles with the muscles
of her private parts'. It was Lola's influence over the king –
who created her Baroness von Rosenthal – that precipitated
the revolution which brought about his abdication. Lola then
returned to England, and sometime afterwards moved on to
America, where she became the mistress of a number of
wealthy men. She died in New York in 1861.

In his film, which was actually made – not dubbed –
in three languages, French, English and German, Ophüls
symbolically interpreted the life of Lola Montès (or Montez),
played by Martine Carol, against a circus in which she was
the main, freak-like, attraction. Ustinov played the arrogant,
monocled ring-master who narrated Lola's life, which was
portrayed – though not properly explained – in flashbacks.
Interestingly enough, an abridged version of the film was
released after completion, though *Lola Montès* – considered to
be a classic – wasn't seen in its entirety until the late 1960s. By
then Max Ophüls, Martine Carol and Anton Walbrook, who
played the King of Bavaria, had all died of heart attacks.

If the present is indicative of the past, Ustinov always
had something of his own on the go while working for others.
Nowadays, the immense amount of paperwork he manages to
cram into his briefcase frequently contains the handwritten
script of a novel, to which he will turn his attention during
intervals in a theatre or breaks between filming. Peter has the
ability to work literally anywhere, regardless of what might or
might not be happening all around him. At the time that his
concentration was disturbed in Los Angeles by the repeated
sound of Sinatra playing Sinatra, Ustinov was in the process
of writing a new play. Romeo and Juliet were brought into the
twentieth century and transplanted from picturesque Verona
to some small, make-believe republic somewhere in the middle
of Europe. They also underwent a change of nationality:
Romeo became Igor Romanoff, son of the Russian Ambassador
to the tiny Ruritanian state, while Juliet Moulsworth was the
daughter of the American Ambassador.

Though delivering the ultimate message that love conquers
all, the play was, of course, a satirical commentary on the relationship between the superpowers, in which Ustinov gently

Above: Peter aged about three, seen with his parents, Klop and Nadia Ustinov. (Courtesy of Peter Ustinov)

Below: The schoolboy Ustinov. Peter at Westminster (above left of Master). (Courtesy of Westminster School)

At the age of nineteen, Peter as Madame Liselotte Beethoven-Fink. (Hulton Picture Company)

Above: Ustinov in uniform: third from right, front row. Circa 1943. (Courtesy of Peter Ustinov)

Below left: Working on *The Way Ahead* with Eric Ambler. (British Film Institute)

Below right: Ustinov with Gladys Gooper looking through the script of *The Indifferent Shepherd*, 1948. (Hulton Picture Company)

Above: Family likeness: Peter Ustinov's first wife, Isolde Denham (left) and their daughter Tamara. (Courtesy of Tamara Ustinov)

Below: Peter and Isolde with Tamara in 1948. (Hulton Picture Company)

Above: Peter with his mother, Nadia Benois, and Roger Livesey, on the set of *Vice-Versa*, 1947. (British Film Institute)

Below: On set discussion: Ustinov making a point to members of the crew. (Syndication International)

Above left: Ustinov making up for *The Love of Four Colonels*, 1951. (Hulton Picture Company)

Above right: As Nero in *Quo Vadis*, 1952. (Syndication International)

Below: Ustinov and Peter Jones as the Grosvenor brothers; *In All Directions,* BBC Radio, 1952. (Hulton Picture Company)

ove left: Ustinov in his play *Romanoff and Juliet*. (Hulton Picture Company)

ove right: As the Prince Regent with Stewart Granger in *Beau Brummel*. (British Film Institute)

ow: With Martine Carol in *Lola Montes*. (British Film Institute)

Above: Peter with Klop and Nadia at home in Chelsea, 1952. (Hulton Picture Company; and courtesy of Peter Ustinov)

Below: Ustinov with his second wife, Suzanne Cloutier, and their daughter Pavla, 1954. (Hulton Picture Company)

Above: Peter Ustinov with Jean Simmons in *Spartacus;* his first Oscar-winning performance. (British Film Institute)

Below: Peter listening to Terence Stamp during the filming of *Billy Budd.* (Syndication International)

Above: Peter gives his second Oscar-winning performance in *Topkapi*. He is seen silencing Akim Tamiroff, 1964. (British Film Institute)

Below: Ustinov with Alec Guinness and Richard Burton in *The Comedians*, 1967. (British Film Institute)

Above: Peter with Elizabeth Taylor during the filming of *Hammersmith Is Out*, 1971. (Rex)

Below: Ustinov in his play *The Unknown Soldier and His Wife*, in London in 1973. (Hulton Picture Company)

Above: In *Death on the Nile*, Peter, as Hercule Poirot, starred with David Niven, George Kennedy, B Davis, Jack Warden, Maggie Smith and Angela Lansbury, 1977. (British Film Institute)

Below: Goodwill Ambassador for UNICEF: Ustinov in Paris with Vietnamese orphans. (Hulton Pi Company)

ve left: Peter and his third wife Hélène, picnic
Richmond Green, 1983 (Terry O'Neill)

ve right: Igor Ustinov in his Paris studio.
urtesy of Igor Ustinov)

w: Peter with Andrea (left) and Tamara, after
first night of *An Evening with Peter Ustinov,* 21
rch 1990. (Alan Davidson)

Above: Peter Ustinov at home in Switzerland. At the door of Au Clos du Château and in the garde overlooking his vineyards.

Below left: Peter clowning with an empty tankard. (Photographs by Christopher Warwick)

Below right: Still joking. With Christopher Warwick at the Savoy, May 1990. (Andrew Mardell)

tain's 'One man beacon of Glasnost', 1990 (Zoë Dominic)

Sir Peter and Lady Ustinov, June 1990. (Chris Harris/*The Times*)

ridiculed the opposing ideologies of East and West. Starring
the playwright himself as the president of the host country,
and Michael David and Katy Vail as the young lovers, *Romanoff
and Juliet* opened at the Piccadilly Theatre on 17 May 1956 to
rapturous acclaim from both critics and audiences. Later that
year, it won the *Evening Standard* Drama Award for Best Play
and subsequently transferred to Broadway. There it delighted
New York theatre-goers for almost a year before going on tour,
and was nominated for the Antoinette Perry Award for Best
Play and Best Performance.

A triumphant new play was not the only cause for jubi-
lation in Ustinov's life, however. For on 30 April 1956, the
very day the production began its pre-West-End run in north
London, Suzanne gave birth to their only son, Igor Nicholas.
'I acted my part euphorically,' Peter was later to say, 'and my
father . . . wept tears of quiet joy.'

In an article for the *Daily Express* ten days later, the proud
father explained some of his ideas about parenthood or, more
accurately, what he saw as the criteria for raising his own
children. Under the headline, *Bringing Up My New Baby*, he
wrote:

> The night that my son . . . was born, I sent a cable
> to my old friend Sam Zimbalist, the Hollywood pro-
> ducer. It said: 'The line is assured.' It's an old family
> joke. But I admit to feeling a trifle patriarchal. I'm no
> authority on bringing up children. But I believe that
> there are some important rules to follow.
>
> The first is that a child of mine must learn to
> challenge everything. Never to accept anything on
> its face value. To dig down for the truth. As far
> as education is concerned, I can't see that formal
> schooling does any harm – so long as the child learns
> to challenge every statement that is made. Of course,
> this inquiry, this continual challenging, can get them
> into trouble. But it's very healthy for the spirit. Travel
> is important too. It helps to winkle out the lies that
> are hidden by the history books. And children must
> learn foreign languages. It is not enough just to make
> yourself understood. I know too many people who

speak half a dozen languages and can say nothing in any of them. But languages break down barriers and we have too many barriers today.

Supervision? I would like my children to stay near enough for me to keep an eye on them. Not that I want to interfere, but I would like to be close enough to put them straight on any problems they might encounter. The enemies of childhood? I'd say that the chief villains were the history books. All that distortion that children swallow wholesale. But if they learn to challenge until it becomes a second nature they won't go far wrong. They'll learn to survive.

TEN

' "The roots of the theatre lie in all-in wrestling . . . ." Whatever I might have expected to hear from Peter Ustinov, it was certainly not a statement of this kind.' Thus wrote Frank Granville Barker for *Plays and Players* in July 1956. But, he went on:

> . . . I was soon reassured. When it comes to matters of the theatre, Peter Ustinov is serious enough. Not in a pompous way, for he has always been the avowed enemy of whatever is pretentious or consciously highbrow; his is the seriousness of someone who loves the theatre and writes for it as a perfectly accomplished craftsman who knows all its possibilities and limitations. It is not always easy for us to understand him, for he has a warmer, more fluid temperament than we British playgoers. His whole imagination, like his sense of humour, often carries him beyond the frontiers of our more down-to-earth taste. And he is often the most serious when he appears to be flippant, which allows him to spring continual surprises on us.
>
> His perpetual striving to achieve delicacy in the texture of his comedies has given them an elegant, thoroughly civilized quality. His current London success, for example, *Romanoff and Juliet*, has [an] unusual artificial air, emphasized in this case by a

formal ending in a style reminiscent of the eighteenth century. The play is completely symmetrical – a fact that we tend to overlook only because the writing has such speed and feathery lightness.

Ustinov thinks that there has been too much insistence on realism, and too much striving on the part of dramatists to be 'profound'. 'What people do not realize,' he went on, 'is that a play that is not in itself profound may have a profound effect on the audience, who are made to do the thinking themselves. I try always to wrap my ideas up in a comedy, a deliberately light play, so that the sugar comes off the pill afterwards – when the audience are on their way home . . . A play should be pure enjoyment at the time of seeing it: it can always be thought about later.

In comedy, particularly . . . spontaneity is essential. Which brought us to those all-in wrestlers. 'Wrestling,' Ustinov told me, 'is excellent theatre. Usually matches are engineered so that the straight man wins, but occasionally, to tease the public, the winner has to be 'heavy'.

At much the same time as the theatre-going public were revelling in the 'feathery lightness' of *Romanoff and Juliet* in the West End, an altogether different Ustinov play had opened at the Bristol Old Vic, starring Peter O'Toole. *The Empty Chair* had a mixed reception and, like *Vice-Versa, The Moment of Truth* and *No Sign of the Dove*, was generally considered to be ahead of its time. Set in the eighteenth century, Peter's inspiration for the play sprang from thoughts of the French Revolution and such characters as Danton, Robespierre, St Just, Barras and Desmoulins. Its essential 'message', for want of a better word, not only highlighted the dangers of Absolutism, but pointed to the way in which revolution tends to destroy its perpetrators.

Talking about it more than thirty years later, Peter says: 'It is a symbolic play. The empty chair is a throne of sorts which people have captured from Versailles, transported to Paris in triumph, neglected, and put in the room where the Cabinet meets. And the three charwomen who have to clean the room before anybody arrives [and through whose eyes the events are really seen] have a legend that whoever sits in the chair is not sure of himself and will therefore be the next for the guillotine. And in every one of the four acts, one of the characters – to emphasize a point or out of fury – sits down in the chair and, in the next act, he is no longer there. At the end, the revolution has spent itself and the charwomen, who are like the witches in *Macbeth* or a Greek chorus, are busy cleaning the chair while thinking, "Well, don't think there's anybody worth sitting in it now." '

Despite its serious tone, *The Empty Chair* was not, nor was it intended to be, an accurate reflection of history. 'There are few things more devitalizing in the theatre than the historical play, in which the sweat of research permeates the hard dramatic substance,' Ustinov said at the time. 'Consequently this play, although based on truth, should not be considered as a mere reproduction of events but rather as a commentary on the psychology of revolution in general.'

The great thing about history, Peter believes, 'is that it is adaptable. It is wide open to interpretation and frequently interpreted wrongly. The French Revolution, for example, is hailed for the good it brought. Actually, very little good came from it. It gave us Napoleon, who was its antithesis. In my view, he was one of the most monstrously egocentric and avaricious men in history.'

In 1956, *The Times* said that *The Empty Chair* was 'a mildly diverting conversation-piece between historical and made-up figures'; while another critic suggested that it was 'sure to be accused of being too wordy, but without much reason for once, since words are the point; the talk has a wealth of indignant wit and even at times a wise passion'.

After its début at Bristol no more was heard of the play in Britain. Some time later it was produced on American television with Ustinov as 'Danton' and George C. Scott as 'Robespierre'. It then disappeared again until the summer of 1989, when, as Peter told me with evident pleasure, 'It opened in Hamburg'. On the first night, the production was plunged into darkness for over half an hour because of an electricity cut, but power failure notwithstanding, the response was tremendously heartening. As Peter put it: 'The leading paper said, "With a great cast, this would probably reveal itself to be a great play. As it is, it is a great success." The review ended by saying, "This is a play you have to see twice in order to capture all its qualities." '

Since he started picking up the threads of his life again at the end of the war, there has scarcely been an inactive moment in Peter Ustinov's life. Whenever possible, he snatches a few days here and there to touch base and simply enjoy being at home. Now and then he even manages to take a break aboard his 'greatest luxury' – the 58-foot ketch he bought from a business acquaintance in the South of France during the mid-1950s. Then known as the *Christina* – which meant it sometimes got confused with Aristotle Onassis' yacht of the same name – Peter rechristened the vessel *Nitchevo* (Russian for 'nothing'). The rest of the time Ustinov is never still. He is addicted to travel; compulsively criss-crossing the globe from West to East and back again. At the end of 1956, however, circumstance put him flat on his back. During a tennis match at the Russian embassy in Kensington, he leapt for the ball and landed awkwardly, dislodging a disc.

Often stubborn to the point of perversity, Peter not only scorned his doctor's advice never to play tennis again but, having worn it only once, discarded the corset that had been specially made to lend support to his back. A museum piece even when new, Peter described it as something that would have found 'immediate favour in the wardrobe of a sado-masochistic transvestite'.

Forced to spend Christmas in bed that year, Peter was cured very shortly afterwards by an acquaintance of Suzanne's who 'had a great knowledge of things oriental, and . . . walked on my spine with all her weight, stubbing out imaginary cigarettes on every vertebra'.

Back on his feet early in the New Year, Ustinov made two films during 1957. The first, shot in Paris for the director Henri-Georges Clouzot, was *Les Espions* (The Spies), in which Martita Hunt, Curt Jürgens, Sam Jaffe and the director's wildly neurotic wife, Vera, who committed suicide not long afterwards, also appeared. The second, called *An Angel Over*

Brooklyn, for the Hungarian director Ladislao Vajda, was set in New York and filmed entirely in Madrid. The Spanish entry at the Venice Film Festival that year, the story was centred on a mean-minded character knows as 'Mr Bossi' – played by Ustinov. In a sense it was a sentimental, 'Scrooge'-like tale of goodness overcoming greed and so on. Whimsical enough to appeal to a wide audience, which at least made it a commercial success, it cannot be said to have taxed Ustinov's abilities to any large extent.

It was also during 1957 that Peter and his family became officially resident in Switzerland. For two or three years, Suzanne had been agitating to leave England, though her reasons were not always clear or even logical. In the past her behaviour had beguiled, as well as confused and exasperated the cast and crew of *Othello*, while the circumstances of her first marriage had certainly troubled Peter himself. There were times when fact still tended to become indistinguishable from fiction, and many of the tales she was apt to tell had to be taken with a large pinch of salt. At one time, for example, Suzanne liked to lay claim to Red Indian descent. She also maintained that her mother had German–Jewish blood and had had to flee to Canada to escape Nazi persecution. Neither story was true.

In the early days of their relationship, Peter had found Suzanne's inventiveness diverting. But within three years, it had started to impose a strain on the marriage which even outsiders couldn't fail to notice. 'Incompatibility was writ large,' said Frank Muir. 'It wasn't a question of what went wrong, but of what went right.'

'I remember having dinner with Peter and Suzanne one night,' Cyril Luckham recalled, 'and, of course, Peter had us absolutely helpless with laughter. But Suzanne – who was known to finish Peter's stories for him – remained po-faced throughout. "You see," she had once told me, "I have absolutely no sense of humour." I was astonished by that. To be married to Peter and to admit she had no sense of humour . . . it was too pathetic.'

Robin Bailey was another dinner-party guest Suzanne surprised. 'She had an extraordinary gift – if gift is the right word – of falling asleep, quite often before the second or third course had been served.'

These and other deeper issues, which gave rise to anxiety and discord, created an undercurrent of tension which, as time went by, Peter found increasingly difficult to cope with. In the meantime, in what he called the role of 'Peacemaker', he arranged for his family to leave London for a rented châlet in Villars-sur-Ollon.

In those days, Switzerland was still renowned for its pecuniary advantages and large numbers of Britons who had had enough of being robbed by the Inland Revenue, chose to become tax exiles. While financial considerations could not be overlooked, they were not responsible for Ustinov's decision to live abroad. Nevertheless, when given the fact that he had made only £5 after surtax for a four-hour television production of *Peer Gynt*, recorded for the BBC, he was not averse to the idea of putting his money to better use elsewhere.

In Hollywood, towards the end of 1958, Peter became part of the impressive cast of *Spartacus*. Produced by Kirk Douglas, who also played the title role, and directed by Stanley Kubrick, the film recreated the remarkable story of the Thracian slave gladiator who, in 74 BC, escaped from Capua and for three years led a slave revolt of massive proportions throughout southern Italy.

Heading a well-organized army composed of an estimated 90,000 men, Spartacus emerged victorious from each of his engagements, until he came up against six legions under the command of the Pro consul Marcus Licinius Crassus. In six months, Crassus' forces vanquished the rebels – some 6,000 of whom were crucified along the Appian Way – while Spartacus himself was finally hacked to death on the battlefield.

Based on the novel by Howard Fast, the film – which decided to crucify the Thracian hero, rather than have him torn apart at the end – cost about $12 million, took well over a year to make, and employed a staggering 8,000 extras. Despite the fact that the filming 'seemed to go on for ever', Peter found 'Batiatus', the slave dealer, an interesting part to play, even though he didn't enjoy having to wear a toga yet again. 'I can't think of any garment less suited to my figure.'

With Kirk Douglas in the lead role, Laurence Olivier was

engaged to play Crassus. John Gavin was cast as Julius Caesar, Tony Curtis as Antoninus and Charles Laughton as Gracchus. Ustinov had, in fact, met Laughton many years earlier, when he and his wife, Elsa Lanchester, visited the Barn Theatre for a performance of *Mariana Pineda*. A little later, they had met again as Peter was crossing Green Park in London, having just been to see Laughton as 'Nero' in *The Sign of the Cross*.

Twenty years later, *Spartacus* re-established that most fleeting of acquaintanceships and led to a comfortable rapport between the two actors. Today, Peter likes to tell a story about the first time his son Igor, who was then no more than three or four years old, met the rotund creator of such memorable characters as King Henry VIII, Captain Bligh and Quasimodo. Because of his role, Laughton was wearing curlers to keep his 'bobbed' Roman hairstyle in shape. Having been formally introduced, Igor turned immediately to his father and asked, 'Who is this lady?' Peter explained that he wasn't a lady, he was a man. 'Then why has he got breasts?' the boy replied.

In *Ustinov in Focus*, Tony Thomas told another amusing Laughton story, which Peter had told him during one of their interviews for the Canadian Broadcasting Corporation in the 1960s.

> Laughton was a priceless man. I remember sitting with him one day in his dressing-room – both of us in our togas – when a middle-aged lady tourist poked her head in the door. She spotted Charlie and yelled, 'I know you! You're the greatest. I loved you in *Cat on a Hot Tin Roof*, where you had cancer and roared at everybody, and that great scene in the basement with all the old furniture.' Laughton screwed his face up and blinked his eyes, muttering, 'Thank you, thank you.' When she left, he said, 'If you disagree with them, they come back.' She came back anyway, full of apologies, 'Now how do you suppose I got you mixed up with that Mr Ives?' Charlie looked balefully at me, then at the woman. Gesturing in my direction he then said, 'Madam, meet Edward G. Robinson.' She shook her head, saying, 'No, he's not Mr Robinson. He's that Walter Hustonov.'

To 'Hustonov's' great relief, *Spartacus* was finally completed in 1960. By then it had been in production for so long that Peter had not only written his first full-length novel, but had also become a father again. On 30 March 1959, Suzanne had given birth to their third child and second daughter, Andrea.

At the Academy Awards in 1951, Ustinov had narrowly missed winning an Oscar for his portrayal of 'Nero' in *Quo Vadis*. Now, ten years later, his second Roman epic changed all that and he was awarded the Oscar for Best Supporting Actor. Putting the first century BC behind him, Ustinov took off for twentieth-century Australia and the sheep-droving outback of the 1920s. *The Sundowners*, based on the novel by Jon Cleary and made by Fred Zinnemann for Warner Brothers, described the nomadic existence of the Irish–Australian Carmody family. 'Paddy', played by Robert Mitchum affecting a highly-believable Australian accent, is content with his carefree lot travelling the outback, while his wife Ida, played by Deborah Kerr, and their fourteen-year-old son Sean, played by Michael Anderson Junior, hanker after a settled existence on a farm of their own.

Attaching himself to this small family group is an almost archetypal English gent, Rupert Venneker, played by Ustinov. 'A sort of superannuated boyscout', Venneker appears as one of life's more endearing drifters. With a vaguely mysterious background – he admits to having been 'cashiered from the 17th Lancers' and to having sailed the China Seas, but to very little else – he is certainly the most eccentric and unexpected of figures to find roaming the Australian wilderness. In one typically Ustinovian exchange, Sean asks Venneker, 'Why do you talk to horses?' and receives the reply, 'Has nobody told you it's rude to listen to other people's conversations?'; while a little later, Venneker tells the boy: 'I've never grown up and you've never had time.'

In preparation for the film, which was superbly photographed by Jack Hildyard – who captured several delightfully evocative sequences of jumping sheep and bounding kangaroos – Fred Zinnemann spent some twelve weeks in Australia, searching out the right locations before the cast and crew arrived in Cooma, New South Wales. As the production got under way, Ustinov grew to like Zinnemann, though only after a somewhat inauspicious encounter. In an interview he gave to the *Sunday Telegraph* at the time of the film's London première, Peter said:

> At the start I didn't see eye to eye with Zinnemann. Then one day something happened. I was walking up and down with a cigarette dangling from my mouth trying to improve on a line. Suddenly Zinnemann snatched the cigarette out of my mouth tearing my lip. 'What did you do that for?' I asked him. 'You can't concentrate with a cigarette in your mouth,' he said. 'You mean you can't concentrate with a cigarette in my mouth,' I said. From then on we understood one another.

Despite the climatic extremes – rain and sleet in the Snowy River Mountains, intense heat and burning winds in Port Augusta – Ustinov's good humour never wavered.

'How many characters – animals, orchestras, opera singers – are wrapped up in this extraordinary man?' asks Deborah Kerr. 'I shall never forget working with Peter on *The Sundowners*, on a very tough location . . . We would meet every morning in the rather thrown-together make-up room in Cooma, and the make-up man could hardly manage to make me sit still and get "my face on" because I was laughing so much at Peter.

'One morning it would be Beethoven's *Eroica* in which he would imitate *all* the instruments of the orchestra perfectly. The next morning – *Madame Butterfly*! Every day he would be a different person: American – Russian – Chinese – Japanese – and so on ad lib! He is possessed of boundless energy. I am filled with admiration for all facets of Peter – the serious side, too – and grateful for the laughter . . . he has given me and countless others.'

During the late summer of 1960, Peter was back in Italy for the film version of his highly-successful play, *Romanoff and Juliet*. Initially under discussion with Universal while he was making *Spartacus*, it had been agreed that Ustinov himself would recreate the role of 'The General', head of the make-believe state of 'Concordia' – which in the film was represented by the eleventh-century village of Todi, about 100 miles north of Rome.

As part of the package Peter accepted from Universal, however, the studio stipulated that two of its own contract players should appear as the besotted offspring of the Soviet and American ambassadors. Though in his opinion the casting was far from ideal, Peter had no choice but to accept John Gavin, who had played Julius Caesar in *Spartacus*, and Sandra Dee – once described as 'Hollywood's first virgin sex-bomb' – for the title roles. One player he did approve of unreservedly, however, was his wife Suzanne, who, in her first acting role since their marriage, was cast as a Russian naval officer who travels to Concordia in search of her boyfriend, Igor Romanoff, only to find herself seduced by a growing taste for life in the West.

That summer in Rome, where part of the film was shot at the Cinecitta Studios, the volume of traffic in the normally congested streets was increased to bursting point when the Olympic Games opened on 25 August. To avoid sweltering in daily traffic jams, Peter hit upon an audacious idea. He explained: 'It used to take hours getting across Rome in a car because of the traffic going to the games. So one day I put the Concordia flag on my car. It was magic. The police stood to attention as we went by, saluted, and escorted us through all the traffic jams. We also had an old Italian Army plane painted in the Concordian colours. One day the pilot was refused permission to land at the military airfield which we used. So he went over Ciampino, the main Rome airport, said he was "Concordia Airlines, Flight 423 from Beirut" and was given permission to land.'

Suzanne Cloutier's appearance in *Romanoff and Juliet* came at a moment of relative calm in her troubled existence. It was also a respite of sorts from the tortuous and unremitting war of nerves which the Ustinov marriage had become; and from which Peter took refuge either in silence or by removing himself entirely at every opportunity.

But for Igor, Andrea and their elder sister Pavla – for whom childhood holds uncomfortable memories of years spent in plaster casts, the result of a youthful bone disorder – Peter would most certainly have ended his second marriage long before events made divorce inevitable. 'One always imagines, fool that one is, that marriages must be kept going for the sake of the children,' he was eventually to write. Yet children, he went on, 'are the first to sniff insincerity and the makeshift harmony of moribund unions. . . . I fondly imagined that by removing myself, I was removing the cause of discord, but this proved to be untrue. I merely buried my head in distant sand instead of being content with the pile on my own front porch.'

To all intents and purposes, Suzanne wanted for nothing. After Villars-sur-Ollon and then Montreux, where their neighbour was the celebrated Vladimir Nabokov, Peter bought a plot of land in the small ski resort of Les Diablerets, near Gstaad, on which he built a châlet. When Suzanne wanted to enjoy life in Paris, Peter rented a property on the rue de Prony. Later on, he rented an even bigger, yet more elegant, four-storey house complete with internal lift, on the rue Edouard Nortier in Neuilly. Here, in her role as hostess and châtelaine, Suzanne seemed to be in her element. With her 'wonderful business brain', as Peter put it, she was responsible for controlling the family finances and for hiring and firing staff, including a succession of nannies and secretaries. In short – and to her great credit – she ran a stylish home, which was always kept full of fresh flowers, highly polished woodwork and shining surfaces, with 'the efficiency of a well-organized company'. She arranged Peter's social life, took care of the children – for whom she planned such things as horse-riding, piano and judo – and, as Igor and Andrea well remember, 'Gave us the most *incredible* birthday parties'. Funfairs would be set up in the garden, jugglers and magicians would come along, and even well-known pop singers would be engaged to entertain the children and their guests. As Igor put it, 'There were times for work and there were also times for fun'.

To others who knew her, Suzanne had 'warmth', 'style' and what has been called 'moral elegance'. She was also capable of enormous kindness. 'At times like Christmas,' said Peter's secretary, 'Suzanne was the sort of person who would always send flowers to people whom she knew couldn't really afford them.' Even so, a life-style that appeared to offer so much, never seemed to be enough. To whatever extent, jealousy of

Peter evidently contributed to Suzanne's unhappiness; so, too, a desperate need for approval and recognition in her own right.

'It must have been terrible to be married to one of the best-loved people in the world,' said Frank Muir. 'How much better to have been married to a gifted swine. At least then people would have preferred you for yourself and him for his gifts.' Another friend, Schuyler Chapin, spoke of a time in New York when, in Peter's presence, 'Suzanne flung herself into my lap, looked up at me and said, "Don't you think I'm adorable?" I looked at Peter. His expression was neutral. He never discussed his problems with *anyone*, though I got the feeling that he'd seen all this before.'

It is frequently said that – as a general rule – there are no heroes or villains in the breakdown of a marriage; that culpability is invalid. In this instance, an unusually large number of factors would seem to have played a part in the gradual erosion of Peter and Suzanne's relationship. That Suzanne was a deeply troubled individual, is beyond doubt. But to what extent Peter acknowledged – or would allow himself to acknowledge – the problems really isn't clear. Even his own admission that he sought escape in silence or in putting hundreds, if not thousands, of miles between Suzanne and himself, albeit in the course of his work, can only be interpreted as a form of denial which inevitably agitated a steadily worsening situation.

The result is a hopelessly fragmented picture, which no amount of conjecture – and certainly no amount of colourful hearsay – is about to piece together, much less clarify.

ELEVEN

Since 1941 – the year in which he completed *House of Regrets* – Peter Ustinov has written twenty-three plays. On the whole, he regards their respective successes and failures philosophically, but is reluctant to set one above another in his own estimation. 'It is difficult to have a favourite,' he says, 'because you always have to tally the ambition of the play. It's very difficult to compare one which hasn't very high ambitions – but which succeeds on one level of entertainment – with another, which had much higher ambitions and which, perhaps, failed to realize them, but which still rose higher than the first.'

Where his film work is concerned, however, Peter's likes and dislikes are more clearly defined. Without hesitation he says that *Billy Budd* – which won the David O. Selznick Silver Laurel Award in Germany and eight nominations in the British equivalent of the Oscars – was his favourite. 'I have always been tempted by things which were seemingly impossible,' he explains, 'and that was terribly difficult, because to dramatize good and evil is practically impossible anyway. It's very difficult to avoid making them dull. Evil can be a *tiny* bit more attractive than good, but they're both pretty difficult. I somehow managed it with the help of some wonderful actors.' He went on, 'It was a rather fruitful period for me . . . I said in some article I wrote, for *Time* I think it was, that I had at last succeeded in fighting my way through to my own heart. *Billy Budd* did that because it was a great challenge to try and instil

135

human feelings into the kind of barren rituals of military life. I loved it.'

Billy Budd, Foretopman, first published in 1924, more than thirty years after the death of its author, was the last work of Herman Melville, the American novelist, whose earlier creations included *Moby Dick*. Widely recognized nowadays as 'one of the earliest of truly modern writers', Melville conceived *Billy Budd* as an essay in morality or, as it has been more dramatically described, as a revision of 'the Christian myth' with Billy presented as a Christ-like figure 'who dies to satisfy an impressive but futile tyranny posing as "law" and "civilization"'.

Set on the high seas at the end of the eighteenth century, this tug of war between good and evil starred Robert Ryan as 'Claggart', the sadistic Master-at-Arms whom Billy unintentionally kills, and Ustinov himself as 'Captain Vere', 'the Pontius Pilate of this Passion', who finds himself torn between the rule of law and the dictates of his own conscience. It was a powerful role, but not one that Peter would normally have chosen for himself. 'I didn't want to play him at all,' he said at the time. 'I don't think I'm straight enough, but it was the only way I could get another name in there without it costing very much. On paper I would have seen a much more English type of Vere. I felt like a kind of land-locked Russian admiral . . . looking at myself with a slightly petulant look.'

Shortly before *Billy* went into production in 1961, at a cost of $1.4 million, it fell to Peter, who was not only a star of the film but also its producer, director and screenplay-writer, to cast the title role. It went to a young unknown from London's East End, called Terence Stamp. In his book *Coming Attractions*, Stamp recalled the screen test for the film which launched his career. He wrote:

> As soon as the camera had stopped rolling, Ustinov came on to the set and drew me conspiratorially into a corner. In a soft voice he explained that he wanted to shoot a little extra. He would insult and provoke me from behind the camera; he would accuse me of things I hadn't done, crimes I hadn't committed.

I, being innocent, would be confused and bewildered by this. Because of a speech impediment, triggered by behaviour I couldn't comprehend, I would be rendered dumb. I was not to speak. Whatever happened, I must not say anything until he said, 'Cut'. He'd patted me on the shoulder and led me back to a . . . chalk mark that had been drawn on the floor in front of the camera. 'Stay near that', he had said, and then, 'Whenever you're ready'. I nodded OK . . . He'd immediately started to harangue me, adopting the tone and manner of the vicious Master-at-Arms, Claggart. I felt as if I was being pelted with gravel. Emotions welled up inside me . . . I couldn't speak. I needed to cry out . . . but, try as I might, not a sound came.

Ustinov kept pushing. Eventually the film ran out and the camera rattled to a halt. Somebody said, 'Cut'. Everyone giggled. Then it was quiet. Ustinov had come forward and rubbed my face. 'Thank you', he'd said. 'That was,' he'd paused, then smiled, 'tumultuous.'

At that moment, Peter had found what he was looking for. 'When Terry Stamp came to see me,' he said later, 'he was so nervous that the more he was sure he wasn't going to get the part, the more sure I was that he was Billy Budd, because he behaved like Billy. I began to feel quite sadistic, because he just sat there looking at nothing, half-mouthing and fidgeting. But he did a remarkable test. You have to be very careful with Billy because that sort of character doesn't really exist. It's also very hard to conceive of a man as black as Claggart. That's why I carefully put in a long confrontation scene in which the two almost convert each other; Billy is made aware of the presence of evil in men, and Claggart becomes tempted towards tenderness.

'If *Billy Budd* has a quality,' Peter says, 'it's the quality of looking you straight in the eye. It is honest and absolutely without artifice. It's a quality I'm most proud of.'

Filmed off the coast of Alicante, on a frigate that had been constructed from an old barque, Peter decided to shoot the picture in black and white because, as he explained, 'I felt colour would clean everything, whereas black and white gives you a better feeling of the texture of splintered wood and of rigging, and a more stark feeling of the sea and the sky. I'm very interested in that period of history, and I wanted to treat the study as a kind of documentary.'

Complementing the principal trio of Ustinov, Ryan and Stamp were, among others, Melvyn Douglas, Paul Rogers, John Neville, David McCallum and Cyril Luckham, nearly all of whom were praised for their parts in a film that merited considerable critical acclaim at the time, and even now continues to be referred to both as Ustinov's 'Masterwork' and 'a minor classic'.

Cyril Luckham, who enjoyed a long and varied career as a character actor of distinction, and who had worked with Peter several times before, spoke to me of Ustinov's strategy as a director. 'He was very entertaining and slightly erratic,' he recalled. 'But it was the only time in my career when I was properly directed. I also have to say that it was due entirely to Peter who, with sheer patience and skill, got such an astonishing performance out of that horrible Stamp boy. To me, Peter's directing was an absolute joy. We had to get up at five o'clock every morning and go to sea in this bloody frigate and, because he was very conscious of the endless waiting around for winds and that sort of thing, he would do everything to keep up our morale.

'Sometimes he would do his full "orchestra" and we'd all be helpless with laughter. Then he'd go off and entertain the Spanish crew and in a moment you'd hear the *yells* of laughter, because he'd be just as funny in Spanish. I well remember that one day he'd direct as if he were a Spanish bullfighter. The next, he'd be Ben Jonson. One day he did the whole thing *à la* Benjamin Britten. He intoned in absolutely accurate Benjamin Britten intervals – and he kept that up all day, too. It was terribly funny.'

If, as Cyril Luckham pointed out, Ustinov's technical ability as a director was supplemented by his skills as an entertainer, in order to help diffuse the boredom experienced by more seasoned actors during some of the long intervals between shooting, his skills as a diplomat, even as a nanny, were also required to soothe the anxieties of his young and in-experienced protégé. Doubtless well aware that he shouldered a not inconsiderable responsibility, Terence Stamp also found himself attempting to cope with the mournful effects of home-sickness, as well as a kind of despair at not knowing how his portrayal of Billy was being received.

In *Double Feature*, the sequel to his first volume of memoirs, Stamp recalled his emotions at that time. He wrote:

> The situation I found myself in during the location shooting . . . was like nothing I had encountered before. In a foreign country for the first time and without old chums to turn to, I had nothing to grab hold of. . . . My sense of presence, that dream-like quality I'd always retained when experiencing a dislocation of environment, was the one constant in the uncontrollable sequence unfolding all around me.
>
> During the first few weeks I clung to this token stability and, once I'd begun to understand the pace dictated by filming, the sheer technicality of the work involved, I noticed odd things thrown up by my psyche which complemented the role I was to play. . . . It turned out my first scene was with Claggart, Robert Ryan himself. In the shot I come upon him unexpectedly, and the surprise causes Billy to stammer, the first evidence of the young sailor's impediment . . . I wanted to portray it as an emotional difficulty and had tried to work out what sort of problem would block speech. When we were all set to go, a wisp of melancholy settled over me which would have been the perfect underlay for the action, but a boat drifted into camera-frame and Robert Krasker [Director of Photography] called a halt to the shot until it sailed on. As we waited, my mood deepened. Before I knew it, I was in tears. . . . Ustinov found me and asked me what had happened. I tried to explain but felt overwhelmed by the thought that I wouldn't be able to capture the moment again when the camera was set. Ustinov

>   appeared to understand. He said, 'Of course you
>   will, and if you're not ready we'll wait until you are.'

Peter's sympathetic approach undoubtedly played its part in
encouraging a performance from Stamp which Dilys Powell,
doyenne of British film critics, later called 'miraculous'. But in
the meantime, it fell to Suzanne Ustinov to reassure the young
actor about her husband's reaction to his work. She told him:
'Peter thinks, as this is your first film, is is better for you not
to see the rushes . . . He feels it might disturb what you are
doing, you might start to change things if you look now,
because you will only be watching you, getting everything out
of proportion. Always remember, Peter is a genius; if you're not
good, he will make you good. . . . If he doesn't speak, this is
the best, it means he is happy with what you do.'
Ustinov's delight in Terence Stamp's performance was duly
echoed by the critics themselves. The only disappointing note
came with the film's distribution. In Britain, where the picture
was handled by the J. Arthur Rank organization, *Billy* enjoyed
considerable success. But in America, where a splendid review had appeared in *Time* magazine, it was handled by a minor
company, whose efficiency left everything to be desired. After
a successful opening in New York, it was, to quote Ustinov himself, 'jammed straight into the circuit. People didn't know
what it was.' Even more vexing was the American distributors'
choice of outlets in Canada where, as Peter was to discover,
it had been 'rushed into all sorts of downtown areas' and put
out 'among the nudie pictures, where it was double-billed
with something like *Swish of the Lash* . . . '.
While *Billy Budd* was still in production, the novel Peter had
written during the filming of *Spartacus* was finally published.
The Loser was, in fact, his third book. His first, a collection
of eight short stories entitled *Add a Dash of Pity*, had been
published two years earlier in 1959, while *Ustinov's Diplomats*,
a picture book in which he spoofed various world statesmen,
appeared the following year.
Set during the Second World War, *The Loser*, which was
republished as recently as 1989, is a frequently harrowing
story, tracing the brief life of a young German soldier, Hans
Winterschild. Under the influence of his father – a soldier of

the old school – and his brother-in-law, a stormtrooper, Hans is turned into a 'hardened little monster', fanatically devoted to the Nazi régime. As the story unfolds, Winterschild, awakened by the stirrings of love, gradually begins to recognize himself for himself but, almost inevitably, the recognition of his own humanity comes far too late.

In asking Ustinov what moved him to write *The Loser*, he said, 'It's a question which is very difficult to answer and be truthful about . . . except that there is an endless over-simplification of things after conflict. Don't forget, I'd already written a play which was more or less about Pétain and Laval. I found the trial of Laval [in the autumn of 1945] absolutely repellent. In many ways it was worse than anything that happened in the war. There was Laval [who had tried to commit suicide by] taking strong barbiturates or whatever they were, and then being brought back by stomach-pump, in order to be in a good condition to shoot! That is a side of human nature that not only makes me rebel, but makes me embarrassed to be part of the same race.

'Of course, I didn't want to try to justify [Hans Winterschild in *The Loser*],' Peter said. 'I never plead in any case, because that suggests that there is some sort of superior worldly authority to which one must pay some kind of homage. I don't think there is. [In *The Loser*] I just wanted to suggest that a man like that could be formed by his environment and might be treated as a ghastly war criminal without himself knowing why . . . It seems to me very alarming that we end certain conflicts with enormous moral capital and then the first thing we have to do is to try and spend it, so that we are on an equal footing again. It seems to me absolutely extraordinary that people will say, "He's a Nazi", without realizing that, in other circumstances, he could have been a very attractive personality, but that "they" just got to him too soon and *he* never gave the matter enough thought. So this was a case of a man whose arteries had hardened prematurely and who didn't have the capacity to react other than the way in which he had been brought up.'

It has been said on occasion that despite Ustinov's openness, his works – and in particular his plays – reveal 'uncommonly little about him'. It has also been claimed that he prefers to be known as a *non*-autobiographical writer. In response, Peter says, 'I don't care what I'm known as. In point of fact, very little of my work is autobiographical and *The Loser* had nothing to do with me in that sense. It's all stuff I've observed. I prefer autobiographies to be autobiographies and fiction to be fiction. I don't really like leaning on myself. . . . People always assume that a first book especially is autobiographical, it almost *has* to be. Well, mine never was.

'I'm not terribly self-analytical, unless it becomes imperative that I should be. In the same way, I find it very difficult to answer questionnaires without being frivolous. Just recently, I was sent one by a magazine and it had questions like, "How would you like to die?" A charming question. I said, "Not before the end of a sentence". And, "Who is your favourite musician?" I put down "Salieri, of whom I am jealous". I can't take those things seriously, so obviously I don't reveal very much.

'But as a playwright,' Peter continued, 'you have to be a Devil's Advocate – and sometimes more than just one – because in order to have any dramatic conflict, you have got to have people expressing opinions that are not your own [so as] to make your own appear. It's really rather true of a novelist as well, although less obviously so. A novelist can intervene more personally in the narrative, and therefore load the dice in full sight of the audience. A playwright cannot really afford to do that.'

Throughout his adulthood Ustinov's acute observations of human behaviour, along with his grasp of international politics, current affairs, and so on, have frequently suggested themes which he has then adapted either for the theatre or as the basis for his novels. The late Peter Daubeny once commented:

All of Peter Ustinov's writing contains a powerful sense of recorded experience conveyed beneath overtones of humour and serio-comic thunderclaps. His sharp ironical wit saves his sense of pity from deteriorating into sentiment. He balances his humour between the earth and the moon, between St Peter and the Devil. In such plays as *House of Regrets*, *The Love of Four Colonels* and *Romanoff and Juliet* his characters move in a hinterland between illusion and reality, failing to dodge a satirical aim which can have the unsparing precision of a well-handled machine-gun.

While certain drama critics, among them J. C. Trewin, share Richard Attenborough's belief that Peter's '*great* play is still to come', the originality of his work – both as a dramatist and novelist – has seldom been brought into question. Indeed, in the spring of 1962 his fifteenth play, *Photo Finish*, which opened in the West End at the same time as *Billy Budd*, was received by the kind of notices that would make any self-respecting playwright break open the champagne. *Photo Finish*, which was described by its author as 'an adventure in biography', marked Peter's return to the London stage after an absence of six years. Preceded by a four-week run at the Gaiety Theatre in Dublin, the play opened at the Saville Theatre on Shaftesbury Avenue on 23 April. In it, Ustinov appeared in the role of 'Sam Kinsale', an eighty-year-old writer who, while working on his autobiography, is joined by himself at the ages of sixty, forty and twenty. With the simultaneous appearance on stage of all four characters re-examining their collective life, it became imperative to find actors who bore at least a passing resemblance to Ustinov himself.

In his memoirs, *My World of Theatre*, Peter Daubeny, who presented the play, wrote:

> Peter and I had already spent three months together in London dissecting sets, examining costumes and auditioning actors. Exploring facial landscapes, intonations, gestures and build, we had sought for germs of resemblance in faces for the three generations that *Photo Finish* required, and felt like plastic surgeons, examining eyes, measuring noses, peering at nostrils.

One by one, the roles were cast: Wensley Pithey as 'Sam Elderly'; Robert Brown as 'Sam Middle-Aged' and Edward Hardwicke, whose youthful appearance belied his thirty years, as 'Sam Young'.

Like *The Banbury Nose* before it, *Photo Finish* explored a subject that has always captivated Ustinov. He says quite simply,

'I am fascinated by the balance of past and future. Civilization today is regarded as being pretty final and it isn't. Values change, people do not.' This was a theme that Peter would return to again some years later, when he wrote a play called *The Unknown Soldier and His Wife*, but for now 'the experimental nature' of *Photo Finish* was clearly as fascinating to the critics and its paying audiences as it was to Ustinov himself.

Writing in the *Daily Telegraph*, W.A. Darlington said:

> One of the chief assets in our theatre's treasury, though we see the glint of its gold too seldom, is Peter Ustinov's sure, light touch in his own kind of fantasy. It was delightfully in evidence . . . in his new play *Photo Finish*. Sam Kinsale . . . is eighty years old and near his death, dragging out an unhappy existence with his nagging old wife Stella [played to much acclaim by Diana Wynyard]. He lies thinking over his past life; and, by Mr Ustinov's magic, he is permitted to observe it again, but from a most unusual angle. This is no commonplace affair of flashbacks. Not merely the people and events of Sam's past years, but Sam's own past selves, are present in his study. . . . More than that, he is able to meet his own father. . . . Now, with the son the elder of the two, they can sit down and discuss life amicably . . . and find what good friends they could have been if fate had not made them father and son.
>
> All this makes a remarkably commodious and smooth-running vehicle for Mr Ustinov's wise, humorous and tolerant views on human relationships. He does not allow his characters to alter the mistakes of the past, but he allows them to understand a little better how the mistakes were made.

Save for *The Times* – which wrote: 'Even if one did not already know Mr Ustinov to be an incomparable impersonator and raconteur, one might suspect that the source of the entertainment was a playwright's virtuosity a little in love with itself' – other critics were delighted with Peter's latest work. Writing in the *Daily Mail*, Robert Muller said, 'When so much that is served in the West End these days is no better than cafeteria fare, one is bound to welcome this succulent theatrical dish ... prepared with great expertise and served by the chef himself.'

Despite the general chorus of approval, *Photo Finish* came up against one – and, by now, an all too familiar – criticism. Its length. Almost to a man the drama critics adjudged it to be too long. *The Illustrated London News*, for instance, expressed the opinion that, 'It is certainly a play of the year; it would be ... a play of any year, though Ustinov might prune a little. He has long been luxuriant; and it would not harm [the play] if it were gently and judiciously trimmed.'

Before long it was, though not by Ustinov. In due course, Paul Rogers took over Peter's role as 'Old Sam' and, between them, he and the director, Nick Garland, deleted certain passages which they considered unworkable. By the time *Photo Finish* transferred to America, however, the deletions had been reinstated. In Boston, where the play opened, the first notices were anything but favourable. 'You might say we got the reviews in the right order, which to Peter was the wrong order,' says Paul Rogers. 'From the doyen of American critics there was a very bad review. Among other things, it complained about the length. Later on, the reviews were shoved under my door at the Ritz, where we were all staying, and I did something I don't normally do. I read them. Just then, the telephone rang and it was Peter. "Paul, are you doing anything? Would you mind coming up?" So I went up and the atmosphere literally hit one. Peter was terrifying. There was Nick Garland, Peter, Peter's then wife, Suzanne ... and a long silence.

'I sat myself very near the door and waited. Then Peter said, "Paul, in London you made some cuts". I said, "Yes", and it was as if I was walking on broken glass, because Peter's "babies" are his "babies" and he doesn't like them to be touched. "Use those cuts", he said. Now, I'm glad he didn't wait for the afternoon papers, because they were rather favourable. But the result was, that by the time we opened in New York, we had a lovely tight production.'

Although Peter says that he is 'getting better' at accepting criticism, his disliking for it, especially where his own work is concerned, has often been intense. 'If Peter has a weakness, and he has, it is that he is too sensitive,' says Paul Rogers. 'You need to have a skin like a rhino. You need to be capable of being hurt and the capability to shrug it off. As they inevitably do, critics hold you up, only to knock you down. When Peter started to get unfavourable notices for his plays, it wounded him terribly . . . it shut the door on the writing, and one can understand it. Not that Peter, as a writer, did much agonizing over the process of creation. But there was a great deal of delight in it, so that when, on occasion, that innocence and delight were met with a dismissiveness and, frankly, unkindness, it struck deep and hurt a hell of a lot.

'There is this enigmatic aspect about him,' Rogers went on, 'so that no one can say, "I *know* Ustinov". When one meets him, it is wonderfully warm, but you are aware that there are areas that you will never, never know. One area that one didn't suspect, was *anger*. That *is* frightening. Extraordinarily enough, Peter can be scary and I think he is quite well aware that, given the circumstances, he can be quite a forbidding person. I have never known him to lose his temper. It doesn't blow. But you know it's boiling there, like a contained volcano.'

Putting Paul Rogers' assessment of the 'angry Ustinov' to him, in order to slot one more piece of this human jigsaw into place, Peter said, 'I am very interested to hear that, because you hear lots of things about yourself on these occasions which you wouldn't hear normally. I'm interested in what Paul said because he watched me direct *Billy Budd* and saw how I cope with anger.

'I always remind myself when I am threatened to go overboard – and I must say it has happened extremely rarely – of a Chinese proverb: "He who loses temper, loses argument". I think there's a lot to it, because even in life I am a great believer in keeping something in reserve. If there is an opportunity to speak, I usually don't take it, because it may come in a little more usefully later on. I think this is probably a very Russian quality. It punctuates the whole of Russian history. They are nothing if not patient. And I feel that kind of patience in myself, thinking, "I'm not nimble as a person because I'm too heavy; I'm fairly nimble as a mind, but one must always keep something in reserve."

'For the same reason, I don't like actors who use all their voice in loud moments because it somehow shouts to me that they can't go any louder. Whereas, if you don't use all your voice, there is always the possibility that you can be twice as loud if you tried. It's all that. I think one should be economical with everything.'

Tolerance and 'economy' are indisputable hallmarks of Ustinov's character, even to the point of being part of his universal popularity. 'In the film industry,' says his London-based agent, Steve Kenis, 'people build themselves up by tearing other people down. Peter is not a subscriber to that. He has always been known as co-operative and very professional. He doesn't see much point in being otherwise, because he knows that isn't the way to deal with people.

If he considers somebody to be foolish or disruptive, he will try to keep his distance, but he won't castigate them. He will just have as little to do with them or with the situation as needs be. Peter is never unkind or malicious. If he doesn't like someone, he will never say so and they will never know. I think he has his own mind's view of life and what he would like it to be. I don't think he is striving towards any kind of perfection, it is simply his "take" on how he thinks he ought to be treating people and how he wished other people would treat him. He follows his instincts. Simple as that.'

For Peter and his mother, 1962 ended on a note of deep, personal sorrow.

With Klop's retirement in the autumn of 1957, he and Nadia had moved to a Tudor cottage, near Cheltenham in Gloucestershire, which – like Barrow Elm, Nadia's wartime home – was owned by their friend, Sir Thomas Bazley. During their last years together, Klop and Nadia led a relatively tranquil life, far removed from their respective and sharply contrasting worlds of espionage and theatrical design.

With or without his family, Peter visited his parents at 49 Eastleach whenever he could, or otherwise met them briefly in London if he was simply passing through. For Nadia, however, that was never enough, especially when the intervals between seeing or hearing from him became increasingly prolonged. 'It's a pity we didn't have more children,' she once remarked to Klop. 'There would have been perhaps one amongst them who would have cared to keep in touch with us.'

'Nonsense!' Klop had replied. 'It's far better as it is. To worry about one is quite sufficient. And what a blessing that it was a boy! I dread to think how it could have been! Fancy us having an ugly daughter whom nobody wanted or, even worse – a very beautiful and attractive one! I would have died long ago worrying and trying to keep her out of trouble.'

By now, Klop was nearing his seventieth birthday: an anniversary he had vowed never to see. In his autobiography, Peter wrote: 'It was during the war . . . that my father suddenly declared, quite out of the blue, that he refused to live over seventy years. His categorical announcement took everyone by surprise, particularly because there was nothing about the conversation to warrant it.'

In 1945, Klop's reaction to the birth of his first granddaughter, Tamara, had been one of shock more than of pleasure, and that, perhaps more than anything else, had reminded him of the inexorable march of time. 'I believe he felt his powers waning,' Peter was to write, 'not only physical powers, but his credibility as a seducer, and he refused a life of mere observation, with the promise of nothing but senility.'

Some time during November 1962, Klop's powers began to fail him altogether. So much so, in fact, that by the end of that month, when he was visited by Nadia's eldest sister, Olga Steiner, or 'Olia' as she was called, it was obvious that he was already close to death. Peter's arrival hot-foot from Paris on the 29th caused Klop to rally momentarily and even to ask for some champagne, of which, as Nadia recalled, he had 'only a very tiny sip'.

Next morning when Peter went into his father's room, Klop told him that he had been dreaming.

'Of me?' Peter asked.

'Yes,' Klop replied. Then, with a puzzled look, he had whispered, *'Je te reconnais de mes rêves'* ('I know you from my dreams').

Klop died on 1 December, the very eve of the birthday he had so stoutly refused to see. Many years later, Peter was to write, 'So vanished a man I never really knew, and whom I, like all sons everywhere, needed to know better.'

TWELVE

For his eighteenth film, *Topkapi*, which United Artists released in 1964, Peter won his second Oscar for Best Supporting Actor. He observed:

> I was reaching the age of compensation. I had, on my desk, two emasculated gentlemen, and two emasculated ladies as well. These were Emmy awards, which I received for playing Dr Johnson and Socrates, and the four of them made for a fine mixed-doubles match. Then I won a third Emmy playing an aged Jewish delicatessen-store owner on Long Island, at grips with racial prejudice in the shape of a proud black boy. . . . We now had an Umpire as well.

Quite where the pair of golden Academy Awards fitted into this unlikely tournament is anyone's guess, though at one time they stared impassively through the doors of a glass cabinet Peter kept in his bathroom. 'I remember David Selznick dining at my house on one occasion, and he came out of my bathroom angry and aghast to find my trophies there displayed,' Ustinov recalls with amusement. 'He said he thought I had desecrated the entire theatrical awards system. He simply didn't understand that it's the one place where you can lock yourself up without hurting anyone's feelings and contemplate your achievements without interruption.'

Nowadays, with one on Peter's desk in the study of his

home in Switzerland, and the other in his Paris apartment, the situation of these cinematic holy of holies can offend the sensibilities of no one.

Topkapi, which was based on Eric Ambler's novel, *The Light of Day*, was made by Jules Dassin on location in Turkey and Greece. It was a highly entertaining and frequently amusing film which told the story of a woman (Melina Mercouri) with a passion for emeralds who, with the help of her lover (Maximilian Schell) and a band of hand-picked amateurs unknown to the police, plans to steal a jewel-encrusted dagger from the museum at the Topkapi Sarayi, former palace of the Ottoman sultans, in Istanbul.

Among the team chosen to carry out the ill-fated theft is 'Arthur Simpson', a fool of an Englishman, who scratches a living as a tourist guide in Greece. Ustinov, as his Oscar nomination testified, breathed full and ridiculous life into this pretentious, yet pitiful, character. 'I love the idea of a man who aims low and misses,' said Peter at the time of the film's release, adding, 'Simpson is the kind of man who wears blazers a little too consistently, the kind with military presumptions, who has to belong to a cricket club. He's a man who hovers between the more reprehensible columns of the *News of the World* and oblivion.'

During the 1960s, Ustinov was seen in no fewer than ten films, not all of them worthy of his time or his abilities. 'When you look at what he's done,' Dilys Powell told me, 'a lot of Peter Ustinov's career has, in a way, diminished him. A lot of it isn't on a level with a man who could write such good comedy and act so well. In *Topkapi* he gave a very good performance in his lighter and more ironic vein. That was one of the best things he has done and it's nice to think he got an Oscar for that. He deserved it. But, on the whole, I think Ustinov belongs to the theatre, not in cinema, and I think that shows.

'During the war, when I saw him in one or two films, I remember thinking, "Hello, he's good, he's interesting", and I hope I said so at the time.'

In common with many critics, however, Dilys Powell believes Peter has often found himself ensnared by roles to which he was profoundly unsuited. She went on, 'A serious comedian is the rarest thing in the world and I think he was that. But then he's been wasted again and again and again. But an actor can get trapped. After all, they have to make a living like everyone else. He's offered a part and he can judge what he can do with the script he is shown. But he doesn't know what he is going to be surrounded by'.

One of Ustinov's most lamentable films was *John Goldfarb, Please Come Home*, which he made immediately after *Topkapi*. Produced by Steve Parker for 20th-Century Fox, it was one of an immense number of what can only be called 'junk' films, churned out by Hollywood during the 60s and 70s in an apparent mood of 'anything goes'. Described as 'doggedly unfunny . . . like a man trying to swim while wearing weighed boots', the film, which cost over $4 million to make, told the story of an American pilot called, not surprisingly, John Goldfarb, played by Richard Crenna, who crashes in the Middle-Eastern kingdom of Fawzia while returning from a spying mission over Russia.

A former footballer, Goldfarb is brought before King Fawz, otherwise Peter Ustinov, and given the choice of either coaching the royal football team or being handed over to the Russian authorities. Peter was joined in this film by Shirley MacLaine – one of the reasons why he agreed to appear in it in the first place – who played the part of an American photo-journalist. In order to get a story about the harem of the football-mad, sex-crazed monarch, she joins his flock of scantily-dressed lovelies, and spends much of her time trying to keep herself out of the king's bed.

John Goldfarb was followed in 1965 by *Lady L*, which Peter not only directed and scripted, but which he also appeared in. Produced for MGM by Carlo Ponti, and starring a cast which included Sophia Loren in the title role, Paul Newman, David Niven and Philippe Noiret, *Lady L*, though more entertaining than its predecessor, fared no better as a commercial proposition.

Two years later, having played an Arabian king in *John Goldfarb* and a Bavarian prince in *Lady L*, Peter found himself demoted to the lowest rung on the ladder of respectability in the first of three films he was to make for the studios of Walt Disney. In *Blackbeard's Ghost* his was the eponymous role of the pirate captain who, in order to redeem his wandering soul, has to perform a good deed. In this picture, directed by Robert Stevenson, who had directed Julie Andrews in *Mary Poppins* three years earlier, Captain Blackbeard of course performs several good deeds. In the end, having seen off the bad guys and created nothing but happiness in the lives of the good, the captain is himself set free, to sail his ship towards more celestial shores. *Blackbeard's Ghost* was pure family entertainment, and with Disney's name attached to it it couldn't fail to succeed.

Yet it is perhaps a sad reflection on the film industry itself that, of the ten pictures Ustinov made during a decade in which films dominated his professional life, few are worthy of recall today. Even *The Comedians*, which was scripted by Graham Greene and in which Peter starred with Elizabeth Taylor and Richard Burton, Alec Guinness and Lilian Gish, met precious little success at the box office, and did virtually nothing to enhance the reputation of its players.

Filmed in Dahomey, West Africa, the closest they could get to Haiti, *The Comedians* set out to expose the régime of 'Papa Doc' Duvalier. But for the intervention of a tiresome love affair between Taylor, as the wife of a long-suffering diplomat, played by Ustinov, and a failed hotelier, played by Burton, it might have succeeded. Though there was scant praise for the film itself, Peter's portrayal of the cuckolded husband did earn applause from fellow actors such as Sir Alec Guinness. In his own autobiography, *Blessings in Disguise*, he was to write: '*The Comedians* was not a particularly successful film but it contained one beautiful performance, unfortunately not properly appreciated by the critics, and that was given by Peter Ustinov. It was a serious, wise and sensitive portrayal of a sad diplomat, full of feeling and superbly well judged.'

Like Alec Guinness, Peter's own feelings about *The Comedians* was one of disappointment. He said later, 'It was too strange and too long . . . . It was one of those mysterious films – *Lady L* was another – that looks marvellous in the daily rushes . . . but when you string the whole thing together, there is a certain feeling of imbalance. This is something about film making that is hard to understand or explain.'

Towards the end of 1967, Peter was back in London to finalize production arrangements for his latest play – a perceptive commentary on the times, entitled *Halfway up the Tree*. By then the West had been enveloped by the cultural and social revolution emanating from Britain. The Beatles – or the 'Fab Four' as they were being called – had firmly established the cult of youth, and London was hailed as the 'Swinging Capital' of the world. London dictated trends in fashion as well as contemporary art and music. Mini-skirted designer Mary Quant had put King's Road, Chelsea, now bourgeoning with boutiques and discotheques, on the map; Barbara Hulanicki and 'Biba' did the same for Kensington; while Glaswegian John Stephens transformed Carnaby Street from a rather shabby thoroughfare on the edge of Soho into a mecca of 'high' fashion.

Liberated by a new ideology – which the media called 'The Pill, Pot and Freedom' – young people almost everywhere shook themselves free, albeit temporarily, from conventional values. Morality became something of a dirty word and 'Flower Power Ruled OK!' With the abolition of the Lord Chamberlain's powers of stage-censorship, the British theatre was revolutionized overnight by the imported American musical *Hair*, complete with four-letter words and full-frontal nudity; while not long afterwards, a bearded, white-robed John Lennon took his new bride, Yoko Ono, to the presidential suite at the Hilton Hotel in Amsterdam, where their honeymoon became a much-publicized 'bed-in' for peace.

All this, though merely the tip of the psychedelic iceberg, provided a veritable feast of ideas for a playwright as receptive as Ustinov. The outcome, in the form of a new comedy, was a light-hearted exploration of the generation gap and the effect the 'new morality' had on the ultra-conservative household of General Sir Mallalieu Fitz-Buttress of the Brigade of Guards – newly returned from a lengthy tour of duty in Malaya – and his – by now – rebellious, hippie offspring.

John Gielgud, who directed the play in London while Ustinov himself went to New York to direct it on Broadway, remembers being given the script to read some time earlier, when he and Peter were occupying adjoining bungalows at the Beverly Hills Hotel. He says, 'I liked *Halfway up the Tree* very much and suggested that Binkie Beaumont, my manager, should buy it for Ralph Richardson; but Richardson refused it.

A year later, Beaumont suggested Robert Morley [for the role of Sir Mallalieu], who agreed to play in it.

'Morley was wonderfully accomplished, but he was very rude to Peter at the first reading. Then Peter left for New York, from where he sent me various amendations. Morley took no notice of them and proceeded to rewrite and add dialogue of his own, incidentally removing all the things which Richardson had disliked when he was offered it. Consequently, I was in some trepidation when Peter returned to see our last rehearsal in London, but to my great surprise and relief he made no objections and, indeed, congratulated us on our work. The play was a great success and had a long run, even though Morley had to leave and Jimmy Edwards took over for the last weeks.'

Jonathan Cecil, then a young comedy actor, had been cast in the role of a gauche scoutmaster, inveigled into marrying the General's already pregnant daughter. He also recalled Robert Morley's inability to leave a fellow playwright's work intact. 'In the last week of the pre-London tour,' he said, 'I had a vivid glimpse of Peter's deadpan humour and also his forbearance. Robert Morley's unique comic gift and audience rapport go hand-in-hand with a compulsion verging on mania to rewrite every line of his own part in his own style. After an absence of six weeks, Peter saw the play . . . by now replete with Morleyisms, and came backstage to congratulate the cast on their performances. Slightly humbled, Robert said, "Good Lord! By this stage of the tour my author has usually stopped speaking to me".

' "You mean," said Peter, "you've stopped talking to yourself"?'

By the time *Halfway up the Tree* was running simultaneously in London, New York and Berlin, it had also opened in Copenhagen and Prague. On his travels to and from those cities, Peter was sometimes accompanied by Suzanne. To the outside world, theirs was still the harmonious partnership of magazine and newspaper stories. Life with Peter, Suzanne maintained, was still 'chaotic but fun', and, no, she hadn't any regrets about giving up her own acting career. 'After all,' she said, 'living is more important than make-believe.'

Despite the calm, united front, Peter and Suzanne's marriage had already entered its final phase; and early in 1968 Peter was forced to acknowledge the fact that separation was his only course of action.

Now his prime concern was the welfare of their children. But since he was in England, in the midst of filming Ira Wallach's *Hot Millions* with Maggie Smith, and the children were at home in Neuilly, ostensibly on their own, Peter took the decision to send each of them to boarding schools in Switzerland. Entrusting the task of making the necessary arrangements to his lawyers, he settled on Château Brillamont for fourteen-year-old Pavla, Le Rosay for Igor, who was now twelve, and Châlet Marie-José for eight-year-old Andrea.

To anyone outside his small and intimate family circle, the end of Peter's marriage to Suzanne Cloutier, as she is again known, and the catalogue of reasons for it, remains an intensely private matter. In his autobiography, Peter made several references to it, some more pointed than others, but as a man of colossal integrity, he reserved the right not to surrender his soul to public scrutiny. At the time of the book's publication, Ustinov's circumspection was criticized by a handful of reviewers, even though he clearly explained his reasons for it when he wrote:

> ... my second marriage is the theme for another book, a book which will never be written. At least, not by me. If one of the children should take it into his or her head to be as crisp and objective as their grandmother was about their grandfather ... that is a legitimate prerogative of a later generation. They may have at their disposal by then psychological insights which were denied me, and which could explain the irrational with greater assurance than I can, and which could analyse with serenity and precision the sources of my despair.

Today, Peter is no less determined not to discuss his second marriage which, when it was finally dissolved in 1971, all but wiped him out, financially as well as emotionally. In order to meet the half-a-million-dollar settlement imposed by the Swiss courts, in what was ironically called a *divorce à l'amiable*, Peter was obliged to sell anything – property, pictures, and so on – that could realize enough to act as a 'down payment'. The rest of the debt – which, with time to pay and accruing interest, amounted to over $1 million – was paid off over a period of several years. During that time Peter undertook television commercials and acting roles from which he derived little or no satisfaction. He did them, 'simply in order to make ends meet, and to contrive to give my children an adolescence as serene as their childhood had been tormented'.

Almost twenty years later, when Peter and I talked about that desolate period in his life, he gave an indication of why the marriage had 'very nearly torpedoed' him.

'It made me not lose confidence in myself,' he said, 'but it maimed – for a time – the necessary objectivity and distance from my work. Gone was the luxury of having moments of relaxation. I am a temperament who needs calm . . . I can't bear tension [even] when I am working. There are people who thrive on it. There are some directors who thrive on it, and those I try to avoid, or tell them not to try it with me because they won't get the results they hoped for.

'But the marriage was like being deprived of sleep. That's what it was really like, and that I found the most hurtful element. It wasn't a question of an attempt of any sort to interfere with my intellect, it was an interference with my stamina. And that, as someone who rations himself very carefully, I found very nearly intolerable.

'These are things I don't think about very often now . . . time provides its own medicine. But I can now talk about them objectively with my children, and that is a tremendous relief because my chief concern was to try and save them. They were all affected by it, of course, but I think the worst is over, [even though] I still see residue, gravel. My "victory" in the whole thing was that I had custody of the children. That must say something to any reasonably intelligent person.'

It is a fact that public 'clowns' often tend to be private depressives. Peter Ustinov is not of their number. For while acting or, more correctly, entertainment, represents the main thrust of Ustinov's life, he is separated from most of his profession not only by intellect, but by the diversity of his activities. As Frank Muir put it: 'Peter is living a life, not working out a career.'

Nor is he what might be called an 'actor's actor'. Award ceremonies, show-business parties, night-clubs, the society of so-called 'beautiful people', and all that palaver, is not to Ustinov's taste.

'I can safely say that I hate show business,' he once told me. 'I hate show business and I hate the words attached to it; "razzamatazz", "glitz", and all that. It doesn't interest me at all.'

That said, Peter's lack of enthusiasm for the more vacuous or superficial aspects of his profession, together with his preference for retiring to his caravan during breaks in filming, rather than lingering idly by on the set, for example, does not reflect an anti-social desire to detach himself from those around him. On the contrary. It is simply that, while remaining accessible to his colleagues, he is invariably concerned with occupying his time with something more constructive, or at least rewarding.

Jonathan Cecil, who has made three or four films with Ustinov, and has seen how he handles working relationships, says, 'Peter has an unselfish enthusiasm for his fellow-actors' abilities, which makes him a joy to work with. In fact, because of the on- and off-set atmosphere he creates, I would call him a model leading man. On set his spontaneity brings out the best in all but the most hidebound actors. He dislikes too many retakes, recognizing his own talent as essentially impromptu and natural – though he is technically dazzling.'

Cecil went on: 'Between takes, and often mischievously in rehearsal, his outstanding gifts as an entertainer keep up a permanent and invaluable party atmosphere . . . . He is adept at breaking tension and rising above trying conditions . . . . In fact, although . . . he has no English blood, he has some of the best qualities of an old-fashioned English gentleman. He treats everyone with the same courtesy, is sensitive to the worries of beginners and is tolerant of others' weaknesses; though by no means without his dislikes. He has an old-world distaste for coarseness and crassness and does not care for the humourless pretensions of certain "stars". Yet his forbearance is admirable. I have seen him tired out, in discomfort, having to suffer fools gladly, but never, never showing impatience.

'One example of his imaginative thought for others springs to mind. During one film he had to go to Ireland for the weekend. Mindful of the onset of winter, he brought back half-a-dozen hand-woven scarves for the actresses, each one carefully chosen for the individual's colouring.

'Peter's ability to bring humour to serious topics and a touch of gravity to humorous ones is a very attractive quality; showing a realistically rounded view of life. When someone asked me, away from the film set, if Peter Ustinov was as brilliantly amusing as he appeared, I replied unhesitatingly, that indeed he was, and even more so; but that I found him most amusing when he was talking seriously.'

It was no doubt for reasons such as these that, in 1968, Peter was invited to become the first Rector of the newly-established University of Dundee. The students, he said, 'may have thought of it as a joke, but . . . for me it was a vital moment in my life, when I bent my mind to new problems, to real problems, compared to the mere careers of plays or films'.

That October, a day or two after members of the university football team had hauled him through the streets of the city in an open carriage, while he obligingly quaffed half a bottle of whisky out of a silver chalice, Ustinov was formally installed as Rector. Dressed in robes of red and blue, he entered the Great Hall to a cacophony of sound, flights of balloons and paper darts, cascades of lavatory paper, and a wave of wolf-whistles – the latter aimed not so much at him, as at the university's Chancellor, Queen Elizabeth the Queen Mother, in whose procession Peter made his way to the podium.

Witnessing the ceremony for *The Times*, Philip Howard wrote:

> A granite, Old Testament patriarch would have had difficulty in surviving the pitfalls of the occasion and of his uniform. Mr Ustinov managed charmingly as if to the rectorial manner born, at the same time exuding an air of rakish Roman emperor and Ruritanian diplomat.
>
> Mr Ustinov used his address to deliver a wry,

very funny, very serious survey of the state of the world, and wistful hymn of hope to youth; a *tour de force* full of his philosophy about the importance of the individual, which runs through his plays. Speaking of the rebellion of students everywhere, the rector asked himself whether youth had rebelled quite enough against the growing grey hopelessness of the modern world. 'Has youth really risen to our expectations of it? All our hopes are invested in it, as the hopes of every disappointed generation are always invested in those who follow them. We wait impatiently to see if the idealism of those at present without responsibility can survive once it emerges into the practical, unprotected realities of competitive existence. . . .

On the horrors of the twentieth century, Philip Howard's report went on, Ustinov said:

The world used to be a place of unanswered questions, and consequently a place of poetry. Man stood under an infinity of sky, minute, naked to his enemies and to the elements, believing in the gods or in God, who represented the colossal question mark of his existence, and asking why in words, music and dance. Soon the world will be a place of answers without questions. Already the most sophisticated computers shower us with answers to questions so complicated that only another computer can put them. Without questions there is no music, no dance; there are no words. A world without questions is the death-knell of gods, of God, ultimately, of man.

People, says Ustinov, are united by their doubts, but divided by their convictions. He adds: 'I am willing to share anybody's doubts, but there are certain convictions I cannot and will not share with anybody.'

During his first three-year term as Rector of Dundee University, Peter came up against a section of the student body which he described as being 'already well versed in all the low tricks of political chicanery'. These were the social sciences Marxists 'who called wildcat meetings amongst themselves' and who were now petitioning for the Rector's resignation; informing him that, in a (secret) ballot, forty were in favour of the motion while only six were against.

This apparent vote of no confidence was stirred up because he had refused to support an illegal strike over government grants. The Rector's response was to initiate a secret ballot on his own behalf, 'sending the forms to the entire student body of the University'. This time the results told a very different story: forty-five in favour of his resignation, but almost 2,000 against.

Recalling the episode in *Dear Me*, Peter wrote:

> There were howls and bleats of unconstitutional behaviour on my part. I ignored them, wrote an article for a leading newspaper, and met the lads in a head-on collision on television. They protested to me in private at having gone to such lengths to defeat them. I informed them that what they wanted above all was publicity, and that, as a good Rector, I had acceded to their request.

At the end of his first term of office, Peter was immediately re-elected for a further three years; and in the light of that recent moment of friction, chose to devote part of his second rectorial address to the greater virtues of reason. He said: 'In our moments of irritation and even anguish ... let us not only dwell vociferously on all that is wrong, but also examine ... that which is not so bad. First of all, let us realize there will always be something wrong ... but let us also pause to reflect that the machinery for dialogue is the most precious asset at our disposal ...

'Let us speak our minds by all means, but for God's sake let us listen too. Let us indulge in a constant dialogue, and arrive at our conclusion through reason, without consideration of rank or age. It is still the best, the only way. And if we are lured by our temperaments to shout or to dissolve into silence, in obedience to the images we have created for ourselves, let us remember that he or she who looks into the mirror is always more important that the he or she who looks back.'

At Dundee today, Peter's six-year tenure as Rector is commemorated by the *Ustinov Room*, which he formally opened in the newly-built Bonar Hall, in May 1979. Designed for receptions and conferences, one of its principal features is a strikingly original portrait of Rector Ustinov in the form of a five-headed bronze by the Venetian sculptor, Erno Plazzotta, which the University acquired in 1968.

Looking back, Peter retains many fond memories of his foray into Academia. But perhaps the most abiding, concerned a letter he received from an anxious parent. It was addressed to 'The Lord Rectum of Dundee University'. That, he says, 'is how I have seen myself ever since in moments of self-doubt'.

THIRTEEN

Ustinov in love has always been boyish, exuberant and ineffably romantic; prone to lovesickness and to bursting into tears – 'for reasons which seem frivolous in retrospect, but which were not so at the time'. Though allegedly diffident in his approach to women, there has never been any shortage of female interest in his life, even though some of his liaisons have been more fleeting – and, in some instances, more painful – than others.

Soon after his separation from Suzanne, for example, an (unidentified) American actress seemed certain to become the third Mrs Ustinov. Who she was and why she suddenly vanished from Peter's life is anyone's guess. But whatever her reasons for it, her abrupt departure hurt Peter very deeply.

Then, as though destiny had lent a helping hand, Hélène du Lau d'Allemans, a vivacious, dark-haired Parisienne with a husky voice and bubbling sense of humour, whom Peter had first met in London during the very early 1950s, re-entered his orbit. Granddaughter of the Marquis de Ludré Frolois, a distinguished Republican Senator and some time Mayor of Normandy, Hélène is also descended from the great French painter, Jacques-Louis David – famous for such works as *The Death of Marat*, the *Coronation of Napoleon*, and the mildly erotic *Madame Récamier*.

Despite their mutual attraction nearly twenty years earlier, marriage was out of the question, at least so far as Hélène was concerned. Originally one of a family of seven children, she and her brothers and sisters had been raised as strict Roman Catholics and, as Hélène put it: 'In my family, you never married a divorcé. Besides, I didn't want to hurt my parents.' By the time she and Peter met again, at a film screening in Paris some fifteen or so years later, Hélène's attitudes had changed. 'Little by little,' she says, 'I realized that by trying to avoid hurting other people, you waste your own life.'

From the moment of their second encounter, Peter and Hélène gradually became inseparable, even to the point where she gave up her work as a freelance political journalist to join Peter in Mexico, during the shooting of his 1969 film, *Viva Max*. In *Dear Me*, he wrote of Hélène: 'She has made me into something approaching the man I once hoped to be, privately and secretly. She came to my rescue at a turning point during that exhausting, terrifying and magnificent journey of self-discovery we call life. And for that, I am endlessly grateful.'

In returning the compliment, Hélène told me: 'Peter is really the happiness of my life. He is an exceptional man. A genius. People like him should live eternally. I believe in friendship and in love and in respect for the other. Like Peter, I had been disappointed, too; but never mind, that's life. But maybe I wouldn't have understood him so well if I hadn't suffered myself.'

Peter and Hélène were married in Corsica on 17 June 1972. Out of deference to the feelings of Peter's children – and those of their mother, whom he had divorced the year before – the wedding, says Hélène, was a lively, but deliberately discreet occasion. The only witnesses were the local Deputy, who married them – and who also happened to be a friend – and members of his family.

'Hélène and I are compatible,' Peter once said, 'because essentially we're both terribly independent people, she out of habit, I out of spirit. More important, we respect each other's independence.' Indeed, one of the reasons why the marriage continues to work as successfully as it does is the very fact that Peter and Hélène aren't always together.

Not long before the Ustinovs married, another famous couple who were not always together – though for entirely different reasons – were Peter's friends, Elizabeth Taylor and

Richard Burton. The last time all three had worked together had been on the unsuccessful Graham Greene film *The Comedians* for MGM. Now they were back in harness for a curious picture that Peter had written and intended to direct.

In his biography of Burton, entitled *Rich*, Melvyn Bragg quoted the actor on the subject of Ustinov's proposed film.

> I read . . . the script called *Hammersmith Is Out* which P Ustinov had sent,' Burton noted in his diary. 'It is very wild and formless but just the kind of thing that I would like to do at the moment. Particularly as it has a splendid part for E[lizabeth] too. . . . The whole thing begins and ends in a lunatic asylum and my role is a deadly and totally insane killer called Hammersmith. The idea is not new. Who are mad? Those inside the bin or those outside? In this case both. . . . It should be wildly funny and fun to do, especially with somebody as congenial as Ustinov and as brilliant, and might be a big commercial success to boot and spur.'

Alas, the film was not a commercial success. A few years later, Peter wrote:

> Having worked with the Burtons . . . on two different occasions . . . I can only confirm my opinion that the chemistry of having them both in a film, regarded as a rare 'coup' by financiers, in fact lacked mystery. Love scenes, and even worse, lust scenes between people who presumably have them anyway in the privacy of their home are inevitably somewhat flat on the screen, and if they happen to be passing through a momentary crisis, such scenes are worse than flat, merely a tribute to their professionalism, and there are few things worse than that.

In recent years, Peter's literary output, whether for the screen, the theatre or the bookshop, had been prodigious. In the same year that *Hammersmith Is Out* was released, Peter's sixth book (and second novel) was published.

Krumnagel, which might almost have been subtitled 'Peter Ustinov's America', was a true *tour de force*, satirizing the absurdities of justice and the law on both sides of the Atlantic. Barton Krumnagel is a coarse, vulgar, fool of a police chief from the American mid-west; a trigger-happy 'cop' whose world is sharply divided into black and white – into good guys and bad guys. To control his hypocritical, crime-ridden city, more concerned with its high level of rape cases than its equally high murder rate, Krumnagel runs a force made up of officers disguised as women provocatively dressed in mini-skirts and 'mincing heels'; as orthodox Jews (or ASPs, short for 'Anti-Semite Patrols); as drug-addicts, perverts, and hippies. Sent by his 'devoted' department on a world tour with his thrice-widowed wife, Edie, who 'had the kind of looks which would have gone far in the days of the silent screen . . . ' Krumnagel arrives in England bringing with him all his horrendous attitudes and values . . . as well as his gun. In a quiet village pub, the cop who once shot a man he saw racing from a jeweller's shop, only to discover he had been running for a bus, draws his gun on an argumentative Scotsman and kills him. The clash between the New World and the Old has begun.

While *Krumnagel*, which was republished in 1989, is generally considered to be the best of Ustinov's books so far, *The Unknown Soldier and His Wife* is widely thought of as his best play. First performed in 1967 at the Lincoln Arts Center in New York, and in Britain at the Chichester Festival Theatre in May 1968, it was the production which was chosen to open officially the New London Theatre in Drury Lane in January 1973. The New Theatre had been built on a site once occupied by a Victorian music hall and, before that, a pub called the *Great Mogul*, frequented by the famous seventeenth-century courtesan, Nell Gwynne.

The Unknown Soldier and His Wife not only allowed Ustinov to re-examine his fascination with time – a theme to which he had given voice in two of his earlier plays, *The Banbury Nose* and *Photo Finish* – but, against the then current backdrop of Vietnam, to express himself dramatically on the stupidity and immorality of war. In essence, the play tells the story of the eternal conscript who, after centuries of unquestioning obedience, ultimately refuses to die for the sake of an authority which, as one of the play's characters puts it, 'has no place . . . in a society advanced enough to destroy itself'.

The eponymous 'Unknown Soldier' is the ordinary man who, throughout history, has been the victim of political cross-fire everywhere and who has had to pay for the folly and vanity of princes, politicians and generals, with his life. He is the ordinary man who, as his wife says, 'was never recognized by anyone'; who is ordered to kill those he would prefer to befriend, and who is ordered to die when all he wants – and eventually learns to demand – is to live.

'Ideas cannot be judged by their success or failure in practice,' says the recurrent voice of rebellion. 'The idea of liberty is really only clear in captivity. Equality is only understandable in an autocracy. Fraternity has a meaning in a civil war. Ideals do not lend themselves to practical application in normal times. They are vibrant only when they are unattainable.'

In *The Unknown Soldier*, Ustinov transports us through 2,000 years of conflict: from the Cretan battlefield where Roman meets Greek, and the Holy Land where Christian Crusader challenges Muslim infidel; to revolution, world war and, ultimately, the threat of something infinitely worse, among the so-called 'civilized' peoples of the modern world.

Of Peter Ustinov's work, one critic wrote:

> An examination of what he has written in books and plays, places him as a fundamental moralist, although he squirms to be recognized as such. 'I try not to be a finger wagger. I don't think I have any right to be. If I do it, then I try to disguise it as much as possible. And you must make that finger attractive so that people don't notice it wagging. I loathe dogma.'

In 1974, a year after Peter, together with his actress daughter, Tamara, appeared on the stage of the New Theatre, he was back on screen in his second Walt Disney picture, *One of*

Our Dinosaurs is Missing. His third and last, *The Treasure of Matecumbe*, was to follow two years later.

Almost as lightweight as anything Disney might have produced, was a film called *Logan's Run*. It is the year 2274 and what is left of humanity, after pollution and war have destroyed the rest of the world, lives in a pristine glass-domed city somewhere outside the ruins of what was once Washington DC. Life within this luxurious twenty-third-century bolt-hole isn't quite as beautiful as it might appear, however. For none of its immaculately-uniformed inhabitants is allowed to live beyond the age of thirty.

Not surprisingly, the thought of enforced euthanasia doesn't appeal to every citizen of bubble-town and, every now and then, someone decides to run; only to be shot down by the police. Two inmates – security guard Logan, played by Michael York, and Jessica, better known as Jenny Agutter – do make a successful bid for freedom and escape into the wilderness. There, surrounded by monumental debris, they discover a lone survivor of the lost world, played by Peter Ustinov. His characterization of a ninety-year-old, cat-loving eccentric – exuding 'charm and idiosyncrasy', as Dilys Powell put it in her review – was one of the very few redeeming features of an otherwise dubious picture.

At the start of 1975, the year in which *Logan's Run* was made, Peter returned to England to be with his dying mother. It had been a little over twelve years since Klop's death, and in that time Nadia had slipped into a state of lugubrious inactivity, just as Peter's father had done not long before his demise in 1962. Nadia Benois, whom *The Times* said 'was greatly loved as a woman as she was admired as an artist', died peacefully at her cottage in Eastleach, Gloucestershire, on 8 February, at the age of seventy-nine.

Throughout Peter's adulthood, Nadia had always been a close observer of her son's achievements, following his career with the sympathy and objectivity of a fellow artist. 'She could be damning in her criticism,' Peter said, 'but her expression of it was always polite and gentle. She knew too well the difficulties of creation to be negligent in her condemnation or unstinting in her praise.'

Had she lived but a few months longer, Nadia would

doubtless have derived a great deal of satisfaction from seeing Peter's 'services to the arts' formally acknowledged. At a ceremony at the British Embassy in Paris that summer, attended by Hélène and a handful of friends, the Ambassador, Sir Edward Tomkins, acting on behalf of the Queen, invested Ustinov with the insignia of the CBE (Commander of the Order of the British Empire).

Yet of all the awards, decorations, medals and diplomas Peter has received through the years, those which mean the most invariably have something to do with his work in aid of the world's children. It has been said that in any kind of cat-and-mouse situation Ustinov will always champion the mouse. In other words, his sympathies lie with the underdog; with the vulnerable, the underprivileged and those most in need. Unicef and Unesco, together with the Red Cross and the Variety Club of Great Britain are chief among the charitable organizations he has actively supported over the past twenty years and more.

There are also occasions when Peter will make time to assist other causes he believes in. In 1989, for example, an appeal he broadcast on behalf of the Royal National Institute for the Deaf brought in donations totalling more than £10,000.

Because of the type of person he is, however, and because people are aware of the respect his name commands around the world, Ustinov is perpetually bombarded with requests to join any number of panels and committees, or to help sponsor all manner of causes and events. Ask him – or any of those around him – what his faults are, and one that immediately springs to mind is his almost pathological inability to say 'no'.

'I find that I often put myself in another person's shoes so thoroughly,' he explains, 'that I say "yes" to all sorts of things I don't want to do at all, because I understand *their* need for it, which is really ridiculous. But there are times when you have to be firm, just from a sense of self-preservation. So, although I find it awfully difficult, I have to stop myself from saying "yes" all the time, because it lessens the credibility of the things I am really interested in.' Then, as an afterthought, Peter adds, 'It also depends on age. You look at yourself in the mirror and you think that "no" is slightly more credible than it used to be. I can now afford to be bad-tempered.

Nobody thinks ill of an old gentleman with white hair, saying "No".'

Peter Ustinov first became involved with Unicef – the United Nations International Children's Fund – in 1968. He has often been quoted as saying, 'There is a side of my character that badly needs to help', and that is precisely what he was given the opportunity of doing when Unicef, at that time an organization he knew little about, invited him to act as Master of Ceremonies at a concert at the Théâtre National de l'Odéon in Paris.

'I couldn't understand how such an organization could get together a concert [featuring three ballet companies, four orchestras and soloists from all round the world] that no commercial manager could possibly afford,' he said later. 'Then I found out that all the hotels and airline fares had been donated, too. I thought it must be a very extraordinary outfit to engender this kind of good will.' Of the concert itself, one of Peter's most enduring memories is of the moment when a dancer with a Polish folk ballet, 'severed my microphone cable with his axe by mistake'. The result was that, as MC, Ustinov had to shout his way through the rest of the evening, ending up 'a hoarser but happier man'.

Since then, Peter has devoted much of his time to helping to promote the aims not only of Unicef, but of its educational and cultural 'twin', the United Nations Educational, Scientific and Cultural Organization, Unesco. As a goodwill ambassador, he has travelled extensively in countries such as China, Egypt, Kenya, Jordan, Thailand, Guatemala, the Philippines, India and Pakistan, on fact-finding missions and 'field' visits. He has also been responsible for helping the industrialized world to understand the needs of developing nations through documentaries, television appeals and commercials, lectures and one-man shows.

Speaking of the amount of work that still needs to be done in most African and Asian countries – particularly in the field of medicine – he has said, 'What we are doing is merely a drop in the ocean; but it is an effort to create a balance in the situation. We are trying to do what the governments of the world ought to do but are neglecting.'

Ustinov's commitment to Unicef, initially motivated by

Léon Davičo, a former journalist seconded to Unicef and now head of public relations at Unesco in Paris, is due in part to the fact that he is 'lucky enough to have four children ... who are more or less presentable, more or less intelligent and more or less agreeable'. So, he says, 'I thought it was time to start paying my debt for that kind of pleasure. If you have managed to get on in the world, your responsibilities increase, they don't diminish.'

Another factor which strengthened Peter's decision to continue with his voluntary work was the realization that the world's *annual* contribution to Unicef was the same as that spent on armaments in the West every *hour and a half*. 'I thought that this statistic was so hideous, so unreasonable, and so silly,' he said, 'that I wanted to do all I could to let people know about Unicef.'

In 1968 the organization had only one 'celebrity' spokesman, the American entertainer Danny Kaye. But although well established as a household name and immediately recognizable all over the world, he wasn't to everyone's taste. 'People either liked him or they didn't,' said Léon Davičo, 'so I suggested that we needed somebody else as well. Right away I thought of Peter Ustinov, not only because he is greatly loved, but because he is extremely sensitive to the problems of all those who suffer, whether they're children, poor people or poor countries. ... Now, quite apart from everything he does for Unicef, which is a hell of a lot, he is also very active for Unesco, which maintains that the first thing to give children in the Third World is a chance to survive. But as soon as they have survived, the next thing to give them is education, because without education, why survive?

'The aims of Unesco ... are therefore wider than those of Unicef. So, Peter works for Unicef to give children the chance to survive, and for Unesco because, as a man of culture, as a writer and so on, he knows what it means to be educated. He has also helped the [United Nations] High Commission for Refugees. Again there are children ... the innocent victims of wars, camps, torture, etcetera. He does all this work with his heart ... and with his intelligence, which is unique!'

Like show-business events, galas do not normally find favour in the Ustinov household; though in the interests of raising money for his charities, Peter agrees to them purely as a means to an end. During the International Year of the Child in 1979, for instance, he flew to Copenhagen for a televised gala performance of *Peter and the Wolf*, which he had perfected in Danish especially for the occasion. Attended by members of Denmark's royal family, that single event raised $5,000,000.

There have also been times when the knowledge of Peter's involvement with Unicef has been enough to move the rich and famous to open their cheque books. In February 1972, Elizabeth Taylor celebrated her fortieth birthday with a lavish, star-studded party in Budapest, at which Richard Burton gave her the now-famous $50,000 heart-shaped Indian diamond that was to make front-page news all over Europe. At the time, he promised to donate the equivalent of the cost of the party to a good cause and, sure enough, five months later Ustinov received Burton's cheque, made out to Unicef, to the tune of $45,000.

Infinitely smaller, but just as generous sums have also passed Peter's way. Not long after he first started to give his services to Unicef he returned home with a sheaf of pamphlets about the organization. 'How much are they?' his children asked. Peter replied, 'Nothing. They are free.' Later that day, Igor, Pavla and Andrea put an amount of money into their father's hand. Unbeknown to him, they had taken the pamphlets and sold them around the neighbourhood.

In March 1978, ten years after he first appeared at the Unicef gala in Paris, Ustinov was presented with the organization's own award for Distinguished Service. Six months earlier, he had been to Warsaw for a similar occasion, but to receive a rather more unusual award: the Order of the Smile. For once, this was an honour that did not originate with adults, but with children or, to be more precise, with one child: a boy patient at the city's Konstancin Hospital, which Unicef had helped furnish with technical equipment. Why, the boy had asked, did adults always give prizes and never children? That question led to the *Kurier Polski* ('Polish Courier') running a children's competition. Their brief was to design a new order which would be awarded to deserving adults. The winning design – a bright sun with blue eyes and a red mouth set in a broad smile – was submitted by Ewa Chrobak, a nine-year-old girl from Glucholazy. Chosen from over 50,000 entries, the smiling sun was made up in the form of a medal suspended from a ribbon. Its first recipient, nominated by the children of Poland, was an eminent orthopaedist. Subsequent nominees included a Russian puppeteer, Finnish, Yugoslavian and Czechoslovakian authors and, in 1977, Peter Ustinov.

Although fluent in several languages, including French, German, Italian and Spanish – with a certain amount of Russian thrown in for good measure – Ustinov came up against a communication problem in countries like Thailand and China. That is, until he hit upon the idea of 'barking' at the children he was taken to see. To begin with, he says, they tended to look startled or bewildered, but 'when they realized that I was rather over-dressed for a dog' they suddenly became relaxed and animated. By that point, Peter was invariably down on all-fours, with excited youngsters clambering all over him. But, as he says, 'It's an immediate contact, a sort of universal language.'

Another successful method of contact with children is through illusion. Not long ago, when visiting a class of oriental infants, Peter impersonated the cooing of a dove. Moments later, he clapped his hands, made the sound of fluttering wings, and all the children looked up at the same time and in the same direction to watch the bird fly away. It was, he says, 'a spine-tingling experience'.

Over the years, Ustinov's involvement with Unicef has led to introductions to many influential world figures, among them Pope John Paul II. Their meeting took place at the Vatican, when he and Léon Davičo visited Rome during the International Year of the Child. It proved to be an easy meeting between men of common interests and shared sympathies, not only in humanitarian issues such as child welfare and the development of poor nations, but also in the theatre and even in tennis.

'I am fascinated by the Pope's position, what he has to do, and so on,' says Peter. 'I did say to him at one point, rather impertinently, "Do you think we get on well because I'm not a Catholic?" and he said, "It's very possible". Of course, our conversation was on a superficial level, but it was very agreeable and open; very uncomplicated.'

After Ustinov had left the Vatican that day, thoughts of another meeting obviously lingered in the mind of the former Archbishop of Cracow. For when Peter arrived in London from Rome he found an urgent message from Bishop John Magee, the Pope's secretary, waiting for him. 'I thought it was very strange,' said Peter, 'so I called him straightaway. He said, "I've just had this message from the Holy Father: if you come back to Rome in the near future, don't forget your tennis racquet." '

Nothing more was ever mentioned about a papal 'tournament' however, for in May 1981 a young Turk shot John Paul four times as he drove through St Peter's Square in his 'Pope-mobile', to bless a huge crowd of pilgrims. The Pope, of course, survived the attempt on his life, but, says Ustinov, 'I think it aged him rather, in the sense of playing games . . . and I haven't seen him since.'

Whenever possible, Ustinov tries to combine his charitable work with his film schedules. For instance, in 1977, having recently completed *The Last Remake of Beau Geste*, with a cast that included its director, Marty Feldman, Ann-Margret and John Cleese; as well as *Purple Taxi*, in which he appeared with Charlotte Rampling and Fred Astaire, Peter left almost immediately for Egypt to star in Agatha Christie's *Death on the Nile*. While in that part of the world, he made a point of meeting Unicef field workers for, as he said, 'It seemed silly to go all that way and not take advantage of the opportunity.'

In *Death on the Nile*, which John Brabourne produced, Anthony Shafer wrote and John Guillermin directed, Peter made his début as Hercule Poirot, and became the latest in an unlikely series of actors – from Austin Trevor and Francis L. Sullivan to Charles Laughton and Albert Finney – to play the famous Belgian sleuth of 'the little grey cells'. According to many of her followers, Agatha Christie based Poirot on a real-life, Austro–Hungarian private detective called Ignatius Paul Pollaky, who operated from an office in Paddington, London, from 1850, and was immortalized by Gilbert and Sullivan in their operetta *Patience*.

Whatever Christie's inspiration, Poirot (like Ustinov himself) made his first appearance in 1921 in *The Mysterious Affair at Styles*. This was not only Agatha Christie's first book – rejected by six publishers before it finally saw the light of day – but the first of thirty-three novels and fifty-six short stories to feature the sharp-witted and ever-resourceful investigator.

Death on the Nile, a hugely entertaining triple-murder mystery, reunited Ustinov with both David Niven and Maggie Smith. It also gave him an opportunity to work with his former sister-in-law, Angela Lansbury (cast as the eccentric Salome Otterbourne, one of the victims) and, for the first and last time, to appear opposite Bette Davis, who played a rich but waspish Washington socialite called Mrs Van Schuyler.

Though Peter says the legendary actress was 'very good to work with', he also found her 'very intimidating', especially on one occasion when the shooting schedule was altered at the last minute and Ustinov discovered that he and David Niven would be sharing a scene with her the very next morning. He told me the story:

'We were all staying in the same hotel in Aswan and, suddenly, at about eight o'clock in the evening, I was told that one of the actors had tonsilitis and the schedule had therefore been changed and David Niven and I would have to play our scene with Bette Davis. I said, "OK" and offered to tell David, who happened to have the room next to mine. So I knocked on his door . . . "A late piece of news . . . Our scene with Bette Davis . . . .'

' "Oh, *No*!" said David.

'I said, "What's the matter? You've worked with her."

'He said, "No, but I used to live in Hollywood and, Christ, everybody knew about her. She is terrifying! She knows your part better than her own. She stops you and asks why you're leaving the commas out!"

'I said, "Oh, my God", and retired to my room. It was extremely hot, and I walked around in my underwear trying to learn this scene. I found it impossible. Anyway, I woke up at about six o'clock in the morning, half-an-hour before our call. I was lying on the bed, still dressed in my underwear, with all the lights still on. I had fallen into a stupor. I felt awful . . . and I still couldn't remember the scene. A little later, I saw David looking as white as a sheet.

' "What the hell's the matter?"

'He said, "Oh, God! I tried until three in the morning to

learn this shit and I can't do it. Eventually I slept for about two hours."

'So off we went. The scene was to be filmed on the boat and I saw Bette Davis walking around and smoking through a veil and as the smoke came back out it splintered into shafts. She looked *terrifying*! We started rehearsing the scene and David and I couldn't remember our lines at all. But Bette didn't know *one word* of her takes and she was very robust about it. She threw her cigarette on to the deck and stamped it out with her tiny foot and said, "Fuck, fuck, fuck . . . ."

'Eventually, we asked, "What's the matter?" and she said, "Oh, God! When I heard that we'd have to play this scene today and I knew I was gonna have to work with two professionals . . . why, I stayed up all night trying to learn this, and . . . ."

'We all had a great laugh and then – by some miracle – we all knew our lines perfectly.'

FOURTEEN

Aided by a lifetime's observation of humanity in all its manifestations, Peter Ustinov – as witnessed by the volume of invitations that pile up in his office – has earned a reputation for being one of the world's foremost raconteurs. He is, of course, in a unique position to add constantly to his repertoire, rotating both stories and characters to suit the occasion.

Old favourites like the ancient cleric, 'Who spoke as though he had a cathedral in the back of his mouth', are revived whenever Peter describes characters from his school days; while a particular kind of crusty old English gent has been known to put in an 'appearance' when life in the United States comes under discussion. He is the type of character who, having been told once too often, in too short a period, to 'Have a nice day' impatiently snaps back, 'I have *other* plans!'

Perhaps not surprisingly, Ustinov has always relished the company of colourful personalities, and in *Dear Me*, which was first published in October 1977, he shares many stories and anecdotes about some of those he has known. A particular favourite was Moura Budberg, an imposing 'Peter the Great' look-alike, who was a friend of Klop and Nadia, and to whom Peter dedicated his first novel. The youngest daughter of a Russian count – who was descended on the wrong side of the blanket from the Empress Elizabeth I – Baroness Budberg spent almost forty years of her life at the centre of London's intellectual, artistic and social set. Not the least of her many claims to fame were long love affairs with Maxim Gorky, H.G. Wells and Sir Robert Bruce Lockhart. For many years, the twice-married baroness was 'at home' to visitors in the early evening, when it was said that she smoked like a chimney and could drink any sailor under the table without blinking an eyelid.

One of Peter's stories about this indomitable woman happened during the Second World War.

> Owing to a circumstance as eccentric as herself, she found herself locked out of her London apartment naked. Instead of doing what most women would have done, which is to call for help while attempting to conceal their modesty, Moura placed a fire-bucket over her head, and went down into the street to solicit assistance.

Another character Ustinov greatly admired was the Labour politician, Ernest Bevin. The illegitimate son of a west country midwife, Mercy Bevin, 'Ernie' not only became Britain's most powerful trade union leader but also war-time Minister of Labour and subsequently Foreign Secretary under the premiership of Clement Attlee. Ustinov was not yet thirty when he and Bevin first met and, as he told me: 'I'd never seen anybody like that in my life before. He was an extraordinary character because he treated the whole of foreign policy as though it was something out of *The Archers*. He would talk to the Russians and say, "Now look 'ere. Someone's goin' through this wicket-gate all the time without paying me. I don't care for it." It was all reduced to that level. His thinking was like that. "Did Stalin speak English, sir?" "Only when it came to 'ow much." That's a direct quote. Everything was an eye-opener and, in a way, a joy, because he'd say, "Reminds me o' the time we was in the . . . in the Boshloi [sic] ballet and we was in the box . . . I was there with . . . with . . . and it come to the end of the ballet and they all start applaudin'. Then the curtain go up and they're all applaudin' us from the stage. This 'appens three or four times and I want to put a stop to it. I don't see who applaudin' who. I don't see any future in it, so I gotta stop it . . . my 'ands gettin' sore too. So behind Stalin's back, I did the Communist salute. Brought the 'ouse down. Got a rocket

from Clem [Attlee] when I got 'ome." That sort of thing was
so endearing. So crazy.

'And immediately things started to get boring, he used
to start singing old music hall duets with his wife. Didn't
matter where they were, with Stalin or whoever. He'd just
say, "Floss," her name was Florence, "D'you remember this
one . . . ", and they'd sing together. It was absolutely flat and
ghastly, but he remembered songs that were forgotten as soon
as they were written. Of course, there were other people who
were impressive, but they weren't as tolerable. He was very
colourful.'

Dear Me did not meet with the unanimous approbation
of book reviewers in Britain. In fact, the notices were very
much a mixed bag. There was applause from both the *Sunday
Times* and *Books and Bookmen*, for instance, who between them
employed adjectives like 'brilliant', 'joyous', 'illuminating' and
'controversial', but there was a sense of disappointment from,
among others, the *Sunday Telegraph*. Its review said: '*Dear Me*
will no doubt be very successful, but it will never be considered one of the great autobiographies.'

Reviewers are, of course, as human as anyone else, which
may or may not mean that they are capable of taking a
properly balanced look at whatever it is they are asked to
review. On occasion, there are those who would seem to
have personal axes to grind or petty jealousies to air, while
others do their job as it should be done, and do it well. Yet, at
the end of the day, even the most friendly or, for that matter,
most vituperative notice, can never amount to more than one
person's 'professional' opinion. The ultimate arbiters are the
book-buying or film- and theatre-going public.

Thus, in Britain, as in Europe and the United States, *Dear
Me* became an instant best seller. In Paris, it won the *Prix de
la Butte* for Best Autobiography of the Year; and when a paper-
back edition was produced in 1978, the immediate sale of half
a million copies led to the first of a long series of reprints, the
nineteenth of which was published as recently as 1987.

Apart from plays and books, Ustinov's particular brand
of satire has long had another, though on the whole less
public, means of expression. As both a cartoonist and a
caricaturist, his likenesses of public figures, fellow actors,

friends and acquaintances, tend to be regarded by all who snap them up as collector's items. In Paris, his secretary Liliane Couturier has a file of sketches, peopled by real and imaginary figures as diverse as Charles de Gaulle, portrayed as a Prussian officer in a spiked helmet, to a pastiche of the cartoon character, Tintin.

During the run of *Photo Finish*, Ustinov dashed off caricatures of Paul Rogers, who says, 'There was a new and extraordinary one for me almost every night,' while Denis Norden remembers how he and Frank Muir 'used to collect Peter's doodles' at the time of their radio series back in the 1950s. More recently, another friend asked for a 'self-portrait' with the intention of auctioning it in aid of a local charity. The sketch, which Peter completed in a matter of seconds, was sold for £600.

From childhood music has played a major part in Peter Ustinov's life, chiefly by way of pleasure, but from time to time as a commercial proposition.

From Hamburg, Professor Rolf Liebermann, the eminent Swiss-born composer and director, wrote to me: 'The world knows of [Peter's] humour, his qualities as a playwright and actor, and as an author. But few probably know how absolutely amazing is his knowledge of the world of music. I actually do not know anybody who has such a comprehensive, almost encyclopaedic knowledge of music, ranging from Monteverdi to Boulez. He has given me the names of eighteenth- and nineteenth-century Swiss composers, whom even I did not know. He constantly surprises me with his knowledge of my field.'

At Westminster four or five decades before, the schoolboy Ustinov's knowledge of music had also surprised his tutor, though his response to certain – and, in retrospect, evidently rhetorical – questions, was thought to be too clever by half and landed him in trouble. When his class was asked to name the greatest composer ever to have lived, Peter replied, Bach. He was instructed that the correct answer was Beethoven; and when in reply to that, he was heard to mutter that, in his opinion, Mozart was superior to Beethoven, he was made to write out one hundred times, 'Beethoven is the greatest composer who ever lived'. Another time, when asked to name 'one Russian composer' Peter suggested Rimsky-Korsakov. He was told the correct answer was Tchaikovsky and berated in front of the entire school for showing off.

In later years, music critics would sometimes echo Peter's schoolmaster's admonitions, when he started to produce, direct, and even to design, opera. If this seemed a rather curious departure, Schuyler Chapin, a former General Manager of the Metropolitan Opera in New York, explains: 'As an impresario, you search the world to find stage and theatrical minds with a knowledge of music like Peter's, because they bring a new perspective to the Art.'

Sir Georg Solti was also clearly inclined towards that point of view, for it was he who invited Peter to direct his first operatic production at Covent Garden. Performed in June 1962 – three months before the American actor Sam Wanamaker designed and produced Verdi's *La Forza del Destino* on the same stage – Ustinov directed Mary Costa, Amy Shuard and Geraint Evans in a triple bill consisting of Ravel's *L'Heure Espagnole*, Schoenberg's *Erwartung*, and Puccini's *Gianni Schicchi*.

Six years later, Georg Solti, under the aegis of Professor Rolf Liebermann, asked Peter to direct *The Magic Flute* in Hamburg. He needed no second bidding. For while his musical tastes embrace everything from Mexican war music to Flamenco, little-known Russian operas and folk melodies to acknowledged classics, Ustinov has always been a Mozart devotee. He says, 'People often ask me what other writer has influenced me and I've really got to say that I don't think any have in that sense. I was very interested in Chekhov and Gorky and those people, but I don't think they actually influenced what I did. *If* anything has influenced me, it's Mozart, because he has what I call the most profound superficiality. He keeps the surface of the water still, so that you can study the complexity of the rocks beneath; which in itself is a splendid achievement, because there's a case of a man who engages you on one level and makes you think on another. And that, I think, is absolutely right.'

Ustinov's treatment of *The Magic Flute* – 'I made this fictitious Egyptian kingdom on the stage look very much like

a university campus . . . like a cross-section of civilization'
– inevitably won admirers. But it also attracted severe criticism, especially from traditionalists. Some time later, when
the same production was staged in Florence, however, the
New York Herald Tribune openly questioned what had displeased
German audiences; adding that it was 'surely respectful of the
text . . . faithful to the music and yet inventive'.

In 1973, Peter worked on two further operatic produc-
tions: Mozart's *Don Giovanni* for Peter Diamand at that year's
Edinburgh Festival – the first time an opera had been created
specifically by and for the Festival; and Massenet's *Don
Quixote*, which he produced, directed and designed for Rolf
Liebermann at the Paris Opera.

Joined in Edinburgh by Daniel Barenboim, who was making
his début as an operatic conductor, Peter chose to produce
Don Giovanni, which was based on the legend of the infamous
Don Juan, as Mozart and his librettist, Lorenzo Da Ponte,
intended. That included the reinstatement of an amusing
final scene, in which two policemen, the *'due ufficiali'* of the
original libretto, arrive from Madrid to arrest Giovanni, only to
find that he has vanished; that the ground beneath his feet has
opened up and, in settlement of a life of lechery and excess,
he has been dragged down to Hell. In most productions, this
light-hearted scene is dropped altogether, leaving the curtain
to fall on Giovanni's awful disappearance.

Yet that approach, as Ustinov pointed out, diminishes
the impact of what both Mozart and Da Ponte conceived
and produced as a *Dramma Giocosa* – a jocular drama. 'It
isn't meant to be tragic,' says Peter. 'I can't imagine that a
man who seduces two thousand women or whatever it is, is
a tragic figure. What he does with one woman is tragic. What
he does with two thousand is risible. But today, *Don Giovanni* is
treated as being a psychologically convoluted thing, which it
isn't. So at the end, I brought on the *due ufficiali* as two Guardia
Civiles – and what are they doing? They are policemen, and the
culprit they were to have arrested for all his wrongdoing has
got away. So now they are measuring the hole through which
he disappeared and are jotting down the measurements in a
notebook, for the report they will have to send to Madrid.

'I was attacked for doing that, but it's *exactly* the spirit in which Mozart intended the thing. It all makes sense if you treat the work as it was written.'

The cast of the Edinburgh Festival's production – for which Peter also designed the costumes, as well as a revolving set which eliminated the intrusion of scene changes – was led by Roger Soyer as Don Giovanni, Geraint Evans as his servant, Leporello, and Heather Harper as Donna Elvira. Yet even so distinguished a company as that did little to inspire enthusiasm among certain reviewers. On this occasion, the prize for 'Un-happiest Critic' went unequivocally to Gillian Widdicombe of the *Financial Times* who, in her five-column review, had praise for almost nothing and no one; denouncing the production as 'slapdash', 'foolish' and full of 'dozens of small petty details', 'diversions' and 'contradictions'.

Fortunately for the morale of all those most directly concerned, reaction elsewhere was more buoyant. Conrad Wilson in the *Scotsman* proffered the opinion that, while there was a time when 'such a *Giovanni* might have been dismissed as wilful, wasteful and irresponsibly eccentric, it was now recognized:

> that there is a place for productions which set out to look at an established masterpiece afresh, to take risks in their treatment of it, to concentrate on certain aspects of it at the expense perhaps of others.
>
> Right or wrong, it is a *Giovanni* with a distinctive point of view. Some people may dislike it very much. I found it compelling . . . the whole conception alive.

Even more rewarding was Ernest Bradbury's notice in the equally respected *Yorkshire Post*. Clearly familiar with the original concept of the opera, he proclaimed Edinburgh's production to be 'an overwhelming triumph . . . not least for the original authors Da Ponte and Mozart'. And, indeed, where the critic from the *Financial Times* had derided the antics of Ustinov's *due ufficiali* and their tape measure in the final scene as no more than 'a jester's idea', the 'ruin [of] the musical finale', the *Yorkshire Post* saw it as 'a wry reminder of the *Comédie Humaine*, while the detectives . . . measuring up the horror story, display accurate knowledge of the script as well as wit.'

Five years later, in 1978, Ustinov's next sortie into what he calls the 'hybrid' world of opera, took him to Berlin to produce and direct Offenbach's *Les Brigands*. In Leningrad the following spring, opera even had a small part to play in a ninety-minute television programme about the Hermitage, which he and Natalie Wood (who was born of Russian parents and whose real name was Natasha Virapaev) co-presented for NBC. However, on that occasion, the roles of director and directed were reversed when, rigged out in eighteenth-century costume, Peter and his son Igor were to be found on the stage of the small theatre in the Winter Palace performing the coughing duet from *The Pretentious Pundit*. Composed by Catherine the Great's court composer, Pasiello, its first performance was given in that very theatre.

Igor, who was then twenty-three and studying biology at university, sculpture at art school, and who was giving English lessons to fellow students in his spare time, as well as fitting in singing lessons, recalls that he and his father had only three days in which to learn and perfect the duet, before it had to be recorded as part of the programme.

Later that year, having completed a new documentary for Unicef; seen the release of his latest film, *Ashanti*, in which he appeared with Michael Caine and Omar Sharif; and watched, transfixed, as twenty-three-year-old Bjorn Borg carried off the men's championship title at Wimbledon for the fourth year in a row, Ustinov was all set to leave for Canada to play the lead in a new production of *King Lear* at Stratford, Ontario.

If, like his foray into opera, Shakespeare or, at all events, *Lear*, seemed an unlikely diversion for the fifty-eight-year-old actor, his characteristic reply was: 'I've got three daughters of my own, which is a more thorough rehearsal for the part than anything Stanislavsky ever suggested.'

Directed by Robin Phillips, Ustinov's *Lear* was to be no dim and distant drama shrouded in ancient shadows. Instead, it was to be set in the 1850s, around the time of the Crimean War. 'I think we use that "Ancient Britain" too much, when we want to make everything rather remote,' said Peter at the time, adding that *Lear* is a play that 'can be adapted to the court life of the last century. It's a military play, a play about hierarchy. It's also a play about protocol, how Lear discovers with immense pain that we're all naked people just dressed differently. I think that Lear's mad in the beginning, not entirely mad, perhaps, but certainly senile . . . He can't remember things and won't admit that he can't remember until he finally comes face to face with himself from the outside, which of course makes him self-pitying.'

Shakespeare's hapless monarch occupied much of Ustinov's time during the autumn of 1979 and again during the autumn of 1980. But for a case of administrative error, it would have continued to do so until the early part of 1981. From Canada, the production was to have transferred to London, opening at the Theatre Royal, Haymarket, for a twelve-week run in December 1980.

In September of that year, however, the Stratford Festival Theatre cancelled that part of the agreement, claiming that it had been unable to confirm a contract with Triumph Productions at the Haymarket until July, by which time at least eight members of the cast had given up hope of a London opening and had signed contracts elsewhere. Ustinov, who had turned down valuable film work in order to be free for the London season, eventually had no other recourse but to sue for breach of contract. 'I hated doing it,' he says, 'and I didn't get very much out of it. We settled out of court and I agreed to a perfectly nominal sum simply because I didn't want to ruin Stratford. . . . It was a moral victory.'

That experience soured neither Peter's feelings towards the Stratford Festival – 'The fact that it was badly run didn't lessen my pleasure at appearing there' – nor his delight in playing Lear. But ask him if he would like to have played more Shakespeare and his reply is, 'No.' He says, 'I am always delighted when people come up to me – and I must say it happens fairly frequently – and say how much pleasure I've given them. I don't think I'd have given them that much pleasure playing Shakespeare. I enjoyed playing King Lear because I've always had a feeling for him, but otherwise, no, I don't think Shakespeare's for me. I can't see myself *pretending* I know what I'm talking about, like so many distinguished English actors . . . . I don't know what the hell they're talking

about – and they don't either. Ralph Richardson was an ace at
that. He always gave the impression that he'd made a study of
the thing and now knew it all, and was going to interpret it for
us . . . .'

After Stratford's plans for the London production of *Lear*
were aborted, Ustinov was not to be seen in the West End for
another three years. Yet in spite of an absence of what was,
by then, ten years, his 'presence' at –ironically – the Theatre
Royal, Haymarket, was still unmistakable when his play,
Overheard, which starred Deborah Kerr and Ian Carmichael,
opened there in 1981. A love story at the heart of a diplomatic
plot, set in the British Embassy in an unnamed Balkan country,
the comedy had already enjoyed successful runs in Paris and
in Germany.

In the meantime, Peter himself focused his attention on
making two more films: *Charlie Chan and the Curse of the Dragon
Queen*, in which he appeared with Angie Dickinson and Lee
Grant; and his second Agatha Christie murder mystery, *Evil
Under the Sun*, in which he again played Hercule Poirot. This
gave him another opportunity to work with the producer John
Brabourne – making only his second film since recovering
from the severe injuries he had sustained in August 1979,
in the IRA bomb attack which killed his father-in-law, Lord
Mountbatten.

Peter and Hélène Ustinov's friendship with John and Patricia
Brabourne (or Countess Mountbatten, as she is now known)
properly began during the filming of *Death on the Nile* in 1977,
in which, according to Lord Brabourne, Ustinov made 'an
absolutely wonderful Poirot. I don't think he was entirely as
everybody thought, but I think he was the nearest for the
Agatha Christie fans.'

Since that time, the Ustinovs and the Brabournes have not
only enjoyed the social aspect of each other's company, but
also one or two occasions of a quasi-public nature, such as
the time when Peter presented prizes – and 'brought the house
down' – at the Norton Knatchbull School in Kent, which was
founded by one of John Brabourne's forbears.

In London, shortly before *Evil Under the Sun* went into

production, the Brabourne's fourth son, Philip Knatchbull, now also a film-maker and producer, had what his father called 'a marvellous experience' with Ustinov.

'While Philip was trying to get a job,' said Lord Brabourne, 'he used his own car and became a private taxi. Peter, who was staying at the Berkeley, had to go and have a medical for the film, after which he wanted to do some shopping. So he rang for a taxi, driven by my son, and they had the most wonderful misunderstanding about what time they were going to meet. Philip was terribly late and he gave us a marvellous description of Peter wedged into a tiny telephone booth, trying to find out where his taxi was. After he had had the medical, Peter went shopping in Bond Street and, as he got out of the car, he said to Philip, "I won't be long. You wait here and I'll come back to you." So my son sat in his orange Peugeot 504 where he waited and waited.

'After a while, he became rather worried and decided to walk up the street. Suddenly he saw a very shame-faced Peter coming towards him. "Oh, what a shock I've just had," he said. It turned out that there was another orange car parked down the road, which Peter had been sitting in until he realized it was the wrong one. After the earlier misunderstanding, he must have been cursing Philip, wondering where on earth he'd disappeared to.'

Late the following year, Ustinov returned to the Edinburgh Festival to direct and appear in *The Marriage*, an unfinished opera which Modest Mussorgsky had based on Nikolai Gogol's comedy of the same name. The history of the production, so far as Ustinov's involvement was concerned, began when La Piccola Scala, Milan, invited him to think of a way of presenting the one and only act of the opera, on which Mussorgsky had started work one rainy day in July 1868 and had abandoned soon afterwards, in favour of a new commission.

Peter's solution was to write a play around it, subtitled *Rehearsal for The Marriage*, in which he brought on a provincial Russian company who were supposed to have been rehearsing the only available act for six years, while waiting for the composer to deliver the rest. In Milan, says Peter, it was performed 'in front of an operatic audience on an operatic occasion, and we got a marvellous press'.

In Edinburgh, where it was staged at the Royal Lyceum Theatre in September 1982, with a cast that included Ustinov's twenty-eight-year-old daughter, Pavla (who, like her half-sister, Tamara, was pursuing a career as an actress and also, in Los Angeles, as a television script-writer) *The Marriage* received a hostile reception. This, in retrospect, was due very largely to the fact that, in a programme of festival events not nearly as richly endowed as in previous years, the promise of a new Ustinovian production was by far and away the most seductive item on offer. But what had not been made clear, in any of the advertising or promotional material, was that *The Marriage* represented a reconstruction of an unfinished opera, not a new play.

'In Edinburgh everybody thought I was being extremely lazy by giving the central part over to an opera,' Peter says today, 'and because it was done in a theatre, audiences thought it wasn't quite adequate as a theatrical piece. But it was an *opera*. That was the whole idea.'

Nevertheless, as if to compound the misunderstanding for all time, the critics on this occasion were merciless in their condemnation. 'In a studio, it might have been mild fun; as a major festival offering, it was emphatically no joke,' wrote Michael Billington in the *Guardian*. 'The whole thing,' said Michael Coveney in the *Financial Times*, was 'an unmitigated disaster'. John Barber of the *Daily Telegraph* was of the opinion that, 'As a highlight of the official Edinburgh Festival drama programme, this *Marriage* can only give wedlock a bad name'; while Jack Tinker of the *Daily Mail* added a more personal note to this chorus of disapproval when he said: 'I have long ceased to be amused by Mr Ustinov's more grotesque flights of impersonation, as he is plainly pleased enough with his performance for both of us.'

Providing at least a vestige of balance to this miasma of scorn and disappointment, Irving Wardle of *The Times* pointed the finger of blame for the controversy at the festival organizers:

> Ustinov . . . paid the penalty of being caught out in a false position. You could say that he contributed to this by agreeing to play in the main house; but it

was the festival society that put him there and capi-
talized on his name, just as . . . they had trumpeted
the news of Irene Worth's appearance on the same
stage to introduce an Italian opera without music. It
was their cupboard, not Ustinov's, that was bare.

FIFTEEN

Today, almost a decade after it was so soundly trounced at Edinburgh, *The Marriage* continues to be performed in opera houses across Europe; something which not unnaturally gives Peter a great deal of personal satisfaction. In 1982 however he put the adverse reaction of his British critics behind him and moved on to an enterprise that had been almost seven years in the making.

Film rights to *Memed, My Hawk*, a novel first published in 1963 by Turkish writer, Yashar Kemal, then belonged to 20th-Century Fox. At that time, Ustinov had been asked by Darryl Zanuck, who ran the studio, to direct a screen adaptation of the story and, but for a script that was more 'John Wayne with a fez' than a reflection of life in rural Turkey during the early 1920s, he might have agreed.

As it was, Peter was not uninterested in preparing a new script for Fox, but before he was able to do anything about it, a series of expensive flops had landed the studio in debt and Zanuck, as company president, was on his way out. The result was that by the late 1970s Ustinov started to buy options on the novel, and his two co-producers, Fuad Kavur and Brian Smedley-Aston, set about trying to find financial backing in order to bring *Memed* to the screen.

In his novel, Nobel-nominated Yashar Kemal told the story of a young and disaffected Anatolian herdsman, Memed, who becomes an outlaw and, ultimately, a folk hero when he leads a gang of bandits in rebellion against the local tyrant, Abdi

Aga. In a sense, the story mirrored actual political events in Turkey at the start of the twenties, as Mustafa Kemal, better known as Kemal Attaturk, gradually assumed supreme power. He toppled Sultan Abdul Mejid II from his marble perch at the rococo Dolmabahce palace in Istanbul and, in 1923, the year in which *Memed* is set, proclaimed himself president of the new Turkish republic.

With a screenplay written by Ustinov, who also played the part of Abdi Aga, and a cast which included Herbert Lom as his millionaire rival landowner, Denis Quilley, Michael Elphick, Rosalie Crutchley and newcomer Simon Dutton as the heroic Memed, filming eventually began in Yugoslavia in October 1982. However, it nearly ground to a halt soon afterwards because, unbeknown to Peter, part of the financial arrangements proved to be unsoundly based, and much of the promised capital had failed to materialize.

With his back to the wall and concerned not only that his personal integrity had been compromised, but that every member of both cast and crew might suddenly find themselves out of work, Ustinov shouldered the responsibility of financing the rest of the picture himself. His London-based agent, Steven Kenis, says, 'So far as I am aware, Peter wasn't on the line *personally*, and he could have walked away from it and just left others holding the bag, as has happened in this business on a few occasions. But because he is Peter Ustinov, he wouldn't let people down. He didn't walk around beating his breast or tearing his clothes; he just very quietly wound up paying the debts for the picture personally.' Those debts took Peter seven years to pay off.

In London, in September 1983, *Memed* was given a royal world première, in aid of Unicef at the ABC cinema, Shaftesbury Avenue, attended by Prince and Princess Michael of Kent. Unfortunately, it was not the success its producers might have hoped for.

Four months earlier, Ustinov had made his first appearance on the West End stage since his play, *The Unknown Soldier and His Wife*, opened the New London Theatre in January 1973. *Beethoven's Tenth*, which he later took to America and which, from the winter of 1987 to the spring of 1988, he played in German in Berlin, opened at the Vaudeville Theatre that May.

In it, Ustinov brought Beethoven, looking like a dusty version of the Prince Regent, back to life and set him down in the London home of a rather self-important music critic, played by Robin Bailey, who happened to be something of an authority on the composer's works. Together, the two characters established what Sheridan Morley, writing in *Punch*, described as a 'sustained double-act of such massive humanity and charm as to be unmissable and unbeatable'.

During his 'visit', Beethoven helped to sort out the differences between the critic and his wife and son, and even settled down to listen to recordings of his complete works with the assistance of a hearing aid, donated by his 'host's' GP. From one or two critics, there was just the vaguest suggestion that the evening was a little long but, on the whole, Ustinov's twenty-third – and still his most recent – play was warmly received.

It was, said the *Observer*, 'A major comic event', while Michael Billington of the *Guardian*, who had recently condemned Ustinov's Edinburgh Festival production of *The Marriage* as 'no joke', now said of *Beethoven's Tenth*, 'the play brings a touch of erudite intelligence and verbal grace to a West End currently steeped in witless nostalgia'.

Peter Ustinov is on record as having said that he 'lives like an Englishman, thinks like a Frenchman and has the soul of a Russian'. This may explain why he has often been asked, 'Where are your roots?'

'Whenever I'm asked that,' he says, 'I reply that I think it is possible to have one's roots in civilized behaviour. I don't want any other "roots" than that.' As if to emphasize the point, he once wrote, 'There has never been an anthem which sets my foot tapping, never an occasion which brings a lump to my throat'. Yet even so, there is one particular aspect of his cosmopolitan inheritance which has never failed to stimulate interest or provoke comment: his links with Russia.

For the past twenty years and more, or perhaps since he first visited Russia in 1963, Ustinov has spent much of his time trying to act as a sort of unofficial go-between in the interests of East–West relations. During one of our earliest conversations on the subject, Peter said, 'I have always been very careful to take a pragmatic and very low profile approach to what I do, otherwise there is the danger of becoming pretentious or in imagining that one has some kind of mission. I have no "mission" whatever, except to suggest that missiles are not the chips we should be playing with, because they do not reflect – democratically – the will of anybody. And if [through that] I have managed to exert, perhaps, a tiny influence on a few people, then that is adequate for me.'

At the start of the eighties, Ustinov's personal desire to see East and West move closer together was one of the reasons why he accepted Harold Macmillan's invitation to write a book about Russia. It was, as he put it, an attempt 'to eradicate some of the misconceptions that have poisoned the atmosphere'. When it was first published by the former prime minister's own London publishing house in 1983, *My Russia* was criticized for being a whitewash. There was, said its critics, 'too much emphasis on Mother Russia and not enough on Uncle Joe Stalin'.

While it is true that human rights and other issues of equal magnitude were not addressed, it was Ustinov's express intention to attempt a broader understanding of Russia by focusing on the more human aspects of the country, its history and inhabitants. His aim, though dismissed in certain quarters as being naïve, was to add at least a dash of contrast to the West's darker view of what Ronald Reagan once called the 'Evil Empire'.

A year after publication, *My Russia* formed the basis of a six-part television series, produced by John McGreevey and his Toronto-based film company, JMP. It was begun during the thirteen-month 'reign' of Konstantin Chernenko, and Ustinov and McGreevey found the Russian leader more than amenable to their requests for permission and facilities to film – in villages, towns and cities as disparate and far-flung as Moscow and Leningrad, Zagorsk, Novgorod and Smolensk in the west, to Novosibirsk and Irkutsk, on the edge of Lake Baykal, deep in Siberia. In all, a distance of some 20,000 miles. By the time filming was wrapped up in 1985, Chernenko was dead and Mikhail Gorbachev had succeeded him.

The series, *Peter Ustinov's Russia*, subtitled *A Personal History* in order to clarify the stance of its author and presenter, was first shown on Canadian television – and subsequently throughout Europe and the United States – to what the magazine *Film Comment* called 'runaway ratings'. It was an illuminating and visually stunning production which – despite one or two asinine remarks from British critics – won both Ustinov and McGreevey considerable praise.

In October 1986, Peter, who is known in the Soviet Union primarily as a playwright, and who is frequently invited to visit writers' unions throughout the USSR, made yet another return to Russia. This time to Kirghizia on the shores of Lake Issyk-Kul in the foothills of the Tien Shan mountains on the border with China. There, along with American writers Arthur Miller and James Baldwin, Unesco's Augusto Forti, French Nobel Prize winner, Claude Simon, the Turkish writer Yashar Kemal, Ethiopian artist Afework Tekle and the American futurologist Alvin Toffler and his philosopher wife Heidi, he was the guest of Chingiz Aitmatov. A distinguished writer, as well as an elected member of the Supreme Soviet of the Kirghiz republic, Aitmatov was described by Arthur Miller as 'possibly the most renowned novelist and playwright in his country', and by Ustinov as 'a visionary'.

It was his idea to gather together a group of what he called 'cultural personalities', united by their common concern for the destiny of civilization, to discuss the future of mankind and, more specifically, the question of how to enter the third millennium without destroying the human race.

For three days, the group's fifteen members, who elected to be known as 'The Issyk-Kul Forum', shared their views with, as Ustinov put it, 'great application and good humour . . . without any trace of outside "guidance" '. They then submitted their 'slim manifesto' to both Mr Gorbachev and President Reagan. The immediate response from the man who would shortly become the Soviet Union's first Executive President was an invitation to meet him at the Kremlin four days later, on 20 October.

'We were told the encounter would be at eleven o'clock sharp, and that it would last precisely one hour,' Peter was to write. 'It turned into a very Russian occasion, starting at

exactly eleven . . . and we left a fraction under three hours
later.'

Recalling the meeting in his autobiography, *Timebends*,
Arthur Miller wrote:

> Unlike his predecessors, Gorbachev did not look
> baggy and bloated with drink; [he] had an eager
> grin and a certain contemporary wit in his eyes.
> An air of haste about him reminded me of John
> Kennedy . . . . Here [in the Kremlin] was the heart of
> darkness or beacon of light and hope, as one chose,
> and Gorbachev's sheer human ordinariness merely
> added to the mystery of power, for I sensed some
> personal need speaking from within him, beneath
> the command of authority.

During the meeting, each member of the forum touched
upon some of the global issues that concerned them as
individuals. Like James Baldwin, who spoke of the Third
World, Ustinov took the opportunity to raise the problems
that besiege developing nations, the formidable tasks that face
relief agencies such as Unicef, and the greater contribution the
rest of the world, Russia included, could make towards their
endeavours.

The progress of science, the necessity for freedom of
information, the need for education, for communication, and
so on, were all included in the range of issues other delegates put to the Soviet leader – as was, inevitably, the
nuclear threat. Part of Gorbachev's response to these matters
was as follows:

> I think that what prompted our desire to meet, was
> our common worries and concerns, our thoughts
> about the world we live in, and about its future.
> There are many reasons for our thinking so much
> about the world's present and future. The Issyk-Kul
> Forum attracted people of different professions and
> points of view, and it is in this that I see its great
> merit. It was a demonstration in miniature of the
> chance the human race has to reach agreement . . . .

Quite different people took part in your forum, and
therein lay its main strength. The participants trans-
cended everything that divided them and reached
accord on what mattered most: the universal responsibility for the future of humanity. That is a lesson
we all need to learn . . . .

Since 1986, the Issyk-Kul Forum has met in Switzerland,
where it was hosted by Peter Ustinov, in Spain and in Mexico.
In 1990 it returned to Russia and a second meeting with the
President. Of its formation – to forge links between intellec-
tuals the world over, through whose influence it was hoped
the forum's deliberations, or 'message', might be carried still
further – Peter says: 'It's a worthy initiative, but I don't know
how much solid good can come out of it. But those things
you can't work out by any effect but erosion. You realize its
importance afterwards . . . . '

Though there has never been any room in his life for anything approaching hero-worship, Ustinov makes no secret of
his admiration for Mikhail Gorbachev. 'He is without doubt *the*
man of the century,' he says. 'Everything that has happened
in Eastern Europe, for better or worse, has derived from him.
He may be more popular outside Russia than within, that is no
more than you would expect, but there is now no road back
from Perestroika. For the sake of us all, he must be allowed to
succeed.'

To that end, Peter's will to help promote the positive aspects
of Russia has never been firmer, particularly when confronted
by the arrogance of certain western politicians. On one occasion in 1986, for instance, while awaiting the Queen's arrival
at some function or other, he found himself standing next to
Margaret Thatcher, whom he admits to finding 'fascinating as
a person' but whose politics he totally opposes.

'I've been thinking about what you said when we last met,'
she remarked apropos nothing Peter could immediately think
of, 'and you know, you're quite wrong.'

When asked what conversation she was referring to and
what point she was attempting to make, she replied, 'There
is no such thing as public opinion in Russia.'

In his surprise, Peter said, 'I suppose, Prime Minister,

that is why the Russians have had two major revolutions
this century, while the British have only had football riots
and a few bitter strikes.'

'Go on, go on,' Mrs Thatcher urged – in itself a surprising
invitation, not extended to many – when, alas, the Queen's
appearance cut short their exchange.

Inflexibility has always exasperated Ustinov. But in the
political arena, especially when it threatens the fundamental
principles of democracy itself, his exasperation turns to anger.
In Britain, the Thatcher administration, 'intoxicated with
monetarism' and assailed by an 'abrasive short-sightedness',
is very much a case in point.

A liberal – temperamentally as well as politically – Peter
has always believed the central position to be 'the true one'.
Throughout his life, he told me, 'I have always had a very
keen sense of balance. Balance was the all-important thing. It's
almost something metaphysical.' But, he says, 'the position in
the centre is always the most difficult to defend. I have always
been liberal, but a *militant* liberal. I don't see why the central
position should be reticent because it's central.

'I'm very retiring in a way and, as you say, shy. But if
somebody gets my goat, I am absolutely relentless in pursuit –
and nothing will shake me out of that attitude. So I am secretly
a very combative person. Yet I believe the central position
to be the true one because, after all, everything in nature is
divided into two halves; even God and the Devil, which are
inseparable in a way. But the high notes on the piano, like the
low notes, are much more dramatic than Middle C; grey is a
drab colour when compared to black and white. That doesn't
lessen its importance. The truth is very often in the middle
of things and it isn't the result of a compromise. It's so small
we can hardly see it, but it's there that I look for it and never
on an extreme.

'No extreme fascinates me. I think it's all wrong because
it's also too easy. These louts, anarchists or whatever they
are, who go out into the streets to riot and break windows,
don't have to think any more. They're following instructions.
Well, that's easy. And the storm-troopers I saw in Germany as
a boy, all shouting "Germany Awake!". It gives them a sense of
communal core, and there's nothing more exhilarating for a

certain clot-like mentality, than the sound of boots marching all together *and-you're-part-of-the-machine – and-it's wonderful*. In point of fact, it's the isolated voice which can't even be heard in the crowd which is really the most vital of all.'

At the same time as the Russian series was in production in 1984–5, Peter began to work on another, spotlighting prominent figures on the world's stage. Called *Peter Ustinov's People*, the series was the brainchild of Sheamus Smith, a former political commentator for Irish television and now Eire's official Film Censor.

'Over lunch one day,' said Sheamus, 'I told Peter that there would be two great advantages to doing such a series. Firstly, everyone likes him and wants to meet him, and secondly, if we did it for Irish television, which isn't like the BBC, people couldn't say it was being done from a British angle.'

The subject of one of the earliest programmes was King Hussein of Jordan, who wrote to me of his 'great personal pleasure' at meeting Peter. 'Though this was our first meeting,' he said, 'Mr Ustinov was by no means a stranger to me [since] for many years he has enriched the film industry and the theatre with his creativity, wit, charm and superb performances.'

Having first met Hussein's fourth wife, the half-American, half-Lebanese Queen Noor, at play with a posse of small royal children in the palace garden in Amman, Ustinov settled down with the King to record what proved to be a refreshingly open and unstilted interview about his life and career as one of the world's last autocratic monarchs.

In October 1984, another programme in the series, entitled *The Fire and the Phoenix*, took Peter to New Delhi to interview the then Indian Prime Minister, Indira Gandhi. Always a controversial figure, Mrs Gandhi had made headline news only four months earlier when, on her orders, troops stormed the Golden Temple at Amritsar, the holiest of Sikh shrines, after a four-day siege of the temple complex by Sikh militants trying to carve out of India an independent Sikh homeland – 'Khalistan'. Over 700 extremists died in the conflict, which led to daily threats against the Prime Minister and members of her family.

That October, as the threats continued unabated, Ustinov, Sheamus Smith, cameraman Rory O'Farrell and the rest of their unit, spent two days preparing preliminary film footage, before recording the interview with the premier herself. That meeting was arranged to take place in the garden of her office at 1 Akbar Road, on the morning of 31 October.

Dressed in saffron – which according to Sikh belief is the colour of martyrdom – Mrs Gandhi left her nearby residence to join Peter who, by that time, said Sheamus Smith, 'was already sitting in his chair next to that set up for the Prime Minister. Her microphone had been wired-up and tea had been ordered.' As she was about to cross the lawn towards them, Mrs Gandhi was shot ten times by her Sikh bodyguards. Sub-Inspector Beant Singh, who had helped protect her for nine years, shot the Prime Minister in the abdomen and, as she fell, Constable Satwant Singh opened fire with his Sten gun.

Eighty yards away, Ustinov and his colleagues heard, but did not see, the assassination. 'I heard three single shots and then the rattle of Bren gun bullets,' Peter told newsmen after he and the rest of the team had been held and questioned by police for five hours.

As pandemonium swept through India and anti-Sikh riots erupted into violence, Peter was beleaguered by representatives of the world's press, every one of them asking him to name his price for his photographs of Mrs Gandhi's murder. 'I don't think they believed me when I said we didn't have any,' he says, 'but how could we? We didn't see it happen.'

A day or two later, in the early hours of the morning, Ustinov was roused from his sleep by a photographer with a quite different request. On 28 October, Princess Anne, as president of the Save the Children Fund, had arrived in India at the start of an official visit. There to cover her activities was Jayne Fincher, famous for her official and unofficial photographs of the royal family. On the morning of the assassination, Jayne followed the Princess to the state of Uttar Pradesh, some 200 miles from Delhi, where she was to visit a Tibetan Home Foundation in Dehra Dun. There, once reports of the Prime Minister's death had been confirmed, a plane was made ready for the royal party's immediate return to the capital, where the Princess was to have had dinner with Mrs Gandhi that evening.

Allowed the use of a British Embassy Land-Rover – but only after Princess Anne's lady-in-waiting had intervened on her behalf – Jayne made the alarmingly hazardous journey back to New Delhi. Next day, unnoticed among the bustling crowd of harassed officials and mourning relations, she managed to take the first pictures of the dead premier after her body had been prepared for the ritual cremation ceremony. Now, Jayne's immediate problem was how to get her film out of India and back to London. Someone suggested she ask Peter Ustinov, who happened to be staying in the same hotel and who was leaving for England that morning.

'I looked at my watch,' Jayne recalls, 'and said, "Ask Peter Ustinov?! At *two* in the morning?!" ' She eventually had no choice if she wanted to pip her competitors to the post, though it was not without a feeling of trepidation that she knocked on his door. When Peter finally responded, he immediately offered to help, adding with a smile, 'I think your contact in London will be able to recognize me'.

Ten months later, Ustinov returned to New Delhi to complete *The Fire and the Phoenix* with the assistance of Rajiv Gandhi who, just a few hours after his mother was slain, had been sworn in as India's new Prime Minister.

Part of the charm of John Brabourne's film versions of Agatha Christie's Poirot mysteries is undoubtedly a feeling for the period in which they were originally set. The lack of authenticity when American companies attempt to bring the stories up to date for glossy, mass-market, television adaptations, is perhaps just one of the reasons why, at least among a large percentage of British viewers, productions such as *13 At Dinner*, *Deadman's Folly* and *Murder in Three Acts*, seem to arouse little real enthusiasm.

Indeed, the image of Poirot speeding along in a mini-moke, joining a bunch of American 'swells' on some paradise island, or watching a 'film-idol' making an adventure movie in London's Docklands, is about as true to Agatha Christie as relocating what was supposed to be the typically English village of St Mary Mead to the edge of the Arizona desert, or wherever, in order to make Helen Hayes' Miss Marple seem a trifle more believable.

Nevertheless, Ustinov played the Belgian detective, ably supported by Jonathan Cecil as his side-kick, Captain Hastings, in each of these television specials.

Immediately before and shortly after them he again teamed up with John McGreevey, to make a two-hour documentary about China. First seen on Global Television in Toronto, *Peter Ustinov in China*, which won the 1987 ACE Award, had been produced under the aegis of Unicef, on whose behalf Peter toured the vast 'People's Republic' in September 1986.

At the start of a solidly-packed twelve-day schedule, which took him from Beijing to Tibet, and thence to Hong Kong for a further two days, Peter was taken to the old imperial Forbidden City, which took fourteen years to build and, when completed in 1420, claimed a staggering 9,000 rooms. He visited the 6,000-kilometre Great Wall, began in the fifth century BC, and still the only man-made structure visible from the moon. He also made an almost obligatory stop at Mao's shrine at the Gate of Heavenly Peace; was taken to the seven-storey Buddhist Pagoda of the Greater Wild Goose in Xi'an, which was built in the year 652, contains 1,897 rooms and, to this day, still has 300 resident monks living in total seclusion; and he saw the 8,000-strong Terracotta Army, a part of which a peasant farmer, digging a well during the great drought, first discovered as recently as 1974. Peter stared at the warriors:

> They remind you in quality of some of the Greek statues of antiquity, where you stand absolutely dumbfounded in front of them, because of their accurate observation of the human physique and of human nature, because the expression on the faces of each one is different. Some are anxious, some are frozen in this position, everybody has a slightly different expression on his face. Some are fearful, some are determined, some are resigned and some are vigorous. Some are frankly lazy. It's a *wonderful* cross-section of human society 2,000 years ago, or, if you look closely enough, now.

Yet seeing the sights wasn't Peter's only function in this, his first visit to China. As the official brief put it, the tour had been arranged 'To give Mr Ustinov the opportunity to learn first-hand about China's development problems, experiences and CSDR actions.' From the glories of its imperial past, Peter was taken to see some of its present-day realities.

In Lanzhou, China's poorest province, with an 'arid, sandy surface, carried by the winds in the form of dust which gives the Yellow River its name', Peter visited Lanzhou City – the capital of Gansu Province. It was once a large garrison city on the famous Silk Road, travelled by Columbus and Marco Polo at a pace which 'gave thought its profundity and ambition its dimension'. Here he saw how the vaccination programme against Cold Chain and polio was produced and administered, and learned of some of the difficulties in getting vaccines to the province's eighty-six counties. With low population density and mountainous terrain, it takes up to two months for Unicef to reach all the villages, by which time some of the vaccines are ineffective.

In Xi Pa village, where no white face had ever been seen before, Peter visited clay-walled houses where there is no electricity and no gas, but where the provincial government has distributed solar burners, one to every family, for cooking. On the border with Vietnam, Ustinov and his party saw the paddy-fields, 'a world of bog and moisture', and went deep into just one of 'China's unique treasury of caves . . . thrown up by the limestone sea-bed millennia ago . . . '. Against surroundings lit an eery green, blue and bronze, Peter said:

> The Chinese have it over the Irish with their leprechauns and the Norwegians with their little people. Here in these enormous caves, like organ lofts . . . one can see all sorts of things. Even as a non-Chinese, one can see strange dragons and creatures from other worlds attacking each other, being playful with one another. The Chinese are very conscious of all sorts of supernatural things . . . here they all become tangible, visible, frightening and friendly, according to your attitude.

Back in Xi'an, Peter watched elementary teacher training and experimental kindergarten activities. He was even taken out in a rowing-boat on the lake of a public park in the grounds of the old imperial palace. What makes that park – which looks no different from any other – so remarkable, is the fact that, in 1956, it was built, voluntarily but physically, by the men, women and children of the city in their spare time, 'so that there would be grace and pleasure in their moments of relaxation'.

From his boat in the middle of the lake, Ustinov addressed the camera:

> I am aware that my enthusiasms may seem slightly insane at times, and I know that I have been accused of being naïve about them. And yet, I think, personally, that they are justified and I might as well explain myself. I think one of the troubles with the world is that we're all at different stages of our development at the same moment of history, and different political systems suit different countries. I can't understand how one can expect democracy in a country which is not literate. Here there is a lot to do. It's a great nation, a very civilized nation, which has had periods of degradation, deprivation and depression, and they've got a system now which they chose out of many others. And now it has a kind of enthusiasm which is infectious; at least, I believe it to be and it is as far as I'm concerned.

SIXTEEN

Peter Ustinov is famous even in China. There he is called 'Pollo', the closest they can get to 'Poirot', and in the teeming streets of Beijing that is the name by which excited Chinese greeted him.

In July 1987, having recently completed *Murder in Three Acts*, the last in the trio of thrillers mentioned earlier, Peter was back in character, back in costume and back in front of the cameras, for his third *cinematic* appearance as Agatha Christie's gentle hero.

Michael Winner's *Appointment with Death*, which was made in Israel, reunited Ustinov with his old friend, Lauren Bacall, as well as with the octogenarian John Gielgud, who says he found the once impatiently ambitious actor 'greatly mellowed and absolutely delightful. His patience and professionalism were exemplary and his mimicry and skills as a raconteur made my days a real delight. How I envy him his extraordinary flair and his intrinsic kindness and good nature.'

Those sentiments, repeated in one way or another time and again, were echoed by Hayley Mills, who worked with Peter for the first time on this occasion, when she said: 'He is a very lovable man . . . enormously well liked by everyone . . . tireless, good humoured and warm. He possesses one of the most fascinating minds I have ever encountered. For all that, he retains his privacy. Somehow one feels he is in his own world, observing us all and storing it all away. Nothing is ever forgotten . . . .'

When not on set, Peter spent much of his time at his hotel in Tel Aviv. There, in a city described by one of his business associates as being 'like Torremolinos with guns', he completed the text – and a number of cartoons – for a new book that was to be published that September to coincide with the first British screening of his television series, *Peter Ustinov in Russia*.

In fact, at around this time, Peter's work tended to be centred almost exclusively on films and television. The theatre, in which he has always had such a great interest, had, as he put it, 'somehow waned'. Sharing Claire Bloom's view of the West End as 'a commercial wasteland', Peter says, 'I've not been as excited by it. There's a widespread sense of mediocrity . . . a spirit of entrepreneurism which is absolutely terrible'.

In the mid-1950s, Mike Todd, to whom Elizabeth Taylor was married when he was tragically killed in 1958, had offered Ustinov the role of Detective Fix in his famous wide-screen version of *Around the World in 80 Days*. To spite the flamboyant film magnate, the Hollywood studio to which Peter was currently contracted refused to release him. Almost thirty years later, a second chance to play the same part came his way when, in 1988, NBC cast their own six-hour television adaptation of Jules Verne's classic novel. At the same time as 'Fix' was chasing Phileas Fogg, alias Pierce Brosnan, round the globe, Ustinov stopped off in Paris to play Mirabeau in an epic reconstruction of the French Revolution, produced by Ariane Films for the then forthcoming bicentennial celebrations.

In the same year, he was also to be found in Rome, starring in an Italian-language film based on the French novel, *Au Bonheur des Chiens*, or 'Dogs' Paradise', by Remo Forlany. Released in Europe in June 1990 under the title *Bow-Wow*, Peter played 'a drunken veterinarian who gave up practising medicine on humans. He drinks because he thinks it will help him get on the canine wavelength . . . and manages to teach forty dogs to sing the chorus from *Nabucco* by Verdi.' It was an ironic – or brave – choice of role for a man who confesses to being frightened of dogs – at least other people's. At home he has owned a succession of big dogs, from 'Dorothy', an Old English Sheepdog, to a Samoyed called 'Olga', who now keeps a watchful eye on callers at Au Clos du Château. All the same, Peter says he has never really been able to conquer his fear and adds, 'I thought I could master my cowardice by buying some ferocious dogs. I discovered that I wasn't afraid of ferocious dogs. I was afraid of *all the others*.'

Towards the end of what had been a typically busy year in his life, an event of no small significance took Peter and almost every member of his immediate family to the palace of Petrodvorets, near Leningrad. The occasion, on 28 September 1988, was the official opening of the Benois Museum in one of the two 'country house' pavilions that Nicholas Benois had built over a century before.

Conceived as an art-gallery-cum-international-centre for exchange students, which now has the backing of Unesco, the museum's forty-five rooms each contain a permanent exhibition dedicated to individual members of the Benois family and their descendants, ranging in scope and versatility from the architects and painters of the mid-nineteenth century to the artistry of Alexandre Benois, his niece Nadia Benois Ustinov, and her son and grandson.

In spite of his famous surname which, at least in France, made it more difficult for him to establish a professional identity in his own right, Igor Ustinov's reputation as a sculptor has steadily grown since his work was first exhibited in Washington DC in 1979. A graduate of the National School of Fine Arts in Paris, Igor's highly idiosyncratic sculptures have formed part of more than twenty collective exhibitions in cities throughout France, Switzerland and North America, interspersed with as many one-man shows in London, Paris, New York, Geneva, Darmstadt and Munster.

Peter's pride in Igor – indeed, in all four of his children – is only too apparent whenever he speaks of them. Yet while he clearly enjoys the role of paterfamilias, the fact that he is rarely in one place for very long inevitably restricts the number of occasions on which he and they meet *en famille*. Nor is the situation much helped by their independent life-styles or by the distances – geographically speaking – which separate them. Igor, his wife Clementine and daughter Clara, who was born in October 1980 while 'Grospapa' was playing Lear in Ontario, live in Paris; Pavla, like her mother, lives in Santa Monica; Andrea in London, and Tammy in the West Country.

It is not altogether surprising, therefore, that Peter and his offspring aren't always familiar with each other's comings and goings. On one occasion, for instance, Andrea called her father when he was in London. Mistaking her voice for Pavla's, he asked, 'When did you arrive?' The penny dropped when Andrea replied, 'I *live* here, remember?'

Three months after their visit to Leningrad, Peter had the additional bonus of another family get-together, this time in Paris. In November 1987 the prestigious Académie des Beaux Arts announced that, 'In recognition of his contribution to a variety of artistic fields', it had elected Ustinov to the Académie as a 'Foreign Associate'.

Composed of fifty 'Ordinary Members' and fifty 'Correspondents', the Académie's membership is complemented by fifteen 'Foreign Associates', which at that time included Salvador Dalí, Federico Fellini, Yehudi Menuhin and former American president Richard Nixon. In a strictly regulated system, a new Foreign Associate can only be elected after the death of his predecessor, and Peter was to succeed Orson Welles, who had died in 1985.

The formal installation took place, as tradition decrees, beneath the ornate marble 'Cupola', high above the circular auditorium at the Institut de France, on 1 February 1989. That afternoon, as television cameras from French news programmes peered down from a high window, and stewards in black tailcoats and gold chains directed several hundred specially-invited guests to their places, Peter's family were shepherded past a grandiose marble statue of Napoleon, his head wreathed in laurel leaves, to their seats near the rostrum. Close by sat such familiar figures and family friends as Georges Wilson, the distinguished film director; Igor's godfather, Alexandre Trauner, one of the world's most celebrated set designers, whose credits include the famous French classic *Les Enfants du Paradis*; and former ballerina Ludmilla Tcherina, whose veritable mane of jet-black hair contrasted starkly with the pale, almost white, make-up that she wore.

With no shrill fanfare, just the slight clinking sound that swords tend to make when worn, Peter – dressed in the dark blue ceremonial uniform Pierre Cardin had made for him, its cut-away coat embroidered with a design of green and gold leaves – was escorted into the auditorium by similarly attired Academicians. In his forty-minute welcoming speech, to which the newest member of l'Académie then responded – speaking French with 'just the perfume of an accent', as one guest put it – the distinguished architect, Roger Taillibert, spoke of Peter's family history, his life and accomplishments, and ended by commending him as 'an inspiration to the Theatre'.

Not quite two hours later, during a sumptuous reception in a large flower-bedecked room in another part of the Institut building, Peter received his Academician's sword. It was presented to him on behalf of his children by Jean d'Ormesson, who is not only a great personal friend, but also one of France's most famous writers and a member of l'Académie Française. Created by Igor and Andrea, who is by profession a jewellery designer, the sword was cast in bronze and white bronze, with the hilt ingeniously incorporating emblems representing Peter's myriad activities.

From the pommel, designed as a microphone, the head of which also symbolized the world, the hand-guard curved like a symbolic river, studded with musical notes. Elsewhere, and all in miniature, were to be found the masks of comedy and tragedy; a pair of pens, symbolizing Ustinov the writer and playwright; the Unicef emblem, which spoke of his concern for humanity; and an aeroplane, representing his travels.

While brandishing it for the benefit of journalists and photographers, Peter joked: 'Me with a sword! Now you've seen it all. Happily, it's only ceremonial. You can't count on me to defend you . . . . '

During the following months Ustinov was, as always, a frequent visitor to London. But that September he returned chiefly to promote his first work of fiction since the publication of *Krumnagel* in 1971. Inspired by the British government's risible, and ultimately futile attempt to suppress Peter Wright's book *Spycatcher*, Ustinov wrote a satirical novella entitled *The Disinformer*. In it, a retired intelligence officer turns *agent provocateur* to indulge in a little skulduggery of his own design, leading to a terrorist shoot-out in the heart of London.

Not long before he finished writing it, Margaret Thatcher asked Peter what he was 'doing these days'. He replied that he was writing the story of a man who was jealous of Peter Wright.

'He's not worth it,' she said.

'How would you know, Prime Minister?' Ustinov responded. 'You've never had a book banned by someone like you.'

By the time Peter and Hélène left Geneva in early December for Cancun in Mexico, where the fourth Issyk-Kul Forum was held, much of the new year had already been mapped out. Starting in March 1990, Peter's first major professional engagement of the new decade would see him back in London for a six-week season of one-man shows, and back in the West End for the first time in seven years.

That February, however, it looked for one moment as though Peter might not be well enough to appear anywhere. In Mexico he had picked up the particularly virulent 'flu virus that had been plaguing Europe since before Christmas. Though recovered from its worst – and even, in some cases, fatal – effects, it had still left him with an extremely severe cough. In Berlin towards the end of the month Peter awoke in the early morning, unable to breathe. With great presence of mind, he boiled a kettle of water, inhaled the steam and was then able to call a business associate, who drove him to hospital for examination. The diagnosis was pneumonia.

It has been said that one of Peter Ustinov's faults is a constant wish to please others without always pleasing himself. His response is that he is aware that he has now reached an age at which he has to be 'more cautious', but this episode was, in fact, very much a case in point. For no sooner had he started to recover from the attack of pneumonia, than he drove into Geneva to attend a Red Cross conference, saying that since he would be sitting down, he could always doze off if he felt tired.

Though he has a mild form of diabetes, controlled by the 'tiny pill' he has to take every morning, and has always suffered from a nervous stomach, one of the reasons why he hates tension, Peter – who is a physically strong man – has always tried to keep himself as fit as possible, notably through his enjoyment of playing tennis. He gave up cigars a few years ago because, he says, 'I used to wake during the night and think I could hear burglars. It was really only my bronchial tubes so I gave up smoking.' But when, as happens from time to time, his doctors advise losing a few kilos because that way he'll live longer, he hears what they say, but points to his great-great-grandfather, Mikhail Adrianovich Ustinov, who was a bigger man by far, and lived to be 108.

Yet while he seems unwilling – or perhaps unable – to rest for long, and admits to being 'very unresigned to a less active life', Peter recognizes the fact that, as he approaches his seventies, he cannot 'work at the same pace or with the same recklessness' that he used to. He still maintains, however, that he 'always holds something in reserve'.

Health matters notwithstanding, Ustinov arrived in London, as he had promised, in early March. A few days later he was playing to capacity audiences at the Palace Theatre in Manchester, where he gave his one-man show a week's run immediately before coming in to the West End. *An Evening with Peter Ustinov* opened with a press night before a specially-invited audience of family, friends, fellow professionals and critics, at the Theatre Royal, Haymarket, on 21 March. For two hours Peter shared reminiscences and anecdotes about his childhood and schooldays, about his career and some of the theatrical 'greats' he has known. Throughout, mimicry and impersonations proliferated: Queen Mary, Charles Laughton, Olivier, Gielgud and Richardson; Ronnie, and even Nancy, Reagan; and Mitterand and Brezhnev, of whom, by means of clever facial distortions, he suddenly became the very image. By way of an encore or two, there were musical impressions: a flamenco guitar, a mandolin . . . ; then the finale . . . a scattering of coins . . . and . . . applause.

That applause not only continued when Peter arrived at the Café Royal for supper afterwards – where he received congratulations from, among others, his daughters Tammy and Andrea, Angela Lansbury, Bob Geldof, Lords Montagu and Brabourne, Ladies Mountbatten and Daubeny, Natalia Makarova, and the Soviet Ambassador – but from the critics the next day, too. *The Times*, for instance, wanted Ustinov to 'go on talking until the small hours'; the *Daily Express* described him as 'the greatest after-dinner speaker in the galaxy'; Jack Tinker, whose review of *The Marriage* at Edinburgh eight years before was not without a trace of venom, now ended his notice for the *Daily Mail* by saying: 'With the world in its present melting-pot, I would readily nominate Ustinov as the next Pope'.

The following Sunday, Kate Kellaway of the *Observer* chose a rather more orthodox compliment when she advised readers of her column, 'If you like good conversation but don't want to do the talking, the Haymarket Theatre's the place for you'. Among those who just might have taken her tip, were Princess Margaret and Prince and Princess Michael of Kent, who joined the audience on separate evenings. By then, however, Ustinov's six-week run, already extended to nine, was fully booked and, from the first night, there were queues for return tickets waiting outside the Theatre Royal.

In the West End, where at that time no fewer than five shows closed in rapid succession through lack of attendance, Peter could scarcely have asked for higher praise.

On 29 May, the lights came down on Ustinov's sixty-first performance, and the London run – soon to be repeated in Australia and New Zealand – was finally over. Though delighted by its success, he told me during the show's penultimate week, 'I'm beginning to feel as though I have just played six sets against Lendl;' then added, 'I'd rather it had been Lendl's father.'

The following day, Peter headed for home – or at least for France, and the Paris opening of his film *Bow-Wow*. With him went an official communication from Downing Street, which the Prime Minister had had delivered to the stage door of the Theatre Royal little more than two weeks earlier. In her letter, Mrs Thatcher formally extended the offer of a knighthood. If Peter accepted, she said, her recommendation would be submitted to Buckingham Palace for royal approval. And if that was given, Britain's newest theatrical knight would receive confirmation via The Queen's Birthday Honours which, in accordance with tradition, were to be announced on the occasion of the Sovereign's Official Birthday on Saturday, 16 June.

In the meantime, Peter was instructed not to mention the accolade to anyone except Hélène. 'When I told her,' he says, 'she had a fit of the giggles.' Later, when she and Peter discovered that the honour's official designation was actually that of a 'Knight Bachelor', Hélène was even more amused. 'A bachelor?' she asked. 'With *three* wives?'

Ustinov himself was, of course, deeply gratified to receive an honour which was widely regarded as being long overdue. Yet of being known as 'Sir Peter,' he told me, 'I'm a little bit like a gun-dog who has always recognized one name. It's a little late in life to recognize a new one.'

Although he is in almost every respect a 'Modern Renaissance Man' or, as Steve Kenis put it, 'A jack of all trades and master of most', Peter Ustinov is by no means easy to define. Sir Alec Guinness wrote to me:

> That he is a fine actor is obvious, but often, he has been underestimated by critics. Perhaps the fact that he is a brilliant comedian has stood in the way of his serious work being recognized at its true value. His genius as an entertainer . . . and raconteur is unparalleled, and with the passing years this appears to be increasingly so.
>
> Peter Sellers excelled in a remarkable way as a vocal mimic but his material lacked the wit, observation and comment which Ustinov always supplies. There is an underlying wisdom and humanity in all he tackles; he is, I expect, the wisest man in our midst who is also an actor. If I had to choose three words to convey his personality, I would use – humane, affable and wise.

Few would deny that Ustinov is one of the most gifted men of our time. Yet he is also one of the most paradoxical. The idea that the entire world knows him personally is, perhaps, the greatest paradox of all. For while he is beyond doubt one of the world's most public figures, he is also one of its most intensely private. And though it is true that he is rarely ever alone, he is at heart a loner.

That, at least, is my view. And it is one that I believe he confirmed in the words he attributed to 'The Inventor', one of the characters in his play *The Unknown Soldier and His Wife*, when he says, 'I walk in my own rhythm'. So, indeed, does Peter Ustinov.

Postscript to the Paperback

In the two years since this book was first published, a number of momentous political events have occurred in various parts of the world. Each of them provided Peter Ustinov with considerable scope for thought, not to mention myriad themes for comment, in the weekly column he has written for the *European* since it was created by the late Robert Maxwell in May 1990.

Of all the recent changes in world politics, the most dramatic have undoubtedly centred on what was the Soviet Union. Though short-lived, the coup in August 1991 was not only a sharp reminder to the West of discontent within the USSR, but more especially of the increasing vulnerability of its president, Mikhail Gorbachev. Though ostensibly restored to office only forty-eight hours after he and his wife, Raisa, had been placed under house arrest at their holiday dacha in the Crimea, Gorbachev's historic rule was moving inexorably towards its close. Four months later, the dissolution of the Union and the emergence of the new, albeit fragile, Commonwealth of Independent States, under the supervision of Boris Yeltsin, sealed Gorbachev's fate. In a word, events had made him redundant and on Christmas Day, having 'achieved his life's work', as he put it, he formally resigned. With the demise of Russia's Communist regime, images of Lenin began to disappear from view. The old tsarist capital, Leningrad, was renamed St Petersburg, while in Moscow, the red flag was lowered from the Kremlin, to be replaced by an unfamiliar red, white and blue tricolour. Another stage in Russia's progression towards democratization had been embarked upon, though the dangers posed by uncertainty and inexperience belied the new sense of optimism.

During a conversation we had early in 1992, Peter Ustinov told me that, while on a recent visit to Canada, he had been asked to comment on the situation in the former Soviet Union. 'I said it was a wonderful relief to talk on a subject where there are no experts left,' he said. 'Nobody, not even Yeltsin, knows what will happen.' But, he went on, events have shown that 'Russia takes herself seriously and doesn't want any more bloodshed'. Of the former president, Peter told me, 'What happened was normal. There was no rush to get rid of Gorbachev. Like toothpaste from a tube, he finally reached his end and was relegated to another shelf. But as a symbol, he is still too valuable to neglect.'

A year earlier, the dissolution of the Soviet Union may have seemed a distant possibility but, for the present at least, an unthinkable development. Much closer to home, drama surrounded another world leader and with breathtaking speed, the 'unthinkable' in British politics became a reality. Having governed Britain in her own distinctly dictatorial manner for eleven and a half years, Margaret Thatcher finally came unstuck, not at the hands of the British electorate, but as the result of mounting disaffection among her own Cabinet colleagues. Writing of what he called 'a peculiarly British affair', Peter Ustinov said,

> The lady herself was acclaimed, by many of those eager to be rid of her, as the greatest of peacetime prime ministers. The distinction was made retrospectively, with a tactfully suppressed sigh of relief, in order not to affect Churchill's position in the history books. It is a curious one for the lady, so personable, kind and considerate in private, was far better known as her alter-ego, the warrior queen of surpassing arrogance and almost risible overstatement.

Sir Peter was, of course, in a fine position to write about Margaret Thatcher from personal experience, having seen her in action at Chequers as well as No. 10 on more than one occasion during the long years of her premiership.

Yet, infinitely more tragic than 'Maggie's' tearful departure from Downing Street, was the murder of Rajiv Gandhi in May 1991; a barbarous act which was described by Ustinov at the time, as 'Madness masquerading as innocence'. I have already dealt at some length with the assassination of Rajiv's mother, Indira, in 1984 and have described how, at the time of her death, Sir Peter had been working on a film portrait of the Indian premier; a film that he eventually completed with the assistance of her son and successor. Thereafter, his contact with Rajiv Gandhi

centred on humanitarian issues of concern to them both. In 1991, for
example, Gandhi had invited Sir Peter to participate in that year's 'Indira
Gandhi Conference on the Challenges of the Twenty-first Century'.
Postponed once because of the Gulf War, the conference had been
rescheduled to take place towards the end of the year. It was an event
Rajiv would not live to see.

On 21 May, the day of his death, Gandhi – who had been prime
minister from 1984 to 1989 – was campaigning for re-election in the
southern state of Tamil Nadu. It was there that his assassin struck. 'My
initial reaction', said Ustinov (who was then appearing in his one-man
show in San Francisco) 'was not so much shock as a feeling of exasperation.
We were again confronted with a situation as horrible, as inevitable as
any Greek tragedy ... And where does such a murder lead? It is like
trying to wound the ocean with a knife. Only an idiot can derive
satisfaction from such a sterile gesture, one with no sense of tomorrow, or
of the day after: a cripple with a castrated mind.'

Peter's sense of outrage, reflected here in characteristically controlled
tone at the death of Rajiv Gandhi, is – as we saw earlier – as easily
aroused by any manifestation of inhumanity or injustice. That is why he
had no hesitation in accepting an invitation to take part in a special
television film about the work of the International Red Cross. Transmitted
throughout Europe in May 1991, *Light the Darkness* focused attention on
the innocent who suffer as a consequence of war, and issued a direct plea
to the world to abide by the Geneva Conventions and Protocols.

Intercut with a live concert from Geneva, *Light the Darkness* highlighted
the poignant fact that, during the forty-three-day war in the Gulf – from
17 January to 28 February 1991 – there were no fewer than thirty-two
other major conflicts happening in the world. It made the point that, since
1945, war has so far claimed twenty million lives and has forced a further
sixty million to flee their homes.

Some two hours later, Sir Peter brought the evening's programme to a
close, by quoting the words of Fyodor Dostoevsky that are inscribed on
the wall of the Red Cross Headquarters in Geneva: 'Each one of us is
responsible to all others for everything.'

A little under a month earlier, on Tuesday, 16 April, Peter Ustinov
celebrated his seventieth birthday. Left to his own devices, he would
probably have chosen to mark the occasion without ceremony, at his
home in Switzerland. Instead, he was the guest of honour at a special gala

evening, held at the Palais de l'Unesco in Paris, where he was fêted in words and music, by royalty, statesmen, actors, opera singers, distinguished musicians and pop stars.

About four years ago, while researching this book, I have to admit that I started to feel a little uneasy about the admiring tone of the material I was gathering together. It wasn't that I doubted the sincerity of any of it. On the contrary. It was simply that, from a biographer's point of view, the lack of any real criticism of Sir Peter from those who know him, suggested that I might have problems balancing the tone of the book when it came to be written. In the meantime, I was, of course, getting to know the man himself very much better, with the result that I, too, came to appreciate why Peter Ustinov is regarded so highly and, indeed, with such genuine affection. It came as no surprise, therefore, that the guest-list for his birthday gala should have read like some kind of International Who's Who.

One by one, either in person or via the giant screen erected in the auditorium, personalities from Britain, France, America, Russia, Germany, Greece and Australia, offered Peter their own distinctive greetings. Montserrat Caballé and Barbara Hendricks, for example, joined forces to sing Puccini, while Yehudi Menuhin with Ivry Gitlis, Stephen Milencovic and Larry Adler, presented 'Jazz from the Classics'. There were tributes from Leslie Caron, Arthur Miller, Tony Curtis and Robert Mitchum; from Klaus Maria Brandauer, Ute Lemper, Kirk Douglas, Stewart Granger and Jean Simmons. There was also a written message from Henry Kissinger. Describing himself as a 'long-time fan', he wound up his greeting by saying, 'You may be sure that I would be even more enthusiastic in my praise if I were not terrified of becoming the subject of one of your devastating impersonations.'

Still from the world of politics, former German Chancellor, Helmut Schmidt, turned pianist to offer a slightly hesitant rendition of *Happy Birthday to You*; while, later in the proceedings, Edward Heath, with what Ustinov was to call a 'broad Handelian sweep', took to the keyboard to deliver a confident version of *For He's a Jolly Good Fellow*. It also fell to the former British prime minister to read out a message from 'Charles and Diana', Prince and Princess of Wales. In apologizing for their absence, Prince Charles said, 'I cannot believe for one moment that we will be missed! Only you could attract such a glittering array of talent. Please accept our heartfelt congratulations as you enter middle age . . .'

At the end of the evening, Peter himself took the stage. 'This,' he told his 1,200-strong audience, 'was supposed to take me by surprise – and I came here yesterday to rehearse being surprised. I don't have a ready tear, I've put them in reverse, but I have been terribly moved tonight, seeing so many friends all in one place.'

Having paused very briefly in Paris to celebrate his birthday – which was also commemorated in London by a season of his films at the National Film Theatre and, incidentally, by the publication of a special edition of the *European* – Ustinov was off on his travels once more.

Following the success of his one-man shows in London a year earlier (which earned him a nomination for an Olivier Award in 1991), as well as in New Zealand and Australia, Peter embarked on a lengthy tour of American cities. That September, he was back in Britain for a three-month round of engagements in England, Ireland and Wales; towards the end of which, Princess Margaret attended a gala performance of *An Evening with Peter Ustinov*, which officially reopened the newly refurbished Theatre on the Green, in Richmond, Surrey.

This tour, punctuated by a variety of other commitments, such as filming a documentary about the Orient Express (which at one point entailed Peter 'commuting' to and from Britain), ended in Cardiff at the beginning of December. By then, arrangements were already well in hand for Peter to present his show in Singapore, Hong Kong and Kuala Lumpur early in the New Year. Since they have no theatres in that part of the world, however, he was to appear instead in chic hotel dining-rooms which, on one occasion, resulted in the imposition of a very firm rule. 'When I received my visa for Malaysia,' Peter told me, 'it stipulated that I was allowed to perform as a "Comedian", but that I was not permitted to *dance* with members of the audience!'

After Christmas with his family at Au Clos du Château, Ustinov and his wife, Hélène, spent the first three weeks of 1992 on holiday in Phuket, Thailand. While they were away, it was announced that Sir Peter had accepted a significant 'academic' position, the offer of which had originally rendered him speechless. Having been Rector of Dundee University from 1968 to 1974, the University of Durham now wanted him to succeed the late Dame Margot Fonteyn, in the loftier role of Chancellor.

'My reaction was first one of surprise,' he told the Faculty, 'then disbelief and now unmitigated delight. One of my great regrets is that I was never able to go to University. The Rectorship and now this seems to me like the gilding of a lily that was never allowed to bloom in my garden.'

After his installation by the Vice-Chancellor, Professor Evelyn Ebsworth, in Durham's imposing eleventh-century cathedral, on 7 May, the university's tenth chancellor, resplendent in black and gold robe and gold-tasselled academic cap, bestowed three honorary degrees on recipients of his own choosing. Alexander Yakovlev, the Russian diplomat and politician, architect of 'Glasnost' and adviser to Mikhail Gorbachev, became an honorary Doctor of Civil Law, as did Lèon Davičo of Unesco; while Glenda Jackson, actress-turned-politician, became an honorary Doctor of Letters.

But for events unforeseen at the end of 1986, when the University Senate first approved the degree, former Beirut hostage, Terry Waite, would have received his doctorate of Civil Law from Chancellor Fonteyn, in 1987. However, on the very day the University announced its list of honorary graduates, Waite was taken captive while acting as the then Archbishop of Canterbury's special envoy in Lebanon. It now fell to Sir Peter to confer the degree on Terry Waite who, like his fellow hostages, John McCarthy and Jackie Mann, was finally released in 1991.

It might appear to be stating the obvious to say there is nothing predictable about Peter Ustinov. But when most of his generation have long since put their feet up and settled for a quieter life, this seemingly ageless man has lost none of his curiosity, much less any of his zest, for life. On the subject of growing older, however, he is on record as having said, 'My thoughts are the same as fifty years ago, but today people listen to me — that changes everything. When I look in the mirror, however, I see a stranger. This body, which I have never paid much attention to, is beginning to lead a life of its own. I don't love this body, I only use it. And I guess it's only loaned out. Like a rental car, I'll have to give it back eventually.'

That day; if Sir Peter himself has any say in the matter, is still some way off. In fact, when issued with a new passport in the spring of 1990, he noted that its expiry date — 11 April 2000 — falls five days short of his seventy-ninth birthday. With a rumble of laughter, he said, 'I now regard it as a matter of honour not to expire before the passport.'

Peter Ustinov: Chronology

Appendix I: Theatre

STAGE APPEARANCES
(with date of production and playwright)

As a student at the London Theatre Studio
Alcestis, Euripides
Wild Decembers, Clemence Dane
The Plain Dealer, William Wycherley

At the Barn Theatre, Shere, Surrey
The Wood Demon, Anton Chekhov
Mariana Pineda, Federico Garcia Lorca
The Rose and the Cross, Alexander Blok, translated
  by Peter Ustinov and Nadia Benois Ustinov

At the Players' Theatre Club
The Bishop of Limpopoland, Peter Ustinov
Madame Liselotte Beethoven-Fink, Peter Ustinov

With the Aylesbury Repertory Theatre
French Without Tears, Terence Rattigan
White Cargo, Ida Vera Simonton

Rookery Nook, Ben Travers
Goodness How Sad, Robert Morley
Laburnum Grove, J.B. Priestley
Pygmalion, George Bernard Shaw

Professional Engagements

Swinging the Gate, Revue (1940), Norman Marshall
Diversion, Revue, (1940), Herbert Farjeon
Diversion 2, Revue (1941), Herbert Farjeon
Crime and Punishment (1946), Dostoevsky
Frenzy (1948), Ingmar Bergman, translated and
    adapted by Peter Ustinov
Love in Albania (1949), Eric Linklater
The Love of Four Colonels (1951), Peter Ustinov
The Love of Four Colonels (USA), 1952)
Romanoff and Juliet (1956), Peter Ustinov
Romanoff and Juliet (USA, 1957)
Photo Finish (1962), Peter Ustinov
Photo Finish (USA, 1963)
The Unknown Soldier and His Wife (USA, 1967) Peter Ustinov
The Unknown Soldier and His Wife, (Chichester, 1968)
The Unknown Soldier and His Wife, (London, 1973)
Who's Who in Hell, (USA, 1974), Peter Ustinov
King Lear (Stratford, Ontario, 1979), William Shakespeare
King Lear (Stratford, Ontario, 1980), William Shakespeare
Beethoven's Tenth (London, 1983), Peter Ustinov
Beethoven's Tenth (USA, 1983–4))
Beethoven's Tenth (Germany, 1987–8)
An Evening with Peter Ustinov (London, 1990)
An Evening with Peter Usintov (Tour of Australia and
    New Zealand, 1990)
An Evening with Peter Ustinov (US Tour, 1991)
An Evening with Peter Ustinov (Far East, 1992)

PLAYS WRITTEN BY
(with date of production)

House of Regrets (1942)
Beyond (1942)

The Banbury Nose (1942)
Blow Your Own Trumpet (1943)
The Tragedy of Good Intentions (1945)
The Indifferent Shepherd (1948)
Frenzy (1948), Ingmar Bergman, translated and adapted
   by Peter Ustinov
The Man in the Raincoat (1949)
The Love of Four Colonels (1951)
The Moment of Truth (1951)
High Balcony (1952)
No Sign of the Dove (1953)
Romanoff and Juliet (1956)
The Empty Chair (1956)
Paris Not So Gay (1958)
Photo Finish (1962)
The Life in My Hands (1964)
Halfway up The Tree (1967)
The Unknown Soldier and His Wife (1967)
Who's Who in Hell (1974)
Overheard (1981)
Beethoven's Tenth (1983)

PLAYS DIRECTED BY
(with date of production and playwright)

Let the People Sing, Dialogue Director, (1940), J.B. Priestley
Squaring the Circle (1941), Valentin Katayev
The Rivals (1942), Sheridan
Love in Albania (1949), Eric Linklater
A Fiddle at the Wedding (1952), Patricia Pakenham-Walsh
No Sign of the Dove (1953), Peter Ustinov
Romanoff and Juliet (1956), Peter Ustinov
Photo Finish (1962), Peter Ustinov
Halfway Up The Tree (1967), Peter Ustinov
The Unknown Soldier and His Wife (1967), Peter Ustinov

Appendix II: Film

FILM APPEARANCES
(with year of film's release and director)

Mein Kampf, (1940)
Hello, Fame!, (1940)
The Goose Steps Out, (1941)
One of Our Aircraft is Missing (1941), Michael Powell
The Way Ahead (1944), Carol Reed
Private Angelo (1949), Peter Ustinov
Odette (1950), Herbert Wilcox
Quo Vadis (1951), Mervyn LeRoy
Hotel Sahara (1951), Ken Annakin
The Magic Box (1952), John Boulting
Beau Brummel (1954), Curtis Bernhardt
The Egyptian (1954), Michael Curtiz
We're No Angels (1954), Michael Curtiz
Lola Montès (1955), Max Ophüls
The Spies (Les Espions) (1957), Henri-Georges Clouzot
An Angel Over Brooklyn (1957), Ladislao Vajda
Spartacus (1960), Stanley Kubrick
The Sundowners (1960), Fred Zinnemann
Romanoff and Juliet (1961), Peter Ustinov
Billy Budd (1962), Peter Ustinov
Topkapi (1964), Jules Dassin

John Goldfarb, Please Come Home (1964), J. Lee Thompson
Lady L (1965), Peter Ustinov
Blackbeard's Ghost (1967), Robert Stevenson
The Comedians (1967), Peter Glenville
Hot Millions (1968), Eric Till
Viva Max (1969), Jerry Paris
Hammersmith Is Out (1971), Peter Ustinov
Big Truck and Poor Clare (1971), Robert Ellis Miller
One of Our Dinosaurs is Missing (1974), Robert Stevenson
Logan's Run (1975), Michael Anderson
The Treasure of Matecumbe (1975), Vincent McEveety
The Last Remake of Beau Geste (1976), Marty Feldman
Purple Taxi (1977), Yves Boisset
Death on the Nile (1978), John Guillermin
The Thief of Baghdad (1978), Clive Donner
Ashanti (1978), Richard Fleisher
Charlie Chan and the Curse of the Dragon Queen (1980),
  Clive Donner
Evil Under the Sun (1982), Guy Hamilton
Memed, My Hawk (1983), Peter Ustinov
Appointment with Death (1988), Michael Winner
The French Revolution (1989), Roberto Enrico
Bow-Wow (1990), Duccio Tessari

FILMS WRITTEN BY
(with year of film's release and director)

The New Lot (with others) (1942), Carol Reed
The Way Ahead (with Eric Ambler) (1944), Carol Reed
The True Glory (with others) (1945), Carol Reed
School for Secrets (1946), Peter Ustinov
Vice-Versa (1947), Peter Ustinov
Private Angelo (1949), Peter Ustinov
Romanoff and Juliet (1961), Peter Ustinov
Billy Budd (with De Witt Bodeen) (1962), Peter Ustinov
Lady L (with Carlo Ponti) (1965), Peter Ustinov
Hot Millions (with Ira Wallach) (1968), Eric Till
Memed, My Hawk (1983), Peter Ustinov

FILMS DIRECTED AND CO-PRODUCED BY
(with year of film's release)

School for Secrets (1946)
Vice-Versa (1947)
Private Angelo (1949)
Romanoff and Juliet (1961)
Billy Budd (1962)
Lady L (1965)
Hammersmith Is Out (1971)
Memed, My Hawk (1983)

Appendix III: Books

BOOKS WRITTEN BY

Add A Dash of Pity, Heinemann, 1960
Ustinov's Diplomats, Cassel, 1960
We Were Only Human, Heinemann, 1961
The Loser, Heinemann, 1961
Frontiers of The Sea, Heinemann, 1966
Krumnagel, Heinemann, 1971
Dear Me, Heinemann, 1977
My Russia, Macmillan, 1983
Ustinov in Russia, Michael O'Mara, 1987
The Disinformer, Michael O'Mara, 1989
The Old Man and Mr Smith, Michael O'Mara, 1990
Ustinov at Large, Michael O'Mara, 1991

Appendix IV: Television and Radio

TELEVISION AND RADIO APPEARANCES

Include many chat show appearances in Britain, in Germany, throughout the rest of Europe and in the United States, hosted by such personalities as Terry Wogan and Clive James (UK) and Jack Parr, Perry Como and Steve Allen (USA)

In All Directions, BBC Radio (1952), with Peter Jones, Frank Muir and Denis Norden

Some Diversions on a Projected Trans-Atlantic Expedition, BBC Radio (1953), with Peter Jones

Some Further Diversions, BBC Radio (1955), with Peter Jones

Omnibus 'The Life of Samuel Johnson', USA TV, (1957) (Emmy Award for Best Performance)

Storm in Summer, USA TV (1970), (Emmy Award for Best Performance)

Barefoot in Athens, USA TV (1966), (Emmy Award for Best Performance)

The Hermitage, Lothar Bock Associates for NBC (1979), with Natalie Wood

The Mighty Continent, BBC TV (1974)

Around the World in Eighty Days, NBC (1988–9), with Pierce Brosnan

Ustinov Ad Lib, BBC (1969)

Einstein's Universe, PBS and BBC (1979)

The Well Tempered Bach, PBS (1984)
Peter Ustinov's Russia, John McGreevey Productions, Toronto, BBC TV (1984–5)
13 at Dinner, CBS (1985)
Deadman's Folly, CBS (1985)
Murder in Three Acts, CBS (1987)
Peter Ustinov in China, Global Television, Canada (1987)
Light the Darkness BBC (1991)

Appendix V: Opera

OPERAS DIRECTED BY

L'Heure Espagnole, Ravel; *Gianna Schicchi*, Puccini; *Erwartung*, Schoenberg (Triple Bill at Covent Garden, 1962)
The Magic Flute, Mozart (Hamburg, 1968)
Don Giovanni, Mozart (Edinburgh Festival, 1973) (Also designed costumes and sets)
Don Quixote, Massenet (Paris, 1973) (Also produced and designed)
Les Brigands, Offenbach (Berlin, 1978) (Also produced)
The Marriage, Mussorgsky, La Piccola Scala, Milan and Edinburgh Festival, 1982) (Also wrote the libretto)
Mavra and *The Flood*, Stravinsky (La Piccola Scala, Milan, 1982)
Katja Kabanowa, Janacek (Hamburg, 1985)
The Marriage of Figaro, Mozart (Mozarteum, Salzburg and Hamburg, 1987)

Appendix VI: Recordings

PETER USTINOV ON RECORD
(recordings include the following)

Mock Mozart and *Phoney Folk Lore*, Parlophone

The Grand Prix of Gibraltar, Orpheum

Peter and the Wolf, with Herbert von Karajan conducting the Philharmonia, London, Angel Records (Grammy Award)

Nutcracker Suite and *Between Birthdays*, Columbia

The Soldier's Tale, (*L'Histoire Du Soldat*) Narration in French with Jean Cocteau, Phillips

Hary Janos, with the London Symphony Orchestra, London Records

The Little Prince narration of the story by Antoine de St Exupery, Argos Records

The Old Man of Lochnagar, Narration of the children's story by the Prince of Wales, Multi Media Tapes

Grandpa, Narration of an original composition by Howard Blake, CBS

Babar and Father Christmas, Random House

Peter and the Wolf, narration, Castle Records

Blackbeard's Ghost, Disney

The Story of Babar, The Little Elephant and *The Story of the Little Tailor*, Angel Records

Appendix VII: Honours and Awards

PETER USTINOV'S HONOURS AND AWARDS

Include the following:

Knighthood (Knight Bachelor), The Queen's Birthday Honours, 1990

Commander of the Order of the British Empire (CBE), 1975

Commandeur des Arts et des Lettres, Paris, 1984

Foreign Associate, l'Académie des Beaux Arts, Paris, 1988

Benjamin Franklin Medal, Royal Society of Arts, 1957

Order of Istiglal, Hashemite Kingdom of Jordan

Order of the Yugoslav Flag

Order of the Smile (from the Children of Poland), 1975

Unicef Award for Distinguished Service, 1978

Gold Medal of the City of Athens, 1990

Distinguished Service Medal, Greek Red Cross, 1990

Prix de la Butte, Paris (for Best Autobiography), 1978

Variety Club of Great Britain Award for Best Actor, 1979

Academy Award (Oscar), and Golden Globe Award for Best Supporting Actor, *Spartacus*, 1961

Academy Award (Oscar) for Best Supporting Actor, *Topkapi*, 1964

Evening Standard Drama Award for Best Play, *Romanoff and Juliet*, London, 1956

Olivier Award (Nomination), 1991, *An Evening with Peter Ustinov*

Guild of Professional Toastmaster's Award for Best After-Dinner Speakers (in 1990), 1991

Rector, University of Dundee, 1968–74

Honorary Doctorate of Music, Cleveland Institute of Music, 1967

Honorary Doctorate of Law, University of Dundee, 1969

Honorary Doctorate of Law, La Salle College of Philadelphia, 1971

Honorary Doctorate of Letters, University of Lancaster, 1972

Honorary Doctorate of Fine Arts, University of Lethbridge, Canada

Honorary Doctorate, University of Toronto, 1984

Honorary Doctorate Humane Letters, Georgetown University, Washington DC, 1988

Chancellor, University of Durham, (elected 1992)

Honorary Doctorate of Letters, University of Durham, 1992

BIBLIOGRAPHY

Benois, Alexandre, *Memoirs*, Chatto & Windus, 1960

Bragg, Melvyn, *Rich: The Life of Richard Burton*, Hodder & Stoughton, 1988

Daubeny, Peter, *My World of Theatre*, Jonathan Cape, 1971

Field, John, *The King's Nurseries*, James & James, 1987

Findlater, Richard, *Michael Redgrave – Actor*, Heinemann, 1956

Finler, Joel W., *The Hollywood Story*, Octopus Books, 1988

Gingold, Hermione, *How to Grow Old Disgracefully*, Gollancz, 1989

Guinness, Alec, *Blessings in Disguise*, Hamish Hamilton, 1985

Hamilton, George Heard, *The Art and Architecture of Russia*, Penguin, 1987

MacDonald, Nesta, *Diaghilev Observed*, Dance Books, 1975

Mac Liammóir, Micheál, *Put Money in Thy Purse*, Methuen, 1952

Miller, Arthur, *Timebends*, Methuen, 1987

Perry, George (ed.), *Dilys Powell – The Golden Screen*, Pavilion, 1989

Roberts, Peter (ed.), *The Best of Plays and Players 1953–1968*, Methuen 1988

Stamp, Terence, *Coming Attractions*, Bloomsbury, 1988

Stamp, Terence, *Double Feature*, Bloomsbury, 1989

Terras, Victor (ed.), *Handbook of Russian Literature*, Yale, 1988

Thomas, Tony, *Ustinov in Focus*, A. Zwemmer, 1971

Unger-Hamilton, Clive (ed.), *The Entertainers*, Pitman House, 1980

Ustinov, Nadia Benois, *Klop and the Ustinov Family*, Sidgwick & Jackson, 1973

Ustinov, Peter, *Dear Me*, Heinemann, 1977

Ustinov, Peter, *Krumnagel*, Heinemann, 1971

Ustinov, Peter (and others), *The Issyk-Kul Forum; A New Way of Thinking*, Novosti, Moscow, 1987

Ustinov, Peter, *The Unknown Soldier and His Wife*, Heinemann, 1968

Ustinov, Peter, *Ustinov in Russia*, Michael O'Mara, 1987

Willans, Geoffrey, *Peter Ustinov*, Peter Owen, 1957

Wright, Peter, *Spycatcher*, Heinemann, Australia, 1987

Newspapers: *Boston Sunday Globe; Daily Express; Daily Mail; Daily Sketch; Daily Telegraph; Edinburgh Evening News; The European; Evening News; Evening Standard; Le Figaro; Financial Times; Gisborne Herald*, New Zealand; *Glasgow Herald; Guardian; International Herald Tribune; Manchester Guardian; New York Herald Tribune; Newcastle Journal; Observer; Scotsman; The Stage; Sunday Dispatch; Sunday Express; Sunday Telegraph; Sunday Times; The Times; The Times Educational Supplement; Yorkshire Post*

Magazines: *ABC Film Review; Books & Bookmen; Cinémonde; Contact* (University of Dundee); *Film Comment; Films & Filming; Film Review; Illustrated; Illustrated London News; Paris Match; Photoplay; Plays and Players; Poland Illustrated Magazine; Punch; Queen; Radio Times; Sketch; Tatler; Telegraph Magazine; Time; Timeout; US News & World Report; Vogue*

INDEX